The Essential Diabetes Cookbook

Antony Worrall Thompson

The Essential Diabetes Cookbook

GOOD HEALTHY EATING FROM AROUND THE WORLD

with Louise Blair BSc

Kyle Books

IMPORTANT NOTE

The information and advice contained in this book are intended as a general guide to dieting and healthy eating and are not specific to individuals or their particular circumstances. This book is not intended to replace treatment by a qualified practitioner. Neither the authors nor the publishers can be held responsible for claims arising from the inappropriate use of any dietary regime. Do not attempt self-diagnosis or self-treatment for serious or long-term conditions without consulting a medical professional or qualified practitioner.

Published in 2010 by Kyle Books,
an imprint of Kyle Cathie Ltd
www.kylebooks.com

Distributed by National Book Network
4501 Forbes Blvd., Suite 200
Lanham, MD 20706
Phone: (800) 462-6420 Fax: (301) 429-5746
custser@nbnbooks.com

10 9 8 7 6 5 4 3 2 1

978-1-906868-15-4

Editor Judith Hannam
Editorial Assistant Vicki Murrell
Designer Jim Smith
Home Economist and Stylist Annie Nichols
Copyeditor Marion Moisy
Recipe Analyis Wendy Doyle
Production Kyle Cathie and Gemma John

Library of Congress Control Number: 2010932221

Color reproduction by Scanhouse
Printed and bound in Singapore by Tien Wah Press

Note about raw eggs and raw fish

It is recommended that eggs should not be eaten raw. Vulnerable people, such as pregnant or nursing mothers, babies, the young, the elderly, and those with reduced immune efficiency, are advised to avoid eating raw or lightly cooked eggs. If you fall into these catagories you should also make sensible choices as to whether to eat raw fish.

Note about saturated fat

The delicious recipes in this book have been written and adapted to make them healthier and use monounsaturated spreads and sunflower oils. Butter can be used in place of these but this will increase the saturated fat content of the dish. If you are watching your weight, refer to the nutritional analysis at the bottom of each recipe. Where the fat content is high, these recipes are probably best kept for special occasions and not eaten every day.

Acknowledgments

Space is short but it's essential that I thank those that have helped in the making of this book, Kyle for having faith in realizing that there is a real need for a comprehensive cookbook. To Diabetes UK who threw their considerable weight behind this idea. Thanks also go to Judith Hannam, my editor, who skillfully edited my work. A thank you to Jonathan Gregson who did justice to my recipes, with the stunning pictures. To David Wilby, Nicola Atherton, and Fiona Lindsay and the team at Limelight. I couldn't forget my wife, Jacinta and children, Toby and Billie for putting up with me. This book is dedicated to all of those with diabetes; food can still be enjoyable.

Contents

Foreword

I have now written four books designed specifically for people with diabetes, all of which have been well received. Many readers have written to me saying they have changed their life—some even that they've enabled them to come off insulin. This is very satisfying, especially as I'm neither a doctor nor a nutritionist. My main message has always been that you can still enjoy great food, it just requires small changes to your food and lifestyle, and keeping one word fixed firmly at the front of your mind: moderation.

If you have been diagnosed with diabetes, recriminations are pointless. "What if I had lost weight," "I should have done more exercise," "My sweet tooth has been my downfall" phrases like this inevitably spring to mind, but it doesn't do any good to look backwards, you need to look to the future. It's positive thinking you need; how am I going to enjoy my future and still have fun and pleasure at mealtimes?

"The fabulous recipes included here come from all over the world and prove that food for diabetes doesn't need to be boring."

Don't get me wrong, you do need to make some lifestyle changes. Diet is one of the most important areas for people with diabetes to understand, as the correct diet will improve long-term glucose control. You must focus on food and its importance to you personally. For many, it's all about losing weight and, more importantly, keeping it off. This a slow process, it won't just happen overnight, but losing 10 percent of your body weight can improve the quality of your life enormously by lowering your blood pressure, reducing fasting blood glucose levels and improving blood fats.

I'm not, though, a fan of the word "diet," as it implies loss and suffering. Having diabetes may mean lifestyle changes, but it doesn't mean having to give up foods you particularly love. It's that word moderation again, and making sensible choices. It's also about eating as wide a variety of foods as possible, about increasing the amount of fruit and vegetables you eat, reducing protein, and eating more beans and lentils.

My aim with this book is to extend your knowledge of world foods. The fabulous recipes included here come from all the continents and prove that food for those with diabetes doesn't need to be boring. Our Western eating habits aren't always the easiest to adapt to diabetes requirements, whereas the everyday diet in some other cultures is much more in line with the diet for diabetes. Why not take our inspiration from there? Just think about all those wonderful vegetables from Asia; lots of interesting spices give these dishes their flavor, without the need for too much animal fat or salt. Just cut out the ghee, add a delicious salad, and you're there. Suddenly it's easy to eat six to eight portions of vegetables a day, plus you have the satisfaction of knowing that you're benefiting your body. World food offers so many ways of enjoying your new life with diabetes and it teaches you to think outside the box. With so many options, the world is your oyster.

Antony Worrall Thompson

Top cooking tips for you at home

- Eat three meals a day
- Include starchy carbohydrates at each meal
- Follow a low-GI diet
- Cut down on saturated fats
- Eat at least five portions of fruit and vegetables a day
- Cut down on sugar
- Slash the salt
- Drink alcohol moderately
- Avoid diabetic foods

Introduction

With more than 23.6 million people in the United States diagnosed with diabetes and 5.7 million who remain undiagnosed, diabetes is one of the major health issues of modern day US and a huge problem worldwide. Numbers are increasing every year. It is estimated that currently diabetes affects some 246 million people worldwide, and according to estimates, this figure is set to increase to 380 million by the year 2025. One in 20 of the world's adult population now has diabetes, according to the latest figures. The predominant reasons for the huge number of Type 2 diabetes is obesity due to sedentary lifestyles and poor diet.

Diabetes is finally being recognized as a global epidemic, with the potential to cause a worldwide healthcare crisis. In the US, total costs of diagnosed diabetes is $174 billion. According to the American Diabetes Association, after adjusting for population age and sex differences, average medical expenditures among people with diagnosed diabetes were 2.3 times higher than what expenditures would be in the absence of diabetes.

What is diabetes?

Diabetes mellitus is a condition where the amount of glucose in the blood is too high, either because the body is not producing any or enough insulin, or the insulin it is producing is not effective enough. Glucose comes from the digestion of carbohydrates in food and drinks and is also produced by the liver. Carbohydrates come from many different sources including bread, potatoes, fruit, some dairy products, sugar, and other sweet foods.

Insulin is a hormone produced by the pancreas and helps the glucose to enter the cells where it is used as fuel for energy so we can work, play, and generally live our lives.

Diabetes types

There are two main types of diabetes. These are:
- Type 1 diabetes
- Type 2 diabetes

Type 1

Type 1 diabetes develops if the body is unable to produce any insulin. This type of diabetes usually appears before the age of 40. Type 1 diabetes is the less common of the two main types and accounts for 10 percent of all people with diabetes. You cannot prevent Type 1 diabetes. It is treated either by insulin injections or a pump, a healthy diet, and physical activity.

Type 2

Type 2 diabetes develops when the body can still make some insulin, but not enough, or when the insulin that is produced does not work properly (known as insulin resistance). In at least 80 percent of cases, this is linked with being overweight and usually appears in people over the age of 40, although it often appears in Asians and African Americans from the age of 25. However, recently, more children are being diagnosed with Type 2, some as young as seven.

Type 2 diabetes is the more common of the two main types and accounts for 90 percent of all people with diabetes. Type 2 diabetes is treated by a healthy diet and physical activity. In addition to this, medication and/or insulin is often required.

What are the signs and symptoms of diabetes?

- Passing urine more frequently
- Increased thirst
- Extreme tiredness
- Genital itching or frequent episodes of thrush
- Slow healing of cuts and wounds
- Blurred vision
- Recurring infections
- Unexplained weight loss

The risk factors of Type 2 diabetes

- A close blood relative has Type 2 diabetes (parent or sibling).
- You are overweight or if your waist is bigger than 31.5 inches for women; 35 inches for Asian men; and 37 inches for white and Black men.
- You have high blood pressure or you've had a heart attack or a stroke.
- You're a woman with polycystic ovary syndrome and you are overweight.
- Raised triglycerides (a type of blood fat).
- If you're a woman and you've had gestational diabetes.
- You have severe mental health problems.
- You've been told you have pre-diabetes impaired glucose tolerance (IGT) or impaired fasting glycemia (IFT).

"The more risk factors that apply to you, the greater your risk of having diabetes."

If you've been told you have pre-diabetes impaired fasting glycemia (IFG) or impaired glucose tolerance (IGT) it means the level of glucose in your blood is higher than normal, but you don't have diabetes. You should follow a healthy diet, lose weight if you need to, and keep active to help reduce the risk of diabetes. But make sure you're regularly tested for diabetes.

According to the American Diabetes Association, 12 percent of African Americans have been diagnosed with diabetes, over 10 percent of Hispanics, 7.5 percent of Asian Americans, and over 6.5 percent of the white population.

What are the complications?

Diabetes can lead to heart disease, stroke, amputations, kidney failure, and blindness and causes more deaths than breast and prostate cancer combined. Because Type 2 diabetes can remain undetected for 10 years or more before someone is diagnosed, by the time they are diagnosed 50 percent of those people will have begun to develop complications.

Around 50 percent of people with diabetes will die from "cardiovascular complications" such as a heart attack or stroke. But by controlling blood glucose levels, blood pressure, blood fats, and leading a healthy lifestyle, the risk can be significantly reduced.

What now?

Bearing these facts in mind, we should all aim to reduce our risk of developing diabetes. If you have diabetes, then you should maintain good blood glucose control and reduce the risk of complications by:

- Losing weight and/or maintaining a healthy weight for your size;
- Getting active;
- Following a healthy diet;
- Quitting smoking.

Weight Loss

I know we have all heard it before … "you need to lose weight." It sounds simple but the thought of dieting can make most of us groan. It's true, achieving and maintaining a healthy weight for your size boasts considerable health benefits. You probably don't need to lose as much as you think—losing between 5 and 10 percent of your weight (that's 10–20lb if you are 200lb) has health benefits such as lowering blood fats, blood pressure, and blood glucose levels.

You don't have to reach an "ideal" weight either—be realistic and aim to lose weight slowly over time (1–2 lb a week).

Stick to it

The key to making changes is surely to make plans that are easy to stick to and are not too drastic. It may seem like a great plan to cut out fat or goodies like sweet foods and pastries, but after a while this can become really miserable and bingo, just one treat leads to two and before you know it you are back where you started!

So, keep it simple and make small changes that you are happy to stick to. Little changes such as using skim milk instead of 2% or whole milk, trimming excess fat from meats before cooking, grilling or baking instead of deep frying, 1 cookie instead of 2, a plain pastry instead of a chocolate one, or better still swapping the cookies or pastries for a piece of fruit instead—these can all add up to significant calorie reductions over time and in turn weight loss and maybe a return to those clothes you grew out of!

Just because you are watching what you eat, it doesn't mean that you need to cook separate meals from the rest of the family; a little healthy eating is good for everyone! Serve yourself a smaller portion and fill yourself up with vegetables or salad. A little bit of dessert on the odd occasion is fine, but generally it is better to have a piece of fruit or low-fat yogurt.

Eat regular meals and healthy snacks—skipping meals means you are more likely to seek out a quick fix, and this can spell disaster.

Most importantly, don't try to go it alone. A little bit of support will often give you the boost you need when you feel like giving up. Your local health practitioner is there to help, so ask for individual advice and support when needed.

Up the activity!

Get moving … it makes sense when you think about it. If you use up more energy than you take in (calories) then you are bound to lose weight. No one is expecting you to take up marathon running if you haven't done exercise for some time. Set yourself a goal each week, then, as the weeks go by, aim to try to do a little more and push yourself just a little further. The main thing is to take up something that you like, something that you want to go and do, and most importantly, something that you will keep up. Why not get together with a partner or friend and do something together—this means you are less likely to opt out as you will be letting them down as well as yourself.

It is recommended that adults take part in 30 minutes of exercise at least 5 times a week. See if any of these inspire you to kick off the slippers and put on the sneakers! You will really notice the difference in the way you feel and look as activity releases endorphins which boost your sense of happiness.

- See what classes your local gym offers. This could be yoga, pilates, or aerobics. Visit a class of an appropriate level to try out something different.
- Take up bowling. Not only are you exercising, but you can probably fit in time for a chat with your friends.
- Try swimming or see if your local pool does aqua aerobics. This is great as the water helps to support your body but gives you a great workout at the same time. Swimming uses every muscle and is great for cardiovascular fitness.
- Walking requires nothing but you and, best

of all, it is free. Put on a pair of comfortable, well-fitting shoes and join a local walking group or simply explore the area you live in. Walk to the store or work instead of going by car/bus. Get off a few stops early if you have a long journey and walk the rest of the way.

- Get on your bike! Cycling gives you fresh air and a great look around your surrounding area. Plus, once you have the equipment then it is free to keep going. No excuses!
- If you are a little less mobile, then don't worry, there are things you can do as well. Try some simple exercises at home to some music—stretching and lunging, maybe a little on-the-spot walking or jogging. Honestly, anything is better than nothing and you will still feel better for it.
- Before you start a new activity, check with your doctor about what impact it may have on your diabetes and any changes that may be needed to your medications.

What should I eat?

Making sensible food choices and adapting your eating habits will help you manage your diabetes and protect your long-term health. The good news is that you should still be able to enjoy a wide variety of food. The diet for diabetes isn't a special diet, because there is nothing that you can't eat. It is just a case of applying some simple rules to your way of eating, trying to stick to them, and getting the balance right.

Follow these steps to a healthy diet and you will be well on your way to a healthier you.

Eat three meals a day

It is really important to eat regularly, particularly if you are on twice-a-day insulin and some other medications. Not only does regular eating mean you help maintain steady blood glucose levels, in turn reducing the risk of developing complications, it also helps you to control your appetite.

- Avoid skipping meals and space out your breakfast, lunch, and evening meal throughout the day.
- If you have a snack between meals, remember to keep it healthy: a piece of fruit, a handful of nut and raisin mix, a low-fat yogurt, or why not try some plain home-popped popcorn, which you could flavor with a little paprika or mixed spices.
- Start the day with a healthy breakfast—cereal with skim or 1% milk and a piece of fruit or granola with some low-fat natural yogurt and sliced fruit, or a glass of juice and maybe some multigrain toast with a little marmalade, jam, or a topping of your choice.
- Lunch could be a healthy sandwich or stuffed pita or something like a pasta, rice, or bean-based salad.
- For dinner, have a form of carbohydrate like pasta, rice, or potatoes and serve with some protein and plenty of vegetables or salad.
- Desserts – if you crave something sweet after your meal, which let's face it, most of us do, then opt for low-fat yogurt, fruit, or a fruit-based dessert which are all healthier choices.

Include starchy carbohydrate foods at each meal

Obviously everyone is different, and if you are trying to lose weight you may be advised to have a little less carbohydrate at each meal, but on the whole carbohydrates should make up about ⅖ of your main meal, examples of which include bread, pasta, chapattis, potatoes, yams, noodles, rice, and cereals. As well as how much, what is important is how quickly carbohydrates are broken down in your body and how quickly they are absorbed. I am sure you have heard of the term Glycemic Index (GI). But what is it and how can it be of help or benefit to you? Basically, GI is a ranking of foods based on their overall effect on blood glucose levels. Slowly absorbed foods have a low GI rating, while foods that are absorbed more quickly will have a higher rating. This is important because choosing slowly absorbed carbohydrates can help even out blood glucose levels when you have diabetes.

Foods are given a GI number according to their effect on blood glucose levels. Glucose is used as the standard reference (GI 100), and other foods are measured against this. It is now known that different carbohydrate-containing foods have different effects on blood glucose levels. For instance, 1oz of bread does not have the same effect as 1oz of fruit. Pasta has a different GI than rice and even boiled potatoes in their skin have a different GI than mashed potatoes.

What are the benefits of slow acting carbohydrates?

Because meals including low GI foods allow you to absorb carbohydrates at a slower rate, they help to maintain even blood glucose levels between meals, which can help you feel fuller for longer. Think about it, if you have a ham sandwich on white bread it will be broken down much quicker than a ham and lettuce sandwich on multigrain bread, making you feel hungry again sooner.

Even for those without diabetes, eating the low GI way may have a role in helping to prevent or reduce the risk of getting Type 2 diabetes in those at risk. Some research has shown that people who have an overall low GI diet have a lower incidence of heart disease.

Lower GI diets have also been associated with improved levels of "good" cholesterol. One or two small changes can make all the difference.

GI lowdown

Individual foods can be categorized into low, medium, and high GI (see the list opposite for a few examples of each). You can see simply which basic foods would make the best GI sense to choose. However, most foods are not eaten on their own. How you cook a food, what you cook and serve it with, the ripeness of a fruit, and the variety of a vegetable will also all affect a food's GI rating. The structure and texture of a carbohydrate have an effect as well.

LOW GI (0–55)
All-bran
Rolled oats
New potatoes
Pearl barley
Nuts and raisins
Milk chocolate
Apple
Multigrain bread
Broccoli

MEDIUM GI (56–69)
Shredded wheat
Baked potatoes
Couscous
Muffins
Mangoes
Pita bread
Beets

HIGH GI (70+)
Cornflakes
Mashed potatoes
Short-grain rice
Scones
Pretzels
Watermelon
French bread

So is it just a case of choosing low GI foods?

To see the whole picture, we also need to look at how much carbohydrate is in a portion of the food, i.e., its Glycemic Load (GL). Where GI tells you how quickly a food is absorbed, it doesn't tell you how much carbohydrate is in it and you need to know both of these to assess exactly how a food is going to affect blood glucose levels. Watermelon, for example, has a high GI but in fact only contains a small amount of high GI carbohydrate so as a result has a relatively low GL. A GL of 20 or more is high, a GL of 11 to 19 inclusive is medium, and a GL of 10 or less is low. To calculate the GL of a food, you multiply the quantity in grams of its carbohydrate per serving by its GI, and then divide by 100.

What else affects GI?

Unfortunately, it is not as simple as just picking low GI foods to follow a healthy diet. Adding fat and protein slows down the absorption of carbohydrates. You can see from the list opposite that milk chocolate has a low GI, and this is because of its fat content. Milk and other dairy products have a low GI because of their high protein content and the fact that they contain fat, so it would not be sensible only to eat foods with a low GI. The GI of a food only tells you how quickly or slowly it raises the blood glucose when the food is eaten on its own. In practice, we usually eat foods in combination as meals—bread is usually eaten with butter or margarine, or as an accompaniment to a meal, for example; potatoes are often eaten with meat and vegetables.

So cutting out all high GI foods is not the answer. The good thing is you can apply the GI concept so that you can lower the overall GI of a meal by including more low GI foods. You need to think about the overall balance of your meals, which should include starchy foods and be low in fat, salt, and sugar.

Putting GI into practice

- Kick start your day with a bowl of oatmeal and some chopped fruit.
- Snack on fruit or dried fruit or try some fruit loaf for something a little more substantial at snack time.
- Add lentils or beans to casseroles or stews or even salads.
- Include more vegetables with your meals.
- Choose wholegrain foods.
- Choose basmati rice, pasta, and sweet potatoes.

Read up on your fat facts

Fat contains more than twice the amount of calories as the same amount of carbohydrate or protein, so by cutting down on fat you will drastically reduce the amount of calories you consume and this in turn can aid weight loss. The type of fat you use can influence your heart health, but remember all fat contains the same amount of calories.

- Cut down on saturated fats—these are hard fats like butter, lard, and fat on meat and in dairy products. Saturated fats have a proven link with raised blood cholesterol and heart disease. Having too much harmful cholesterol in the blood increases the risk of coronary heart disease—one of the biggest killers in the US.

No more than 30g saturated fat for men and 20g per day for women is recommended.

- Trans fats or hydrogenated fats are chemically altered vegetable oils that change liquid oil into a solid fat. Trans fats have also been linked to high cholesterol and are found in cakes, cookies, and pastries. So it is a good idea to cut down on these too.
- Look out for unsaturated fats that are high in monounsaturates, like olive oil, canola oil, and fats that come from some plant sources; these are a much better choice and can even have health benefits like lowering blood cholesterol.
- Omega-3 – research shows that eating a diet rich in long-chain Omega 3 fatty acids, which is found in oily fish like salmon, fresh tuna, herring, and sardines, can help protect against heart disease, has anti-inflammatory properties, and is good for joints. Omega 3 is essential to human health but cannot be manufactured by the body. For this reason, Omega 3 fatty acids must be obtained from food. Aim to eat at least two portions of oily fish per week.

Top tips to cut down on fat

- Finely grate strong cheese like cheddar or Parmesan as it has a strong flavor and you will need less, or use a reduced-fat version.
- Swap whole milk for skim or 1% milk.
- Invest in an oil sprayer for light frying.
- Make sure the oil you use is really hot before you start cooking. Quickly cooking the outside will help reduce the amount of fat it will absorb.

- Remove all visible fat from food before and after cooking—especially chicken skin which can cut the amount of saturated fat by at least one third.
- Choose low-fat spreads and salad dressings.

Go for 5 a day

We all know that the FDA recommends we eat at least five portions of fruit and vegetables a day, but how many of us can say that we actually do? It may seem like a lot but with a little planning you can improve your diet by including more fruit and vegetables.

- Have a sliced banana or other fruit on your cereal with a glass of juice—that's two portions before you've even stepped out of the door!
- A handful of dried fruit for a morning snack.
- A piece of fruit with lunch.
- A large bowl of salad or vegetables with your evening meal and you will have managed to fit in at least 5 portions easily.
  Remember though … go for a variety of fruit and vegetables in a range of colors to give you a good range of vitamins and antioxidants.

Cut down on sugar

You don't need to eliminate sweet foods and sugar from your diet, but cut down and make sensible choices. Do you really need a cookie or cupcake when you would be much better off having a piece of fruit? There is no reason why you can't use ordinary sugar in baking and desserts; good blood glucose control can still be achieved when sugar and sugar-containing foods are eaten, just try to use less or have smaller portions.

Slash the salt

According to the FDA, most of us are consuming up to twice as much as the recommended 6g or less of salt per day.

Evidence shows that a high salt intake is linked to many diseases including high blood pressure, heart disease, and strokes, and may be linked to osteoporosis, cancer of the stomach, asthma attacks, and kidney stones.

If the nutritional label only gives the value of sodium (which is the part of salt associated with health risks) multiply that amount by two and a half to get the salt content, e.g.,: 0.5g sodium x 2.5 = 1.25g salt. The rule of thumb is that a food item containing 0.1g of sodium or less is considered low in salt and a food containing more than 0.6g of sodium is considered high, but it can depend on how much and how often you eat this food.

Roughly 80 percent of the salt we eat is hiding in processed foods and prepared meals or takeout. Only 20 percent comes from the salt we add while cooking or at the table.

Over a third of the salt we eat comes from cereal and cereal products like bread, breakfast cereals, cookies, and cakes so try and choose lower salt varieties of these.

Cut down on salt by using other flavorings like lemon juice, herbs, spices, and garlic. Most bouillon cubes, soy sauces, and prepared soups are high in salt. Sea salt, rock salt, garlic salt, and natural salt are all forms of salt and contain sodium, so try to cut down on all of these to improve your health.

Drink sensibly

It is recommended that women consume no more than two units of alcohol per day, and for men this figure is three units. It may seem like a lot, but the units quickly mount up . . . a unit may be half a pint of ordinary strength lager, beer, or cider, or a single measure of spirits. A small glass of wine (6oz) can contain as much as two units.

- Intersperse your alcoholic drinks with something non-alcoholic like soda water or a low calorie soda.
- Try and spread your alcohol throughout the week instead of having a huge blowout!
- And try also to have a few alcohol-free days.
- Never drink on an empty stomach, as alcohol can make hypoglycemia (low blood glucose levels) more likely to occur for some people on certain diabetes medication.
- Cut back on alcohol if you are trying to lose weight, as alcohol contains empty calories.

Avoid diabetic foods

They sound great—treats for people with diabetes without the guilt. But in reality, diabetic foods still raise blood glucose levels, they contain just as much fat and calories as their ordinary counterparts, they can have a laxative effect, and they are expensive. If you crave a treat once in a while, have a small amount of an ordinary treat.

Shop smarter

So, you now know the basics, but putting it all into practice can seem daunting and a little mind boggling. Try not to worry—all things new can seem hard when you first start out and something that has been so routine for so long like shopping, preparing food, and eating may seem onerous. By following these tips, you should find things easier.

Planning ahead

What I have always found is that a little planning makes everything from shopping to cooking so much easier and cheaper too. Making detailed shopping lists helps prevent impulse buying and picking up extras, and keeps you from throwing as much away that wasn't used or needed.

- Write down a weekly menu plan, from packed lunches to snacks and main meals. Obviously if your weekly plans change slightly, don't worry—just refigure the menu or make and freeze a dish for another day and continue!
- When you are planning, try to think about how you might use leftovers or excess ingredients another day. For example, if you are having a roast chicken one day, then you could make a delicious stock with the carcass. Then, together with any leftover meat, they could both be used in a tasty risotto the next day, along with some added veggies.
- Also, if you have the oven on for some baked potatoes, could you prepare a casserole for the next day at the same time? Where appropriate, could you double up on recipes so you can pop half in the freezer for another day?
- Keep your shopping lists from week to week. This way you can use them again, making adjustments where necessary. If you are shopping online, you can often refer to previous purchases you have made and quickly add things to your cart from these.
- Try to make the most of coupons, freeze extra portions, or even shop with a friend and do some swaps on your bargains!
- Make the most of seasonal ingredients—not only are they cheaper when in season, they often have a far better flavor. Also look out for locally produced goods to keep down those food miles! Take some time to look around your local farmers markets for really good quality, honest fresh food—you'll be amazed at how good it tastes.

Look at the label

You have read all the advice and made your shopping list, so don't let panic set in once you start looking at the labels. There are a number of ways foods may be labeled.

Those labeled as a healthy choice or with a particular health claim like "low salt" may seem like the perfect choice, but you need to look a little deeper than the claim on the package and assess whether it will really be of benefit to you. Some foods may be highlighted as being low in fat, but they could still be high in sugar to maintain a good and acceptable flavor.

Just because something is labeled reduced fat, it doesn't mean that it is necessarily a healthy choice. It simply means it has a lower fat count than the ordinary version which can still be high. It may be easier and more beneficial to look at the other labels as well.

Traffic light labeling

Probably the easiest way to tell whether you are making a healthy food choice is by looking at the traffic light labeling, which many supermarkets and food manufacturers have adopted on their packaging. Look at the package and you can see whether the food you are choosing has high (red), medium (yellow) or low (green) amounts of different nutrients like fats, saturates, sugars, and salts. And it is a great way of comparing different products at a glance.

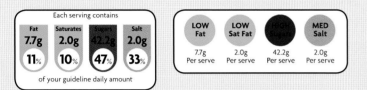

You can see that a red light indicates there is a high amount of an ingredient we should be cutting down on—this would be a food that we shouldn't be having on a regular basis.

A yellow light means that the food is an okay choice, but you would be better choosing something with a green light.

Green lights indicate that the food is a low source of either fat, saturates, or sugar so would be a good choice for healthy eating.

Always aim to choose foods that predominantly have green lights and maybe a little yellow, but as part of sensible eating, you can include foods with red lights but remember not to choose them every time.

Guideline daily amounts

Not all manufacturers use the traffic light system so you may see a Recommended Daily Allowance (RDA) label on some of the foods you buy, such as the example below:

RDA labeling is not quite as simple to use as traffic light labeling as it does require a little calculating and interpreting to see whether this is a good food choice. The label provides you with calories, total fat, sodium, total carbohydrate, fiber, sugar alcohol, and a list of ingredients, and how much, proportionally, that food goes toward your RDA. Choose a food product with a low amount of saturated fat, cholesterol, and sodium and try to select foods with more fiber.

Adapting your own recipes

Being diagnosed with diabetes doesn't mean that you have to banish all your favorite recipes. With a little modification, most recipes can be made healthier and more suited to someone with diabetes, and you won't need to cook separate dishes for the rest of the family either. You can modify your usual recipes by:

- Reducing the amount of fat and type of fat you use.
- Cutting down on the salt.
- Cut down on the amount of sugar they contain—try replacing some sugar with dried fruit in baking.
- Increasing the amount of fiber by using more legumes, fruits and vegetables, and whole wheat and multigrain ingredients.

Make your pantry and fridge work for you

Having a well and imaginatively stocked pantry and fridge makes life in the kitchen so much easier. Add a few things each time you go to the store, then you should never be stuck for something to cook. Some of the recipes in this book use ingredients you may not have heard of or have on hand. Take a look around the larger supermarkets that have fantastic selections of weird and wonderful ingredients from all around the world. Alternatively, visit specialty shops—it really is worth making the effort as it makes the end dishes superb.

Rice
Different types of rice are suited for different dishes.
- Short-grain rice such as arborio or risotto rice and paella rice. Giving risotto rice a stir during cooking releases some of the starch and creates a fabulously creamy dish. The Japanese use short-grain rice, which when cooked becomes sticky and this is great for sushi and other dishes.
- Long-grain rice—the best is probably basmati, giving fluffy individual grains when cooked. Brown basmati is delicious and is higher in fiber.
- Wild rice (which is actually a grain) gives a delicious nutty texture and taste to dishes and is great in salads too.

Pasta
Different shapes are suited to different dishes and sauces.
- The best pasta is made from durum (whole) wheat. Buy the shapes you like or those specified in a recipe. I find if you have lots of different types of pasta in the cupboard you seem to end up with lots of extra with not quite enough for a serving and each with slightly different cooking times!

Noodles
- Rice and egg noodles are quick and easy to prepare—an important player in Asian cuisine.
- Udon noodles are a must for Japanese cooking.

Legumes
- Beans and lentils are a great addition to stews and salads. Dried or canned are great, but obviously for convenience, canned are much quicker.
- Lentils don't require pre-soaking so are quick and easy. Puy lentils are wonderful with a deep earthy flavor and nutty texture and are wonderful in salads and with grilled meat or fish.

Oily fish
- Canned fish in spring water or oil is great for a quick lunch with salad and bread.
- Anchovies can be very salty, but a little can add great depth of flavor to dishes, especially pasta sauces.

Sauces
- Fish sauce (*nam pla*) is an essential in Thai and Vietnamese cooking. It is very salty, so you only need a little.
- Soy sauce and Worcestershire sauce is great for

adding flavor. Again, they are quite salty, so only use a little or use a lower salt version.

- *Ketjap manis* – an Indonesian thick, sweet soy sauce. It can be used as a dip, and also as a substitute for soy sauce in recipes.

Grains

- Bulgar – a staple of the Middle East. Once the grains are soaked and softened, they are a wonderful addition to salads and as an accompaniment to main dishes.
- Couscous – an essential in Moroccan and north African cuisine, simple to prepare and a must with tagines to soak up those fragrant juices.
- Polenta (cornmeal) – a staple in the Italian kitchen, it can either be served served hot—known as wet polenta—or left to cool and set in a dish, and then cut into squares or slices which are fried or grilled to give a light crust.

Herbs and spices

Buy in small quantities as they don't keep their freshness once opened.

Fabulous fridge

Light crème fraiche – a great standby for sweet or savory dishes. It also doesn't split on heating, and so is perfect for sauces.

Parmesan – a little goes a long way as it has such a good strong flavor.

Cottage cheese – virtually fat free, is great mixed with other ingredients like tuna and onion, or a little pesto and grilled bacon for a super healthy lunch on a sandwich.

Eggs – always a great standby for omelets or scrambled eggs—a meal in moments.

And from the freezer ...

Keep a few frozen veggies on standby for those days when the fridge is bare or you are feeling lazy. Frozen berries too for super smoothies and instant desserts.

Diets from around the world

Within each country and continent there are a huge range of cultures and traditions when it comes to food and its relationship within society. It is fascinating to see how different countries embrace their recipes passed down from generation to generation, and to see how these recipes are interpreted across the globe. But with time at an all time premium, many traditions are being eroded by the arrival of ready-made foods that potentially can be much less healthy for you.

India

Spices in all their glory and variety form an intrinsic part of cooking and life itself. Indians take their food very seriously. Cooking is considered an art, and mothers usually begin to teach their daughters and pass down family recipes from an early age. Mealtimes are important occasions for family to get together. Most meals are comprised of several dishes ranging from staples like rice and breads to meat and vegetables and rounded off with a dessert.

In a lot of Indian homes, foods are made from scratch with fresh ingredients. This is changing in bigger cities where people have increasingly hectic lives and ready made ingredients are more readily used. The different regions of India have varying dishes that use the staples and produce that their particular climate and terrain determine.

In the north of India where summers are hot and winters cold, there is an abundance of fruit and vegetables that are used in a huge array of vegetarian dishes. North Indian curries tend to be quite thick and creamy and are usually served with the preferred breads like naan, parathas, and kulchas. Rice is popular in dishes like pilafs and biryanis.

Eastern India is the biggest rice-growing region due to the fact that it has a huge annual rainfall, so most dishes are based around rice, and dishes are kept simple with fish being used on the coast and pork more inland. The people from Eastern India love their sweet foods and desserts!

People from Southern India have a love of hot spicy dishes based on rice.

Over to the west, a *Thaali*, or large plate of mixed foods, is usually served with rices, breads, meat, and vegetable dishes and usually something sweet too! Again, coastal areas use an abundance of the wonderful fresh fish and seafood on offer, where inland the style is a little more frugal.

Indian food at home

Whether you are eating out or you are cooking at home, there are a few tips you should keep in mind to keep the fat and calories down. Indian food is renowned for its use of ghee (clarified butter) which is high in fat and saturates, so use just a little oil instead. If you are dining out, you could ask them to use less or just opt for healthier dishes like tandoori (cooked in a clay oven), tikka, or grilled kebab dishes. Choose plain rice, as pilau rice is fried in oil. Also, ask for your naan plain before it is brushed with ghee.

Eastern Asian diets

The cooking of Japan, Korea, China, and Vietnam are among the most exotic in the world. Looking around our towns and cities, we can see a huge number of restaurants offering these foods showing how popular this way of cooking has become.

In China there are many styles of cooking, but the majority use a simple base of flavorings like, ginger, garlic, scallions, and soy sauce. Northern China is a great producer of wheat, so many meals are based on noodles.

To the East, rice is more plentiful and more widely used. In Southern China, seafood is plentiful and used in many fabulous dishes, including many steamed delicacies.

Think of Japanese food and you probably think of sushi, rice, and a filling wrapped in wafer-thin pieces of seaweed—a really healthy dish as it is almost fat free. But there are a myriad of other techniques and traditions using many ingredients unfamiliar to most of us. Soy beans, made into tofu, miso, and soy sauce are main players in Japanese cuisine. It is thought that Japanese fondness for soy products explains why they have much lower risk of heart disease and cancer than other countries. Rice and noodles are the main staples. Meals generally consist of a variety of dishes with meat each prepared in a different way from raw, grilled, steamed, or deep fried. These dishes are served with rice (or noodles), a light soup, and pickles. While rice is the staple food, several kinds of noodles (udon, soba, and ramen) are cheap and very popular for light meals.

As an island nation, the Japanese take great pride in their seafood. A wide variety of fish, squid, octopus, eel, and shellfish appear in all kinds of dishes from sushi to tempura.

Tips for healthier Asian foods at home

The Chinese use so many different cooking techniques from baking, stewing, and braising to steaming and poaching, some of which are obviously very healthy as they use little or no fat. Stir-frying is what many of us think about when we think of Chinese food and this is a great way to cook healthily. Heat a wok with a little oil until smoking, then quickly add your finely prepared ingredients and cook for a few minutes and then flavor. Don't be tempted to add more oil—if it is looking a little dry, add a little stock or flavorings instead. If eating out, opt for steamed dishes with steamed rice instead of fried ones.

The Americas

America is a true melting pot of food cultures. The traditional basic American foods are now heavily influenced by Italian, Mexican, and Chinese which have become so ingrained in the diet.

Immigrants from Europe stamped their mark on much of North America, each wave of new arrivals making recipes from their native countries, using the ingredients they found available.

Further South, food becomes more soulful— a wonderful blend of native Indian, European, Caribbean, and African cultures with such dishes as jambalayas epitomizing great American recipes.

Cooking the American way at home

South American foods from countries like Mexico, Peru, and Brazil are dominated by spice and, in particular chilli, which seems to appear at the table at every meal in one form or another. The main staples of rice and beans are also a common thread that runs through this vast land.

When many people think of American food, visions of burgers and fries usually come to mind, but even these staples can be good for you. If you are making this at home, use these tips to keep things healthy.

Grill or broil your burger instead of frying, allowing the fat to drip away during cooking. Try not to add cheese and sauces, as this piles on the calories too. Fill the bun with plenty of lettuce and tomato, and if you really must have fries, go for oven-baked ones or make your own thick cut fries by brushing with a little oil and baking until crispy.

Beware if you have a large burger and regular fries at "you know where,"—you could tip the balance and be consuming a whopping 700 plus calories and over 40g fat!

Down Under

In the past 30 years or so, Australian and New Zealand cooking and cuisine has exploded from good basic and staple foods to the ultra modern style it is today and to what is referred to as "Pacific Rim." Influences are gleaned from all over the world, but it is Thailand, Malaysia, Indonesia, and Japan where it draws most of its ideas. Adding spice and flavorings to great seafood and meats and adding twists on recipes from home and southern Europe is its mainstay.

Middle East

Morocco evokes thoughts of spices and plentiful fruits, vegetables, dried fruits, and nuts. Fragrant tagines with couscous is the North African staple.

Further on into Egypt, there is less use of fruits and vegetables but a wider use of legumes and salads and bread becoming a main staple mainly in the form of pita. On to Turkey, where the fertile land provides an abundance of fresh fruit and vegetables and where meals take the form of meze or mixed plates with lots of different salads, purées, and breads to whet the appetite.

Magical Mediterranean

So many countries constitute the Mediterranean that there is no single country's diet to follow. It is really just using the common characteristics and putting them into practice.

It has been scientifically proven that the Mediterranean diet offers many healthy benefits, including helping to protect against arthritis, obesity, diabetes, asthma, and cardiovascular disease.

The Mediterranean diet prides itself on simplicity and freshness. It is not all about superfoods; it is about combining many wonderful foods for a long-term overall health benefit.

There is an abundance and huge array of legumes to even out blood glucose levels. Fresh fruit and vegetables and salads contain many health-giving properties including antioxidants which are found in vitamins A, C and E, lycopene, and beta carotene. Antioxidants are chemical compounds that can bind to free oxygen radicals which are produced naturally in the body, and preventing these radicals from damaging healthy cells.

Most dishes use onions and garlic, and this may help to thin the blood and in turn reduce blood pressure and fight infections.

Fish and seafood are plentiful and are eaten several times a week. It is the good oils (omega-3) in the oily fish combined with the fact that the diet is low in red meat and dairy products which helps to reduce the incidence of heart disease.

Probably the biggest difference between the Mediterranean diet and that of the rest of the world is the source of fat. Roughly 40 percent of the daily calorie intake in the Mediterranean comes from fat, but it is mainly from plant sources such as avocados and of course olive oil. It is these monounsaturated oils that lower bad cholesterol, lower blood pressure, contain antioxidants to help fight cancer, and protect against ulcers.

Let's not forget that the people of the Mediterranean know how to enjoy a glass of red wine. Raising a glass is not only enjoyable, but by stroke of luck also has hidden benefits. Apart from the obvious relaxing and de-stressing qualities we all know the odd drink can give, red wine aids digestion and it contains the antioxidant flavonoid which has an anti-clotting effect and may prevent the oxidation of LDL cholesterol in the blood. One small glass of wine a day can have significant health benefits. But remember—drink alcohol in moderation!

Top Mediterranean tips for you at home

- Use tomatoes frequently—in pasta sauces, on homemade pizzas, fresh in salads, or anyway you can to boost your antioxidant intake.
- Use olive oil in cooking or in dressings.
- Include pasta, wholegrains, and legumes where you can on a daily basis. Try replacing some red meat in dishes with beans for less saturated fat and lower GI too!
- Aim for more oily fish in the diet in place of meat. It has been shown that even ¾ oz of oily fish per day can have significant benefit in the fight against heart disease and can also be good for those who have already suffered from heart attacks.
- Use fresh herbs for flavor instead of salt.

All the information in this book is general. Before undertaking any lifestyle and dietary changes, it important that you liaise with your local doctor, who will give you specific advice tailored to your needs.

Grilled Field Mushrooms Egg White Omelet with Asparagus Textured Kedgeree Hot Herring on Toast *Pa Amb Tomaque* sh Soft Style Muesli Fruit and Nut Nibble Strawberry Oatmea Grilled Field Mushrooms Egg White Omelet with Asparagus Textured Kedgeree Hot Herring on Toast *Pa Amb Tomaque* sh Soft Style Muesli Fruit and Nut Nibble Strawberry Oatmea Grilled Field Mushrooms Egg White Omelet with Asparagus Textured Kedgeree Hot Herring on Toast *Pa Amb Tomaque* sh Soft Style Muesli Fruit and Nut Nibble Strawberry Oatmea Grilled Field Mushrooms Egg White Omelet with Asparagus

matoes on Toast A Textured Kedgeree Hot Herring on Toast Bread Fruity Fresh Soft Style Muesli Fruit and Nut Nibble Str sh Soft Style Muesli Fruit and Nut Nibble Strawberry Oatmea Grilled Field Mushrooms Egg White Omelet with Asparagus Textured Kedgeree Hot Herring on Toast *Pa Amb Tomaque* sh Soft Style Muesli Fruit and Nut Nibble Strawberry Oatmea Grilled Field Mushrooms Egg White Omelet with Asparagus Textured Kedgeree Hot Herring on Toast *Pa Amb Tomaque* sh Soft Style Muesli Fruit and Nut Nibble Strawberry Oatmea Grilled Field Mushrooms Egg White Omelet with Asparagus

d Herbs An Omelet with a Touch of India French Toast with a
Catalan Tomato Bread) Seeded Fig and Walnut Loaf Back-Yo
with Oat Bran, Honey, and Sunflower Seeds Red and Brown Bi
d Herbs An Omelet with a Touch of India French Toast with a
Catalan Tomato Bread) Seeded Fig and Walnut Loaf Back-Yo
with Oat Bran, Honey, and Sunflower Seeds Red and Brown Bi
d Herbs An Omelet with a Touch of India French Toast with a
Catalan Tomato Bread) Seeded Fig and Walnut Loaf Back-Yo
with Oat Bran, Honey, and Sunflower Seeds Red and Brown Bi
d Herbs An Omelet with a Touch of India French Toast with a

Breakfasts and Breads

Amb Tomaquet (Catalan Tomato Bread) Seeded Fig and Wa
vberry Oatmeal with Oat Bran, Honey, and Sunflower Seeds
vith Oat Bran, Honey, and Sunflower Seeds Red and Brown Bi
d Herbs An Omelet with a Touch of India French Toast with a
Catalan Tomato Bread) Seeded Fig and Walnut Loaf Back-Yo
with Oat Bran, Honey, and Sunflower Seeds Red and Brown Bi
d Herbs An Omelet with a Touch of India French Toast with a
Catalan Tomato Bread) Seeded Fig and Walnut Loaf Back-Yo
with Oat Bran, Honey, and Sunflower Seeds Red and Brown Bi
d Herbs An Omelet with a Touch of India French Toast with a

Fruity Fresh Soft-Style Muesli

The Swiss tend to soak their muesli the night before and pop it in the fridge so that it is ready for the morning. Are you that organized? If so, this one's for you.

Serves 2 to 3
⅓ cup rolled oats
⅓ cup toasted wheat flakes
⅓ cup bran flakes
¼ cup mixed seeds (sesame, sunflower, pumpkin)
2 tablespoons dried blueberries
1 dessert apple (McIntosh, Granny Smith, Braeburn)
¼ cup grated carrot
2 teaspoons cider vinegar
½ cup unsweetened apple juice
6 tablespoons low-fat natural yogurt

1 In a bowl combine the rolled oats, wheat and bran flakes, seeds, and dried blueberries.

2 Grate the apple, unpeeled, into the bowl. Mix in the grated carrot and the cider vinegar (this prevents the apple from browning).

3 Beat together the apple juice and yogurt and mix well with the muesli and apple mixture. The muesli is now ready . . . for the morning. Cover and refrigerate until then.

Amount per portion (for 2)
Energy 305 cals, Protein 9.5g, Fat 7.5g, Saturated fat 1.5g, Carbohydrate 53.0g, Total sugars 26.9g, Fiber 6.2g, Salt 0.53g, Sodium 209mg

Amount per portion (for 3)
Energy 203 cals, Protein 6.4g, Fat 5.0g, Saturated fat 1.0g, Carbohydrate 35.3g, Total sugars 17.9g, Fiber 4.1g, Salt 0.35g, Sodium 139mg

Fruit and Nut Nibble

Useful as a snacky pick-me-up or as a topping for your oatmeal or muesli. It's easy to make—and just as easy to eat, so moderation please.

Serves 4
12 dried apricots, chopped
2oz dried cherries
2 tablespoons dried goji berries
½ cup chopped cashews
3 tablespoons whole almonds
3 tablespoons Brazil nuts, chopped
6 tablespoons pine nuts
2 tablespoons vegetable oil
2 tablespoons honey
grated zest and juice of ½ lemon
¾ in piece of fresh ginger, peeled and coarsely chopped

1 Mix together the fruits and nuts. Heat the oil in a frying pan, add the fruit and nut mixture, and cook over low heat for 3 minutes, stirring often. Add the honey and lemon zest and juice.

2 With a garlic press, squeeze the juice from the ginger over the mix and stir well. Store in a glass jar.

Amount per portion
Energy 483 cals, Protein 10.2g, Fat 34.3g, Saturated fat 4.4g, Carbohydrate 35.5g, Total sugars 20.5g, Fiber 4.6g, Salt 0.05g, Sodium 22mg

RIGHT Fruity Fresh Soft Style Muesli

Strawberry Oatmeal with Oat Bran, Honey, and Sunflower Seeds

Oatmeal is the perfect low GI breakfast food, but let's not get too frugal—add some fruit and seeds for extra pleasure.

Serves 2
1 cup whole rolled oats
2 tablespoons oat bran
2 tablespoons sunflower seeds, toasted
1 tablespoon honey
¾ cup strawberries, hulled and coarsely chopped
3 to 4 tablespoons skim milk

1 Put the oats and oat bran in a small saucepan with 1¾ cups of cold water. Bring to a simmer then simmer for 5 minutes, stirring occasionally, until thickened. Add a little more water if you prefer a runnier oatmeal.

2 Divide the oatmeal between two individual bowls, sprinkle with the sunflower seeds, and drizzle with honey. Top with the strawberries and milk and serve.

Variation You can vary the berries to suit your taste.

Amount per portion
Energy 344 cals, Protein 14.0g, Fat 10.5g, Saturated fat 1.6g, Carbohydrate 51.5g, Total sugars 10.1g, Fiber 6.6g, Salt 0.05g, Sodium 19mg

Red and Brown Breakfast Bar

Of course, we always intend to have a good, substantial breakfast, but we often end up eating on the run instead. So, if you're going to have a fruit and nut bar for breakfast, it's got to be better knowing what's in it, and this recipe is just fabulous.

Makes 12 bars
2oz dried cranberries
2oz dried cherries
1oz candied citrus peel
2oz dark chocolate chips
2oz unsweetened muesli
¾oz sunflower seeds
¾oz rice cereal
3oz brazil nuts, chopped
3oz flaked almonds
3 tablespoons honey
5 tablespoons pomegranate juice

1 Preheat the oven to 350°F. Line a rectangular jelly roll pan with parchment paper.

2 In a bowl, mix together all the dry ingredients, then mix in the honey and juice. Transfer the mixture to the prepared pan and smooth to an even thickness.

3 Bake for 15 to 20 minutes until golden, checking from time to time that the mix is not burning. Leave to cool, then refrigerate overnight. Cut into 12 bars and store in an air-tight container in the fridge.

Amount per portion
Energy 178 cals, Protein 3.3g, Fat 10.7g, Saturated fat 2.2g, Carbohydrate 18.4g, Total sugars 13.7g, Fiber 1.5g, Salt 0.02g, Sodium 11mg

Scrambled Eggs on Grilled Field Mushrooms

Taking breakfast just a little bit further, this is a lovely weekend dish.

Serves 2
2 large field mushrooms,
   3 to 4oz each, wiped clean
spray olive oil
freshly ground white pepper
½ teaspoon chopped fresh thyme leaves
4 eggs, lightly beaten
½ teaspoon chopped fresh tarragon
1 teaspoon chopped fresh parsley
1 teaspoon chopped fresh chives
1 tablespoon monounsaturated spread

1 Preheat the broiler. Spray the mushrooms on both sides with a little oil, season generously with pepper, and sprinkle with thyme. Place the mushrooms in an ovenproof pan and add 1 tablespoon of water. Cook under the broiler for 8 to 10 minutes until tender, turning once.

2 Meanwhile, combine the eggs with the tarragon, parsley, and chives and season with pepper. Just before the mushrooms are ready, place a non-stick saucepan or frying pan over low heat and melt the butter substitute. Add the eggs, stir for 30 seconds, then draw the sides of the egg mixture to the center, creating lumpy curds. Cook until done to your liking.

3 Place a mushroom on two separate plates, then spoon the scrambled eggs over the top and serve immediately.

Tips If you have any leftover tarragon, immerse it in a bottle of white wine vinegar or cider vinegar for a delicious splash over grilled fish and chicken, or a soup.
Some people prefer scrambled eggs French style, very smooth with no lumps—very much like baby food—but if you're one of those people, use a whisk instead of a spoon when cooking.

Amount per portion
Energy 235 cals, Protein 17.0g, Fat 19.0g, Saturated fat 4.7g, Carbohydrate 1.0g, Total sugars 0.3g, Fiber 1.0g, Salt 0.53g, Sodium 209mg

Egg White Omelet with Asparagus and Herbs

Egg-white omelets are very popular with health-conscious crowds. By using only the egg whites, you remove almost all the fat content of the egg, as that is concentrated in the yolk.

Serves 2
4 egg whites
1 tablespoon finely chopped fresh mixed
    herbs (chives, tarragon, chervil)
salt and freshly ground black pepper
1 tablespoon monounsaturated spread
8 asparagus spears, cooked, cut into
    1in pieces and kept warm
2 slices wholegrain bread, toasted
cherry tomatoes, halved, to serve

1 Whisk the egg whites with a fork and add the herbs, a pinch of salt, and some pepper.

2 Melt half the spread in a small non-stick omelet pan over medium heat. Pour half the egg whites into the pan and quickly pull the edges to the center with a fork so the omelet cooks evenly. When the omelet is cooked but still soft, place half the warm asparagus in the center and leave on the heat for a second longer. Then fold the omelet in half, giving the pan a light tap to loosen the omelet.

3 Slide the omelet out on to a slice of warm toast and serve with halved cherry tomatoes. Melt the remaining butter substitute and cook the remaining egg whites in the same way.

Amount per portion
Energy 196 cals, Protein 14.0g, Fat 6.0g, Saturated fat 1.2g, Carbohydrate 22.0g, Total sugars 3.3g, Fiber 4.1g, Salt 1.42g, Sodium 559mg

An Omelet with a Touch of India

An omelet is a perfect vehicle to carry a wealth of flavors, as shown here.

Serves 4
8 eggs
5 tablespoons low-fat coconut milk
salt
1 tablespoon sunflower oil
1 onion, finely chopped
3oz button mushrooms, sliced
2 mild green chiles, seeded
    and sliced
4 tomatoes, seeded and diced
1 teaspoon ground cumin
1 teaspoon ground coriander
½ teaspoon ground turmeric
3 tablespoons non-fat yogurt
2 tablespoons chopped fresh cilantro

1 Beat together the eggs and coconut milk, leaving some viscosity in the eggs, and season with a little salt.

2 Place a non-stick omelet pan over medium heat, add the onion, and cook for 6 minutes. Add the mushrooms and chiles, increase the temperature, and cook until the mushrooms have browned. Add the tomatoes and spices and cook for another 3 minutes.

3 Remove three quarters of the vegetable mixture and set aside. Leave the remainder of the mixture in the pan on the heat. Add a quarter of the egg mixture and start drawing the edges to the center, creating eggy curds. When cooked to your liking, add a quarter of the yogurt to the center and sprinkle with a little fresh cilantro. Fold or roll it together, remove it from the pan, and keep warm.

4 Make the other three omelets in the same way, and serve warm.

Amount per portion
Energy 268 cals, Protein 17.6g, Fat 19.0g, Saturated fat 5.7g, Carbohydrate 7.2g, Total sugars 5.5g, Fiber 1.6g, Salt 1.15g, Sodium 456mg

French Toast with a Crunch

Everyone loves egg-dipped French toast, and by using a multigrain bread and muesli, you can make it extra healthy as you are lowering the GI.

Serves 4
1 egg white, lightly beaten
¼ cup skim milk
juice and grated zest of 1 lime
1 teaspoon sugar or low-calorie granulated sweetener
½ cup unsweetened muesli
2 tablespoons dried cranberries, finely chopped
4 slices multigrain bread, each slice halved
1 tablespoon olive oil

1 In a bowl, whisk together the egg white, milk, lime juice and zest, and sweetener. Place the muesli and cranberries on a flat plate and stir to mix well. Dip each piece of bread into the liquid and then into the muesli.

2 Heat half the oil in a large frying pan over low to medium heat. Place half the bread in the pan and gently cook for 3 minutes on each side. Heat the remaining oil and cook the remaining bread in the same way.

Variations Have some fun and instead of cranberries use any other dried berries, such as blueberries or raspberries, or bing cherries. You can also substitute orange for the lime.

Amount per portion
Energy 197 cals, Protein 7.0g, Fat 5.0g, Saturated fat 0.9g, Carbohydrate 33.0g, Total sugars 8.8g, Fiber 3.6g, Salt 0.59g, Sodium 235mg

Spiced Tomatoes on Toast

These spices give fresh tomatoes that extra little kick of flavor, because, let's be honest, unless you grow your own, they can be very bland.

Serves 2
spray olive oil
¼ teaspoon ground coriander
¼ teaspoon fennel seeds
2 scallions, sliced
½ teaspoon ground cumin
2 garlic cloves, sliced
½ teaspoon chili powder
4 medium tomatoes, each cut into 3 thick slices
2 slices multigrain bread, toasted
chopped fresh cilantro, to garnish

1 Spray a frying pan with oil and place over medium heat. Add the ground coriander, fennel seeds, scallions, ground cumin, and garlic, and stir-fry until the spices start releasing their fragrant bouquet. Add the chili powder and the tomatoes and cook for 3 minutes or until the tomatoes start to soften.

2 With a slotted spoon, arrange the tomato slices on top of the toast, retaining the tomato juices. Garnish the tomatoes with chopped cilantro and drizzle with the tomato juices.

Amount per portion
Energy 136 cals, Protein 5.2g, Fat 2.4g, Saturated fat 0.4g, Carbohydrate 24.9g, Total sugars 5.7g, Fiber 3.8g, Salt 0.47g, Sodium 185mg

A Textured Kedgeree

This colonial dish, invented in India to be eaten by the Brits, makes a great weekend brunch. Here I've made a few add-ons to improve the GI rating and by chance, they also heighten the flavor.

Serves 4
1 teaspoon sunflower oil
1 onion, finely diced
1 red chile, seeded and diced
2 teaspoons hot curry paste
1½ cups quick-cook brown rice
2 tomatoes, seeded and diced
10oz hot-smoked salmon, flaked
1 teaspoon ground turmeric
1 tablespoon coarsely chopped
    pistachio nuts
1 tablespoon chopped fresh cilantro
1 teaspoon chopped fresh mint
2 teaspoons chile seeds (spiced seeds)
3 tablespoons non-fat natural
    Greek yogurt
salt and freshly ground black pepper

1 Heat the oil in a frying pan over low heat and cook the onion, chile, and curry paste for approximately 8 minutes.
2 Meanwhile, cook the rice according to the instructions on the package.
3 Add the cooked rice to the spiced onions in the frying pan. Increase the heat and stir in the tomatoes, salmon, turmeric, and pistachios—do this gently so as not to pulp the salmon.
4 Add in the remaining ingredients and mix. Season to taste with salt and pepper and serve warm.

Amount per portion
Energy 407 cals, Protein 23.9g, Fat 10.4g, Saturated fat 2.2g, Carbohydrate 58.2g, Total sugars 4.8g, Fiber 2.9g, Salt 2.52g, Sodium 994mg

Hot Herring on Toast

Called "kippers" in the UK, these herring snacks are delicious and make a great breakfast.

Serves 2
2 herring fillets
2 tablespoons low-fat cream cheese
¼ cup strong Cheddar cheese, grated
½ teaspoon Worcestershire sauce
2 tablespoons non-fat natural
    Greek yogurt
1 tablespoon monounsaturated spread,
    softened
2 slices multigrain bread
freshly ground black pepper

1 Preheat the broiler. Place the herring in a bowl, pour some boiling water over the top, and leave for 4 minutes. Remove the herring and allow to cool, then mash together with the cream cheese, Cheddar, Worcestershire sauce, and yogurt.
2 Butter one side of each piece of bread and season the buttered side with pepper. Set on the grill rack, buttered side up, and grill until brown.
3 Spread the herring mixture on the un-toasted sides and grill until bubbling. Serve with a hot cup of tea.

Tip While I am boiling the water for the tea, I always fill my mug or teapot with hot water—this keeps the tea hot just that little bit longer.

Amount per portion
Energy 443 cals, Protein 27.0g, Fat 29.0g, Saturated fat 7.5g, Carbohydrate 20.0g, Total sugars 2.4g, Fiber 2.1g, Salt 3.03g, Sodium 1193mg

Pa Amb Tomaquet (Catalan Tomato Bread)

Tomato bread, served all over Spain, makes a great breakfast or mid-morning snack. This recipe uses multigrain bread to improve the GI rating, but you could go for a rustic country bread instead if you feel it would give a more authentic result.

Serves 2
2 slices multigrain bread
1 garlic clove
2 large tomatoes, halved
salt and freshly ground pepper
2 teaspoons extra virgin olive oil

1 Toast the bread, then rub the garlic all over—the toast's rough surface will act as a grater. Then rub the cut sides of the tomatoes over the toast until you are left with the skin, which you can discard. Season to taste with salt and pepper, then drizzle modestly with the olive oil.

Variations For an extra treat, a little scattering of crispy bacon would be nice, or if you're on your best behavior, scatter with a few of your favorite seeds—sunflower or pumpkin work well.

Amount per portion
Energy 153 cals, Protein 4.3g, Fat 5.4g, Saturated fat 0.8g, Carbohydrate 23.2g, Total sugars 5.1g, Fiber 3.5g, Salt 1.06g, Sodium 417mg

Seeded Fig and Walnut Loaf

It's a cliché, but you can't beat the smell of freshly baked bread, and you certainly can't beat that touchy-feely experience of hand-crafting loaves. This recipe makes a lovely, dense, crunchy loaf.

Serves 4
1¼ cups unbleached white bread flour, plus extra for dusting
½ cup whole wheat flour
½ oz fast-acting dried yeast
½ teaspoon salt
1 teaspoon superfine sugar
½ cup lukewarm water
¼ cup chopped dried figs
¼ cup mixed seeds (sunflower, flaxseed)
¼ cup chopped walnuts

1 Put both flours, the yeast, salt, and sugar in the bowl of a mixer or food processor with the dough hook attached. Turn the machine on and slowly add the water. When a dough forms, fold in the fruit, seeds, and nuts.
2 Turn out on to a lightly floured work surface, then start kneading and continue for 10 minutes (give yourself a short break from time to time). Shape into a loaf, place on a baking sheet, and leave in a warm spot until it has doubled in size. Meanwhile, preheat the oven to 375°F.
3 When the dough has risen, dust the surface of the loaf with a light snowfall of white flour and bake for 35 to 40 minutes depending on the shape of the loaf; when cooked, the loaf will sound hollow when tapped on the base. Transfer to a rack and leave to cool.

Amount per portion
Energy cals 308, Protein 10.9g, Fat 9.2g, Saturated fat 1.2g, Carbohydrate 48.6g, Total sugars 6.5g, Fiber 3.8g, Salt 0.64g, Sodium 256mg

Bake-Your-Own Multigrain Bread

This delicious nutty multigrain bread is fantastic—it doesn't need to rise so is quick to make, there is no heavy kneading, and it contains loads of slow-release nuts and seeds for lower GI.

Makes 1 small loaf (serves 4)
4 cups spelt flour
½ oz fast-acting dried yeast
¼ teaspoon salt
¼ cup chopped walnuts
3 tablespoons sesame seeds
3 tablespoons hemp seeds
3 tablespoons flax seed
3 tablespoons pumpkin seeds
½ oz dried seaweed, chopped (optional)
1¾ cups warm water

1 Preheat the oven to 400°F and lightly grease a 2 pound loaf pan. Combine all the dry ingredients in a large bowl, then gradually add the water, drawing in the sides of the flour mixture until the dough comes together.

2 Transfer the dough to the prepared pan (no, you don't need to let it rise first; that all happens in the oven). Slash the surface, pop in the oven, and bake for 1 hour. The bread will rise nicely and come away from the sides of the pan. The base of the loaf will sound hollow when cooked.

3 Remove the loaf from the pan and set on a rack to cool. Alternatively, if you prefer crisp sides, take the loaf out of its tin and return it to the oven for 6 to 8 minutes.

Variations Many types of seeds are available; you don't have to follow this formula. Feel free to play around a bit—you could even add a little dried fruit.

Amount per portion
Energy 573,cals, Protein 24.2g, Fat 16.7g, Saturated fat 2.4g, Carbohydrate 86.9g, Total sugars 8.9g, Fiber 8.2g, Salt 0.49g, Sodium 194mg

Carpaccio with Cucumber and Leaves Little Ham Pots Ch
and Rosemary Bruschetta Fried Chicken Livers with Herb
Hot Stuffed Grape Leaves Little Ham Pots Cheese Stuffed
Cod, White Bean, and Honey Eggplant, Red Pepper, and Her
oiled Eggs with Mustard Beans Curried Pickled Eggs Delhi
ice Balls) Asian Surf and Turf Crêpes A Sort of Tom Yam Spic
Squash Soup with Crushed Chickpeas Quick Sweet and Sor
with Borlotti Beans Pistou Harira Avgolemono Soup Fassou
gs with Asparagus Soldiers Spicy Mushrooms on Toast with
Fried Chicken Livers with Herbs and Chile Moutabel with
aves Little

agus with Egg and Cauliflower Sauce Boiled Eggs with Asp
r and Leaves Little Ham Pots Cheese Stuffed Apricots Prese
Fried Chicken Livers with Herbs and Chile Moutabel with
aves Little Ham Pots Cheese Stuffed Apricots Preserved Ora
y Eggplant, Red Pepper, and Herb Salsa Caribbean Salmon
eans Curried Pickled Eggs Delhi Mix The Ultimate Chicken
urf Crêpes A Sort of Tom Yam Spiced Tomato and Coconut S
Chickpeas Quick Sweet and Sour Chicken Soup Fava Bean
ira Avgolemono Soup Fassoulada Spinach and Red Peppe

Snacks, Appetizers, and Soups

Spinach and Red Pepper Omelet Roll

This Korean roll is so versatile—it makes a great snack or supper dish, and is also good for breakfast, although it would probably be best to make it ahead of time as it requires some preparation.

Serves 4
8oz frozen spinach, defrosted
3 roasted red peppers from a jar, drained
    and chopped
1 tablespoon sesame oil
1 tablespoon sesame seeds
2 garlic cloves, crushed to a paste
2 mild green chiles, seeded
    and finely chopped
½ teaspoon chili powder
2 scallions, finely chopped
3 tablespoons reduced-salt soy sauce
6 eggs, beaten
1 tablespoon dry sherry
salt and freshly ground black pepper
spray oil, for frying

1 Squeeze excess liquid from the spinach, then chop it. In a bowl, mix it with the roasted red peppers, sesame oil and seeds, garlic, chile and chili powder, scallions, and half the soy sauce. Set aside. In another bowl, mix together the eggs, remaining soy sauce, and sherry, and season to taste with salt and pepper.

2 Place a non-stick frying pan over low-medium heat and spray with a light coating of oil. Spoon or pour in a quarter of the egg mix, immediately tipping the pan so the egg covers the whole pan in a thin layer. Gently cook for 1½ minutes until cooked all the way through, then transfer it to a clean work surface or plate. Cook the remaining egg mix in the same manner, in three batches.

3 Spread a quarter of the spinach mixture carefully over one of the "omelets" and roll it up into a tight cylinder, then cut it into ¾-inch lengths. Repeat the process with the other rolls.

Tip The rolls can be eaten either at room temperature or hot—warm them up in the microwave or wrap them in foil and pop into the oven. For breakfast, serve it on multigrain toast, and for a more substantial meal, accompany it with new potatoes and a salad.

Amount per portion
Energy 241 cals, Protein 15.0g, Fat 18.0g, Saturated fat 3.7g, Carbohydrate 5.0g, Total sugars 3.7g, Fiber 2.9g, Salt 3.08g, Sodium 1211mg

Asparagus with Egg and Cauliflower Sauce

Australians have fabulous produce and some particularly inventive chefs, such as Bill Granger and Donna Hay, who inspired this dish. This recipe would be delicious served with toasted whole wheat pita bread.

Serves 4

1 cup cauliflower, broken into tiny florets
16 asparagus spears, trimmed
3 eggs
2 anchovy fillets
½ teaspoon chopped fresh rosemary
¼ cup aged sherry vinegar
¼ cup extra virgin olive oil
1 teaspoon snipped fresh chives

1 In a large pot of boiling water, cook the cauliflower florets for 3 minutes. Remove the cauliflower with a slotted spoon, cover to keep warm, and set aside. Plunge the asparagus into the pan and cook for a few minutes (5 to 6 minutes for thick spears), then drain and set aside.

2 Bring a smaller pan of water to a boil and cook the eggs for precisely 4 minutes (set the timer). While the eggs are cooking, chop the anchovy together with the rosemary into a cohesive paste, then place in a warm bowl and beat in the vinegar and the olive oil. Set aside.

3 Once the eggs have cooked, and working quickly, lift them out and hold each with a cloth. Break them in half with the back of a spoon or knife and scoop the contents into the anchovy dressing. Mash together, leaving some texture to the egg white, then fold in the cauliflower.

4 Divide the asparagus between four warmed plates, add the chives to the egg and cauliflower sauce, and spoon over the top of the asparagus. Serve immediately.

Amount per portion
Energy 229 cals, Protein 10.1g, Fat 19.7g, Saturated fat 3.3g, Carbohydrate 3.0g, Total sugars 2.7g, Fiber 2.2g, Salt 0.38g, Sodium 148mg

Soft-Boiled Eggs with Asparagus Soldiers

Soft-boiled eggs are a great fast food, packed with nutrients—a real superfood. Egg and "toast soldiers" (which are just strips of toast) are a popular English breakfast, but here they are wonderfully partnered with crunchy asparagus instead. Serve with a slice or two of toast for extra carbohydrates.

Serves 4
salt
24 thick asparagus spears, trimmed
8 large eggs
2oz Dukkah (see page 257)

1 Bring one large and one medium pan of water to a boil and lightly salt the large pan. Set your timer for 4 minutes 30 seconds, then place the eggs gently into the non-salted water and the asparagus into the salted water. Start the timer.

2 When ready, drain the asparagus and pop the eggs into egg cups (available online or at speciality kitchen stores), allowing 2 eggs per person. Immediately cut the tops off the shells, revealing runny eggs. Place 6 asparagus spears beside each pair of eggs, and serve with a little pot of dukkah. To serve, get the gang to dip the asparagus into the egg yolk then roll it in the dukkah—delicious.

Tip It's important not to overcook the asparagus, so that it remains green and crunchy; floppy asparagus makes for a messy, dribbly experience.

Amount per portion
Energy 298 cals, Protein 22.3g, Fat 20.9g, Saturated fat 4.1g, Carbohydrate 5.5g, Total sugars 3.7g, Fiber 3.7g, Salt 0.44g, Sodium 175mg

Spicy Mushrooms on Toast with Asian Salad

Mushrooms on toast are always a safe bet, but sometimes they cry out for a little extra. Here it is.

Serves 2
1 teaspoon sesame oil
1 teaspoon sunflower oil
1 onion, finely diced
1 teaspoon grated fresh ginger
1 garlic clove, finely chopped
1 fresh chile, seeded and finely chopped
10oz button mushrooms, quartered
½ cup vegetable stock
2 tablespoons *ketjap manis*
     (Indonesian sweet soy sauce)
salt and freshly ground black pepper
2 slices whole-grain bread

For the salad
juice of 1 lime
1 teaspoon sugar
1 teaspoon fish sauce (*nam pla*)
8 cherry tomatoes, halved
2 scallions, sliced
1 tablespoon chopped fresh cilantro
1 tablespoon chopped fresh mint

1 Heat the oil over medium heat, add the onion, ginger, garlic, and chile, and cook until the onion is soft. Increase the heat, add the mushrooms, and cook for 5 minutes. Add the stock and *ketjap manis* and cook for another 5 minutes. Season to taste with salt and pepper.

2 Meanwhile, make the salad. Mix together the lime juice, sugar, and fish sauce, then toss with the rest of the salad ingredients. Toast the bread.

3 With a slotted spoon, remove the mushrooms and place them on the toast. Boil the juices remaining in the pan until no more than 4 tablespoons remain. Pour these juices over the mushrooms and serve with the salad and a slice of lime.

Tip When preparing mushrooms, treat them gently as they are fragile; unless they are old, they rarely need peeling.

Amount per portion
Energy 184 cals, Protein 9.0g, Fat 5.0g, Saturated fat 0.8g, Carbohydrate 27.0g, Total sugars 8.7g, Fiber 4.8g, Salt 2.43g, Sodium 959mg

Tuna Carpaccio with Cucumber and Yogurt

This is a lovely healthy appetizer or light lunch dish, but make sure you use sustainable yellow fin tuna, never blue fin.

Serves 4
11½ oz good-quality tuna
3 tablespoons non-fat natural
     Greek yogurt
1 garlic clove, crushed to a paste
     with a little salt
2 teaspoons chopped fresh mint
salt and freshly ground black pepper
grated zest and juice of 2 lemons
2 tablespoons extra virgin olive oil
½ English cucumber, cut into ½ in dice
multigrain bread, to serve

1 Freeze the tuna for 1 hour—this makes it easier to slice it really thinly. While it is in the freezer, mix together the yogurt, garlic, and mint. Season with a little salt and black pepper and loosen with a little of the lemon juice.

2 With a sharp knife, cut the fish into very thin slices. Arrange the slices onto individual cold plates and drizzle each plate with olive oil and the remaining lemon juice. Scatter the diced cucumber and lemon zest over the top, then dot with the minted yogurt. Serve with a multigrain bread.

Amount per portion
Energy 173 cals, Protein 21.0g, Fat 9.0g, Saturated fat 1.6g, Carbohydrate 2.0g, Total sugars 1.2g, Fiber 0.3g, Salt 0.75g, Sodium 293mg

RIGHT Spicy Mushrooms on Toast with Asian Salad

White Bean and Rosemary Bruschetta

There are plenty of times when you need a good comforting carbohydrate snack, and this Italian one checks all the boxes. Personally, I prefer not to soak dried beans and then cook them, especially when there are so many different varieties of canned beans and legumes available that are all perfectly cooked and ready to use.

Serves 4
4 garlic cloves
½ tablespoon fresh rosemary leaves
1 tablespoon fresh parsley leaves
1 tablespoon extra virgin olive oil
1 (14-oz) can cannellini beans, drained
2 scallions, chopped
3 tablespoons frozen *petit pois* (small peas), defrosted
4 thick slices multigrain bread
freshly ground black pepper

1 With a mortar and pestle or in a small food processor, crush or process together 3 garlic cloves, the rosemary, and the parsley with the olive oil and a splash of water.

2 Cook half the garlic-rosemary paste in a non-stick frying pan over low heat for 3 minutes. Add the beans and toss to coat thoroughly, then cook until heated through. With a fork or a potato masher, coarsely crush the beans, leaving some whole. Fold in the scallions and peas.

3 Toast the bread, then rub each slice with the remaining garlic clove. Spread with the bean mash, then top each slice with a little of the remaining garlic-rosemary paste.

Amount per portion
Energy 219 cals, Protein 9.8g, Fat 4.8g, Saturated fat 0.7g, Carbohydrate 36.3g, Total sugars 3.5g, Fiber 6.6g, Salt 1.16g, Sodium 457mg

Fried Chicken Livers with Herbs and Chile

India meets Italy—big flavors, lovely appetizer.

Serves 4
7oz chicken livers, cleaned and cut in half
1 teaspoon grated ginger
2 teaspoons finely chopped garlic
¼ teaspoon ground turmeric
¼ teaspoon ground cumin
¼ teaspoon ground coriander
1 tablespoon lemon juice
1 tablespoon sunflower oil
1 small red onion, sliced
2 handfuls of baby spinach
2 tablespoons chopped fresh cilantro
2 teaspoons chopped fresh mint
1 tablespoon pine nuts
2 green chiles, seeded and sliced
salt
4 thick slices multigrain country loaf, toasted

1 In a bowl, mix together the chicken livers, ginger, garlic, turmeric, cumin, coriander, and lemon juice. Leave to marinate for 10 minutes.

2 Heat the oil in a frying pan, then add the livers and cook them for 3 minutes on each side, turning once only. Remove them from the pan and keep warm. Add the onion to the pan and cook for 3 minutes, then add the spinach, cilantro, and mint and cook until wilted.

3 Add the livers, pine nuts, and chiles. Adjust the seasoning to taste, adding a little salt if necessary, and toss to combine. Spoon on to the toasted bread and serve immediately.

Amount per portion
Energy 220 cals, Protein 14.5g, Fat 7.3g, Saturated fat 1.2g, Carbohydrate 25.9g, Total sugars 2.8g, Fiber 3.4g, Salt 1.30g, Sodium 514mg

LEFT White Bean and
Rosemary Bruschetta

Moutabel with Chickpeas and Hazelnuts

Moutabel is a bit like that other Middle Eastern eggplant purée, baba ganoush—very addictive, and even more so with my addition of chickpeas and hazelnuts. Serve with vegetable crudités or warm whole wheat pita bread to scoop up this delicious dip.

Serves 4 to 6
2 large eggplants
2 garlic cloves
4 tablespoons tahini (sesame paste)
juice of 1 lemon
2 tablespoons non-fat natural
  Greek yogurt
1 tablespoon extra virgin olive oil
1 (14-oz) can chickpeas, drained
½ cup chopped hazelnuts
freshly ground black pepper

To garnish
2 tablespoons pomegranate seeds
½ teaspoon sweet paprika
chopped fresh parsley

1 Preheat the oven to 450°F. Set the eggplants on a baking sheet and cook for 25 minutes, turning every 5 minutes, until the skin is charred. Transfer the eggplants to a bowl, cover with plastic wrap, and set aside to cool. When cool enough to handle, peel off the skin under running water.

2 In a food processor, blend together the eggplant flesh and garlic until smooth, then add the tahini, lemon juice, yogurt, and olive oil. Pulse briefly to combine. Spoon into a bowl, then fold in the chickpeas and hazelnuts and season with pepper. Serve scattered with pomegranate seeds, paprika, and parsley.

Tip For the best flavor, it's important that the eggplants are well charred.

Amount per portion
Energy 317 cals, Protein 12.0g, Fat 23.0g, Saturated fat 2.3g, Carbohydrate 16.7g, Total sugars 5.9g, Fiber 8.9g, Salt 0.37g, Sodium 146mg

Tzatziki

This yogurt and cucumber mixture is a staple of Greek *mezes*. The various brands available in supermarkets are usually very high in fat, so why buy it when it is so easy to make?

Serves 4 as part of a *meze*
1 cucumber, peeled, seeded, and
  grated or diced
1 teaspoon salt
1 tablespoon extra virgin olive oil
2 to 3 garlic cloves, crushed with a little salt
2 teaspoons white wine vinegar
¼ teaspoon freshly ground black pepper
8oz non-fat natural Greek yogurt
12 mint leaves, chopped
pita bread, to serve

1 Place the cucumber in a colander, sprinkle with the salt, mix well, then set aside for 30 minutes to drain some of the cucumbers' natural liquid. Rinse and pat dry with paper towels.

2 Meanwhile, combine the oil with the garlic, vinegar, and pepper. Whisk in the yogurt and fold in the cucumber and chopped mint. Taste and adjust the seasoning as needed and serve with pita bread.

Tip The easiest way to seed a cucumber is to cut it in half lengthwise and run a teaspoon down the center of each half.

Amount per portion
Energy 66 cals, Protein 6.4g, Fat 2.9g, Saturated fat 0.4g, Carbohydrate 3.9g, Total sugars 2.8g, Fiber 0.5g, Salt 0.36g, Sodium 141mg

Sweet Pea and White Bean Guacamole

I produced this dish on the fly when I was confronted with a bag of frozen peas.
It's rather good, even if I do say so myself, and makes a great dip or accompaniment
to a bowl of chili con carne.

Serves 4
1 tablespoon extra virgin olive oil
2 tablespoons lime juice
2 tablespoons fresh cilantro
2 hot red chiles, seeded and diced
18oz cooked frozen peas, drained
½ teaspoon ground cumin
½ teaspoon ground coriander
1 teaspoon salt
½ teaspoon freshly ground black pepper
2 plum tomatoes, seeded and diced
½ red onion, peeled and finely diced
1 (14-oz) can cannellini beans or other white
    beans, drained and rinsed

1 In a food processor, blend together the oil, lime juice,
cilantro, and chiles until reasonably smooth. Add the peas,
spices, salt, and pepper and blend until smooth (a few
lumps may remain).
2 Transfer the mixture to a bowl and fold in the tomatoes,
onion, and beans. Adjust the seasoning to taste.

Variation Fold in 4 tablespoons of non-fat yogurt along
with the beans at the end.

Amount per portion
Energy 196 cals, Protein 13.2g, Fat 4.9g, Saturated fat 0.4g, Carbohydrate 26.6g,
Total sugars 7.2g, Fiber 10.3g, Salt 2.21g, Sodium 871mg

Hot Stuffed Grape Leaves

I know these won't be everyone's cup of tea, but there is a certain satisfaction in making your own *dolmades*, especially when you can make them to your own personal specification.

Serves 4
½ cup long-grain brown rice
½ lb lean ground beef or lamb
1 (8-oz) can chopped tomatoes
1 small onion, finely chopped
1 teaspoon dried oregano
3 tablespoons finely chopped fresh parsley
3 tablespoons finely chopped celery
salt and freshly ground black pepper
1 tablespoon tomato paste
12 preserved grape leaves, drained
2 tomatoes, sliced
2 garlic cloves, sliced
juice of 1 lemon, or more to taste

1 Preheat the oven to 350°F. Mix together the rice, meat, chopped tomatoes, onion, oregano, parsley, celery, and some salt and pepper. Fold in the tomato paste.

2 Place a grape leaf on a plate, vein-side up. Put a heaping teaspoon of the rice and meat filling in the center, near the stem edge. Fold the stem end up over the filling, then fold both sides toward the middle and roll up like a small cigar. Don't roll too tightly, as the rice will need room to expand. Repeat the process with the remaining filling and leaves.

3 Line the bottom of an ovenproof dish with a layer of tomato slices (or leftover grape leaves) to prevent the stuffed leaves from sticking to the pan and burning. Place the stuffed leaves in layers over the top, pushing slices of garlic here and there between them. Sprinkle with lemon juice and pour over about 1 cup water. Cover with greased aluminum foil.

4 Cook in the preheated oven for 45 minutes or until tender, adding extra water if necessary. Serve as part of a *meze* selection.

Tip Grape leaves are usually sold vacuum-packed, but if you can't find them, try cabbage leaves or spring greens.

Amount per portion
Energy 264 cals, Protein 15.1g, Fat 10.3g, Saturated fat 4.3g, Carbohydrate 29.7g, Total sugars 4.5g, Fiber 2.2g, Salt 1.36g, Sodium 536mg

Little Ham Pots

Classic flavors, lovely finish. This makes a perfect snack with some toasted multigrain bread, or a scrumptious appetizer before dinner. With the exception of the ham and yogurt, you can leave out any of the other ingredients without a problem.

Serves 4

1 cup green beans, cut into ½ in pieces
1 cup frozen *petit pois* (small peas), defrosted
½ lb thickly cut cooked ham, cut in strips or diced
4 cornichons (baby gherkins), quartered
8 baby white pickled onions
1 shallot, diced
1 teaspoon nonpareil capers (baby capers), drained and rinsed
1 tablespoon chopped fresh parsley
freshly ground black pepper
4oz non-fat natural Greek yogurt
2 teaspoons Dijon mustard
1 egg, hard-boiled and chopped
leaf salad and multigrain toast, to serve

1 In a pan of lightly salted boiling water, cook the beans for 3 minutes, then add the peas and cook for another minute. Drain and refresh under cold running water.

2 In a bowl, mix together the ham, beans, peas, cornichons, pickled onions, shallot, capers, and parsley, and season with pepper. In another bowl, combine the yogurt with the mustard, stir in the chopped egg and the ham mixture, and adjust the seasoning to taste. Spoon the mixture into four ramekins and serve with a leaf salad and multigrain toast.

Amount per portion
Energy 148 cals, Protein 19.5g, Fat 5.1g, Saturated fat 1.6g, Carbohydrate 6.4g, Total sugars 3.5g, Fiber 2.5g, Salt 2.13g, Sodium 838mg

Cheese-Stuffed Apricots

This is a typical Australian dish, appropriated from a variety of influences—here, Italy and Greece. It's quick and easy to prepare and makes a great addition to your list of snacks.

Serves 4

8 dried ready-to-eat or fresh apricots, halved
½ cup low-fat ricotta cheese
1 teaspoon chopped fresh mint
1 tablespoon chopped pine nuts
½ mild red chile, seeded and finely chopped
salt and freshly ground black pepper

1 Lay the 16 pieces of apricot, cut-side up, on a work surface. Mix together the remaining ingredients in a bowl. Spoon the mixture into the apricot halves and serve.

Variation If you are feeling a little bit naughty (and everyone needs that moment), a mere whisper of honey drizzled over each apricot is a welcomed addition.

Amount per portion
Energy 80 cals, Protein 4g, Fat 4g, Saturated fat 1.3g, Carbohydrate 8g, Total sugars 8g, Fiber 1.3g, Salt 0.71g, Sodium 280mg

Preserved Orange Duck with Hazelnuts

Preserving food by sealing it in a pot with a layer of fat is a classic tradition. The "authentic" method uses too much fat for a healthy diet, so I've worked out a leaner version.

Serves 8
the raw meat from 6 duck legs, skin and fat removed
¾ cup orange liqueur (Cointreau, Grand Marnier)
grated zest of 2 oranges
1 cup chopped toasted hazelnuts
1 teaspoon green peppercorns in brine
½ lb duck or chicken livers, trimmed
2 egg yolks
2 tablespoons chopped fresh parsley
2 teaspoons chopped fresh mint
freshly ground black pepper
sunflower oil, for greasing
multigrain bread, pickles, and green salad, to serve

1 In a food processor, dice half the duck meat using the pulse setting. Transfer to a bowl and mix with half the liqueur, all the orange zest, the hazelnuts, and peppercorns. In the food processor, grind the remaining meat together with the duck livers and egg yolks. Transfer to a clean bowl, add the parsley and mint, plenty of pepper, and the remaining liqueur, and combine using your hands. Cover both bowls and leave to marinate for 2 hours.

2 Preheat the oven to 350°F. Lightly oil a 25oz terrine mold or terracotta bowl. Place half the ground mixture in the bottom of the terrine mold, then add all of the diced duck, then layer on the remaining ground meat. Cover with foil, put the dish in a deep roasting pan, and pour in enough hot water around the dish to come halfway up its side. Pop the dish in the preheated oven and cook for 1 hour 15 minutes.

3 Remove the dish from the oven, cover with a plate or similar item that fits inside the mold and rests on the preserved duck, and weigh the plate down with a couple of canned goods. Allow to cool, then refrigerate until ready to serve. Serve with fresh multigrain bread, crunchy pickles, and a green salad.

Tip When the preserved duck is ready, it should have shrunk from the sides of the mold.

Amount per portion
Energy 316 cals, Protein 22.5g, Fat 17.0g, Saturated fat 2.7g, Carbohydrate 6.3g, Total sugars 5.9g, Fiber 1.0g, Sodium 124mg

Potato, Garlic, and Shrimp Fritters

By using new potatoes instead of floury ones, and coating the fritters in a nutty dukkah mix instead of the usual batter, you improve on the G.I. rating of traditional fritters. And there's no deep-frying, either—this Indian-influenced version is delicious oven-baked or lightly fried and served with a salad.

Serves 4
1¼ lb new potatoes, quartered
1 tablespoon sunflower oil

For the dukkah spice mix
2 tablespoons sunflower seeds
2 scallions, finely sliced
½ teaspoon ground turmeric
2 garlic cloves, finely chopped
1 teaspoon black mustard seeds
2 tablespoons chopped fresh cilantro
1 teaspoon chopped fresh mint
¼ teaspoon asafoetida powder (optional)
1 teaspoon curry leaves, broken
    or finely chopped
¼ lb cooked shrimp, shells removed
1 egg yolk
2 tablespoons Dukkah (see page 257)
crunchy salad, to serve

1 Cook the new potatoes in boiling salted water until tender, about 20 minutes. Drain, then mash half the potatoes with a fork or masher and lightly crush the remainder. Keep warm.

2 Meanwhile, make the spice mix. Heat the oil in a saucepan over low heat, then add the sunflower seeds, scallions, turmeric, garlic, and mustard seeds. Cook very gently for 4 minutes, stirring often. Add the cilantro, mint, asafoetida (if using), and curry leaves and mix well. Add the spice mix to the potatoes while both are still warm, then leave to cool.

3 Fold the shrimp into the potatoes, then mix in the egg yolk to help bind the mix. Shape into 4 cakes, squeezing them firmly. Refrigerate them for an hour or so to firm up.

4 If baking the fritters, preheat the oven to 350°F. Dip the cakes top and bottom in the Dukkah, pushing the seeds in well. Bake for 20 minutes, turning once. Serve with a crunchy salad made with lots of cucumber, carrots, and radishes.

Amount per portion
Energy 248 cals, Protein 12g, Fat 12g, Saturated fat 1.4g, Carbohydrate 25g, Total sugars 2.2g, Fiber 2.2g, Salt 0.5g, Sodium 197mg

Smoked Cod, White Bean, and Honey

Think of smoked cod in the same way as you would smoked salmon. It's good value, and because it has a "cooked" texture, it is extremely easy to use and makes for a lovely appetizer or supper ingredient, as in this easy Spanish recipe.

Serves 4

13oz undyed smoked cod, skinned and cut into small dice

1 (8-oz) can white beans, drained and rinsed

3 tomatoes, seeded and diced

1 small red onion, thinly sliced

1 tablespoon extra virgin olive oil

1 teaspoon sherry vinegar or balsamic vinegar

2 teaspoons medium sherry (such as Amontillado)

1 teaspoon honey

8 gem lettuce leaves

salt and freshly ground black pepper

crusty multigrain bread, to serve

1 Mix together all the ingredients except the lettuce leaves, and season to taste. Spoon the mixture into the lettuce leaves, and serve with crusty multigrain bread.

Amount per portion

Energy 159 cals, Protein 21.0g, Fat 3.9g, Saturated fat 0.5g, Carbohydrate 10.1g, Total sugars 4.8g, Fiber 2.6g, Salt 2.77g, Sodium 1093mg

Eggplant, Red Pepper, and Herb Salsa

This delicious Thai recipe makes a refreshing salad when tossed with a few jumbo shrimp and some greens, but it also forms a great partnership with plain grilled fish. Serve with crusty bread for extra carbohydrates.

Serves 4

1 large eggplant
1 tablespoon sunflower oil
6 tablespoons reduced-salt soy sauce
6 tablespoons rice vinegar
2 red bell peppers, roasted, peeled, seeded, and cut into 1in dice
2 tablespoons fish sauce (*nam pla*)
1 tablespoon dark brown sugar
1 teaspoon hot chile sauce
4 scallions, finely sliced
1 tablespoon grated fresh ginger
2 tablespoons chopped fresh cilantro
1 tablespoon chopped fresh mint
2 tablespoons chopped fresh flat-leaf parsley
3 garlic cloves, finely chopped
1 teaspoon finely grated lemon zest

1 Cut the eggplant into ¼-inch slices. Mix together the oil, soy sauce, and vinegar. Marinate the eggplant in this mix for 1 hour, turning and basting regularly. Drain well over a bowl to catch any marinade.

2 Cook the eggplant slices—ideally on a grill, but failing that over high heat in a griddle pan or frying pan, for 4 to 5 minutes each side. The eggplant slices should be very dark and thoroughly cooked. Leave to cool.

3 Cut the eggplant slices to match the red pepper dice. Mix all the remaining ingredients together with any remaining marinade, then mix in the eggplant and red pepper. Refrigerate until just before you wish to use, then bring up to room temperature.

Amount per portion
Energy 115 cals, Protein 3.2g, Fat 6.6g, Saturated fat 0.8g, Carbohydrate 11.4g, Total sugars 9.4g, Fiber 3.0g, Salt 3.75g, Sodium 1480mg

Caribbean Salmon Tartare

In the past I would have used tuna or swordfish for this, but as they are potentially threatened with extinction, it's best to use a sustainable fish.

Serves 4 as a starter, or 8 for *meze*
11½ oz raw salmon fillet, finely diced
4 scallions, finely chopped
2 tablespoons lime juice
1 teaspoon finely diced fresh red chile
2 tablespoons avocado oil
1 teaspoon honey
2 tablespoons finely chopped fresh cilantro
1 teaspoon grated ginger
1 mango, cut into small dice
¼ pineapple, peeled and finely diced
fresh cilantro, to garnish
lime wedges, to serve

1 About 1 hour 30 minutes before serving, combine all the ingredients except the cilantro garnish and lime wedges.
2 Place an oiled ring mold onto an individual plate and push a quarter of the mixture into the mold (or an eighth if serving as *meze*), then remove the mold. Repeat with the remaining tartare mixture. Serve garnished with cilantro and lime wedges and bread on the side.

Tip Rubbing your hands with oil will protect them from the heat of the chiles.

Amount per portion
Energy 484 cals, Protein 36.5g, Fat 30.6g, Saturated fat 4.1g, Carbohydrate 16.6g, Total sugars 16.1g, Fiber 2.5g, Salt 0.21g, Sodium 84mg

Salmon Tartare

Based on that French classic, steak tartare, this is a great starter or light lunch served with toasted multigrain bread for an added crunch.

Serves 4
11½ oz very fresh salmon, skinned
    and finely diced
1 teaspoon English mustard
    (such as Colman's)
2 teaspoons capers, rinsed and
    finely chopped
2 scallions, finely chopped
1 sweet gherkin, finely diced
1 teaspoon Worcestershire sauce
½ teaspoon Tabasco sauce
juice of 1 lemon
1 tablespoon good-quality olive oil
2 teaspoons chopped fresh parsley
freshly ground black pepper
multigrain bread, to serve

1 Combine all the ingredients, mixing well to combine the flavors, and season to taste. Line 4 molds with plastic wrap and fill with the mixture, then refrigerate for 20 minutes to set the shape. Turn out on to chilled plates and serve with multigrain bread or toast.

Variations To take the powerful ingredients, you need a strongly flavored fish with an oily base, so very fresh tuna or mackerel also work well.

Amount per portion
Energy 178 cals, Protein 16.8g, Fat 11.9g, Saturated fat 2.2g, Carbohydrate 0.9g, Total sugars 0.6g, Fiber 0.2g, Salt 0.33g, Sodium 131mg

RIGHT Caribbean
Salmon Tartare

Sea Bass, Fennel, and Citrus Ceviche

Raw fish must be über fresh to be delicious. With this recipe and its marinade, there is a cooked effect, so you don't even have to tell your friends it's raw. Serve with bread for extra carbohydrate.

Serves 4
2 fresh sea bass fillets, about 11½ oz in total, skinned and pin-boned
½ teaspoon salt
juice of 2 limes
2 mild fresh red chiles, seeded and cut into thin strips
1 garlic clove, crushed to a paste with a little salt
1 pink grapefruit
1 navel orange
½ red onion, very thinly sliced
1 fennel bulb, very thinly sliced
freshly ground black pepper
1 tablespoon shredded fresh mint leaves, to garnish
2 teaspoons extra virgin olive oil

1 Slice the bass fillets into ½-inch wide strips. Place them in a bowl and sprinkle over the salt, then set aside for 20 minutes during which time the fish will "tighten" and start to "cook." Rinse and dry them well with paper towels, return them to a clean bowl, and add the lime juice, chiles, and garlic. Toss to coat all the fish pieces and leave for 15 minutes to "cook" by marinating in the acid lime juice.

2 Meanwhile, peel the grapefruit and orange. Hold the fruit over a bowl to catch the juice and with a small sharp knife, cut down both sides of each segment as close to the membrane as you can, then ease the flesh out into the bowl. Squeeze the membranes over the bowl to release any remaining juice. Mix in the onion and fennel.

3 Just before serving, add the citrus fruit mix to the fish and its juices and season with pepper. Arrange between 4 cold plates, scatter with mint, and drizzle with olive oil.

Variations Use any really fresh fish, such as salmon or mackerel. A few sprouting seeds (mung beans) scattered over the top of the ceviche makes for good GI.

Amount per portion
Energy 143 cals, Protein 17.3g, Fat 4.3g, Saturated fat 0.7g, Carbohydrate 9.4g, Total sugars 8.8g, Fiber 2.5g, Salt 0.79g, Sodium 310mg

Soft Boiled Eggs with Mustard Beans

This variation on a great British tradition is so simple but so delicious, especially if you grow your own beans in the garden. Just be sure not to overcook the eggs—you want semi-runny yolks to bring a gooey sunshine to the plate.

Serves 4

4 large eggs
⅓ lb extra fine green beans or thinly
    sliced runner beans
2 shallots, thinly sliced
4 radishes, thinly sliced
3 tablespoons toasted chopped hazelnuts

For the dressing

2 tablespoons extra virgin olive oil
2 tablespoons non-fat natural
    Greek yogurt
1 tablespoon Dijon mustard
1 tablespoon cider vinegar
salt and freshly ground black pepper

1 In a pot of boiling water, cook the eggs for 5 minutes 30 seconds. Drain, refresh under cold running water, and peel when cool enough to handle.

2 In another pot of boiling salted water, cook the beans for 4 minutes, then drain but do not refresh. While the beans are still hot, toss in the shallots, radishes, and hazelnuts.

3 Make the dressing by whisking together all the ingredients; add a little water if necessary to thin down. Stir the dressing into the beans and arrange on to individual plates. Cut the eggs in half and place on top of the beans. This is excellent served as a bruschetta on multigrain toast.

Tip If you're a fan of the runner bean, as I am, buy yourself a bean slicer—the perfect little gadget for slicing beans in a couple of moves.

Amount per portion

Energy 206 cals, Protein 10.6g, Fat 16.8g, Saturated fat 2.9g, Carbohydrate 3.3g, Total sugars 2.4g, Fiber 1.8g, Salt 1.14g, Sodium 448mg

Curried Pickled Eggs

I'm a bit of a pickled egg fan, but most readily available ones are submerged in a boring vinegar solution, so this recipe will produce a snack egg that says, "Hello," and "Wow!"

Makes 12, serves 4
2 cups cider vinegar
2 dried chiles
6 green cardamom pods
2 tablespoons coriander seeds
½ teaspoon celery seeds
½ teaspoon yellow mustard seeds
1 teaspoon curry paste or powder
2 cloves
1 teaspoon ground turmeric
6 garlic cloves, lightly crushed
½ teaspoon sugar
¼ teaspoon salt
1 red onion, sliced into rings
12 eggs, hard-boiled and peeled

1 In a non-reactive saucepan, combine all the ingredients except the onion and eggs. Bring to a boil and simmer for 10 minutes. Set aside to cool.

2 Meanwhile, layer the onion rings and eggs in a large clean preserving jar. Strain the vinegar on to the eggs to cover completely, topping off if necessary with extra vinegar. Seal tightly and allow the flavors to develop for at least 1 week before eating. Refrigerate after opening.

Variation Quail's eggs make a nice cocktail snack (they are hard-boiled in 5 minutes). Allow four quail's eggs for every hen's egg.

Amount per portion
Energy 318 cals, Protein 24.7g, Fat 21.2g, Saturated fat 5.5g, Carbohydrate 7.6g, Total sugars 3.1g, Fiber 0.6g, Salt 1.09g, Sodium 428mg

Delhi Mix

This delicious snack mix with an Indian influence is nothing like the well-known Bombay or Punjabi mix. The recipe makes loads; in an airtight container, it will keep for a couple of months—you'll finish it off much quicker than that, but limit yourself to a handful a day.

Serves 4
2oz unsweetened puffed rice
6 tablespoons chopped pine nuts
5 tablespoons chopped dried figs
3oz unsalted plain potato chips, crushed
5 tablespoons coarsely chopped cashew nuts
3 tablespoons brazil nuts, coarsely chopped
2 tablespoons sunflower oil
¼ teaspoon asafoetida powder (optional)
1 teaspoon garlic powder
1 teaspoon ground turmeric
1 teaspoon chili powder
1 teaspoon dried parsley
1 teaspoon confectioners' sugar
½ teaspoon salt

1 Mix together the puffed rice, pine nuts, dried figs, chips, cashews, and brazil nuts. Heat the oil in a frying pan, add the spices and dried parsley, and cook gently for 1 minute. Pour the mixture over the dry mix. Place everything in a plastic container or bag, along with the sugar and salt, and shake well. Store until needed.

Amount per portion
Energy 462 cals, Protein 9.1g, Fat 31.8g, Saturated fat 5.4g, Carbohydrate 37.4g, Total sugars 12.8g, Fiber 3.2g, Salt 0.77g, Sodium 306mg

The Ultimate Chicken Sandwich

This is a delicious sandwich, but to make it you'll have to stock your pantry with a couple of Middle Eastern products. Sumac and za'atar are well worth having, and can be found in Middle Eastern speciality stores or via the internet.

Serves 4
2 chicken breasts, thinly sliced
2 small red onions, thinly sliced
½ tablespoon harissa paste
3 garlic cloves, crushed to a paste
    with a little sea salt
1 teaspoon allspice
½ teaspoon ground cinnamon
1 tablespoon sumac
2 tablespoons extra virgin olive oil
grated zest and juice of ½ lemon
salt and freshly ground black pepper
1 tablespoon za'atar

To serve
4 whole wheat pita breads
a handful of arugula
2 tomatoes, thinly sliced
2 tablespoons non-fat natural
    Greek yogurt
3 tablespoons toasted pine nuts

1 In a large bowl, mix together the chicken slices, onions, harissa, garlic, spices, oil, lemon juice and zest, and add salt and pepper to taste. Leave to marinate for a couple of hours or overnight, if possible.

2 Heat a large frying pan and cook the chicken and its marinade over medium heat for 8 to 10 minutes, stirring regularly, until caramelized with lovely brown onions. Sprinkle with za'atar.

3 Just before the chicken is ready, toast or warm the pita bread, and cut a pocket along the side of each. Place a little arugula in each, along with a few slices of tomato. Spoon in the chicken mix and top with a bit of yogurt and a few pine nuts. Serve immediately.

Amount per portion
Energy 352 cals, Protein 26g, Fat 13g, Saturated fat 2g, Carbohydrate 35g, Total sugars 5.2g, Fiber 4.4g, Salt 2.63g, Sodium 1034mg

Chicken, Bacon, and Avocado Sandwich

Avocado is a misunderstood fruit—it is certainly not low in calories, but it has good monounsaturated fat and its superfood benefits (it's rich in antioxidants and high in potassium) must surely outweigh its downside. In any case, for this classic sandwich, I'm only using a quarter avocado per person, so no need to worry.

Serves 4

1 ripe avocado
7oz canned chickpeas, drained and rinsed
½ teaspoon ground cumin
juice of 1 lime
2 tomatoes, seeded and diced
1 red chile, seeded and finely chopped
1 teaspoon chopped fresh cilantro, plus
    4 sprigs to garnish
salt and freshly ground black pepper
4 slices bacon
1 cooked chicken breast, sliced into
    8 pieces
4 slices country-style multigrain bread

1 Mash the avocado, leaving a little texture. Fold in the chickpeas, cumin, lime juice, tomatoes, chile, and cilantro and season to taste with salt and pepper. Cover tightly with plastic wrap and set aside to let the flavors develop.

2 Grill the bacon until crisp, and cut each into 4 pieces. Spoon the avocado mixture on to the bread slices, scatter the bacon over the top, and place 2 pieces of chicken on each. Garnish with a sprig of cilantro.

Amount per portion
Energy 307 cals, Protein 21.5g, Fat 12.6g, Saturated fat 2.4g, Carbohydrate 28.6g, Total sugars 3.3g, Fiber 5.3g, Salt 2.27g, Sodium 896mg

Arrancine (Stuffed Rice Balls)

There's something very satisfying about crispy rice balls with a surprise filling, and a bonus is that they represent good value. This version of Italian rice balls does require a bit of preparation, so it's best to prepare the mixture in advance. Also, they are quite high in calories, so should probably be limited to special occasions.

Serves 4
1¾ cups brown rice, rinsed
3 eggs, beaten
¼ cup grated Parmesan
salt and freshly ground black pepper
1 tablespoon olive oil
1 onion, finely diced
1 garlic clove, chopped
1 chile, seeded and finely diced
1 celery rib, finely diced
6oz ground beef
1 tablespoon tomato paste
½ cup tomato sauce
½ cup red wine
½ teaspoon chopped fresh thyme
pinch of ground cinnamon
7oz canned lentils, drained
1 cup flour, seasoned with salt and pepper
1 cup breadcrumbs
2 tablespoons linseed or flax seed oil
spray sunflower oil
pasta or new potatoes and salad, to serve

1 Cook the rice in salted boiling water according to the instructions on the package. Drain well, then turn it out on to a cool work surface or large flat platter. Fold in a third of the beaten egg and all the cheese, along with some salt and pepper. Mix well and set aside to cool.

2 Meanwhile, heat the oil in a large pan and cook the onions, garlic, chile, and celery for 8 to 10 minutes. Add the ground beef and brown all over, stirring it into the onion mix. Add the tomato paste, sauce, wine, thyme, and cinnamon. Simmer until thick, about 20 to 30 minutes. Fold in the lentils, adjust the seasoning to taste, and let cool.

3 When both the rice mix and the meat mixture have cooled, put the seasoned flour, remaining beaten eggs, and breadcrumbs into three separate flat bowls. Grab a small amount of rice in one hand and make an indent in the center. Fill the hole with a large teaspoonful of meat mixture, then carefully cover the hole by shaping the rice around the filling, sealing it completely. Your stuffed rice balls should be approximately 3 inches in diameter. Roll the ball in the flour, then the egg (coating completely), and then in the breadcrumbs. Refrigerate while you make the remainder.

4 Preheat the oven to 350°F. Spray the rice balls lightly with oil, set them on a baking sheet, and transfer to the oven. Cook for 20 minutes, turning at least twice. Serve with pasta or new potatoes, and a salad.

Amount per portion
Energy 766 cals, Protein 31.6g, Fat 22.1g, Saturated fat 7.1g, Carbohydrate 115.1g, Total sugars 7.8g, Fiber 6.6g, Salt 1.88g, Sodium 742mg

Asian Surf and Turf Crêpes

Crêpes are always a useful (not to mention healthy) package for all sorts of fillings. Asian flavors make this a very addictive dish.

Serves 8 as an appetizer or 4 as a main

For the batter
⅔ cup cornstarch
2 cups rice flour
1¼ cups low-fat coconut milk
1 cup water

For the filling
6oz pork fillet, thinly cut
16 raw tiger shrimp, shell-off,
    deveined, and split in half lengthwise
2 tablespoons fish sauce (*nam pla*)
1 teaspoon crushed garlic
2 shallots, finely chopped
4 scallions, finely sliced
1 cup sprouting seeds (mung beans)
1 tablespoon superfine sugar or granulated
    low-calorie sweetener
1 teaspoon freshly ground black pepper
2 tablespoons sunflower oil
½ cup beansprouts
½ cup frozen peas, defrosted
1¼ cups button mushrooms, sliced

To serve
baby gem lettuce leaves
fresh mint leaves
fresh cilantro
Vietnamese dipping sauce (see page 107)

1 To make the batter, put all the batter ingredients in a food processor. Process until smooth, then pass through a fine sieve into a bowl and set aside.

2 Put the pork and shrimp together in a large bowl. Add the fish sauce, garlic, shallots, scallions, mung beans, sugar, and pepper and mix well. Set aside to marinate for at least 30 minutes.

3 Heat 1 tablespoon of the oil in a frying pan. Add the pork and shrimp mix and stir-fry over high heat for 2 minutes. Transfer the pork and shrimp to a flat dish and divide into 8 portions.

4 Heat the remaining oil in a small frying pan. Quickly whisk the batter, then pour a small amount into the pan and swirl to cover the base. Immediately add one-eighth of the pork and shrimp and a scattering of the vegetables. Reduce the heat to low, cover with a lid, and cook for 5 minutes. Fold the crêpe in half and then in half again, and slide it onto a plate and keep warm. Repeat the process to make 8 stuffed crêpes.

5 To eat, rip off a piece of crêpe, pop in a piece of lettuce, top with mint and cilantro, and drizzle with dipping sauce.

Amount per portion (sugar)
Energy 626 cals, Protein 29g, Fat 19g, Saturated fat 10g, Carbohydrate 90g, Total sugars 6.6g, Fiber 3.2g, Salt 1.78g, Sodium 1080mg

Amount per portion (low-calorie sweetener)
Energy 613 cals, Protein 29g, Fat 19g, Saturated fat 10g, Carbohydrate 87g, Total sugars 3.1g, Fiber 3.2g, Salt 1.78g, Sodium 1079mg

A Sort of Tom Yam

I say sort of, because to make this classic Asian soup more GI-friendly, I've added a few extra ingredients—but it's just as delicious as the original.

Serves 4

4 boneless skinless chicken thighs, each cut into 6 pieces
1½ quarts chicken stock
2 stalks of lemongrass, heavily bruised with the back of a knife
¾ in piece of galangal (optional), bruised
¾ in piece of fresh ginger, peeled and bruised
1 large onion, coarsely chopped
1 sweet potato, cut into ½ in dice
1 carrot, cut into thin rounds
1 cup cauliflower, broken into small florets
1 (14-oz) can white cannellini beans, drained and rinsed
6 baby sweetcorn, halved
2 bird's-eye chiles, seeded and finely chopped
4 kaffir lime leaves
3 tablespoons chopped fresh cilantro
2 scallions, sliced
1 tablespoon fish sauce (*nam pla*)
2 tablespoons lime juice

1 Wash the chicken pieces then place them in a large saucepan with the stock, lemongrass, galangal if using, ginger, onion, sweet potato, and carrot. Bring to a boil then reduce the heat and simmer for 15 minutes.

2 Add the cauliflower, beans, sweetcorn, chiles, and kaffir lime leaves, and cook for another 8 minutes. Remove the lemongrass, galangal, and ginger and discard.

3 Add the cilantro, scallions, fish sauce, and lime juice, and serve immediately.

Amount per portion
Energy 358 cals, Protein 48.8g, Fat 5.6g, Saturated fat 1.6g, Carbohydrate 30.3g, Total sugars 10.1g, Fiber 7.3g, Salt 2.75g, Sodium 1086mg

Spiced Tomato and Coconut Soup

An unusual and delicious soup with a strong Indian background. The coconut makes it quite high in fat but it is quick and easy to make, so maybe save it for special occasions.

Serves 4
1 cup desiccated coconut
1 cup warm water
1 tablespoon sunflower oil
1 large onion, finely chopped
1 small carrot, cut into ½ in dice
2 garlic cloves, finely chopped
1 teaspoon brown mustard seeds
1 teaspoon cumin seeds
¼ teaspoon asafoetida powder (optional)
8 curry leaves, crumbled
2 (14-oz) cans chopped tomatoes
1 (14-oz) can navy beans, rinsed and
    drained
1 teaspoon chili powder
1 teaspoon ground turmeric
1 teaspoon garam masala
1 teaspoon superfine sugar
salt and freshly ground black pepper
crusty multigrain bread, to serve

1 Soak the desiccated coconut in the warm water for 20 minutes.
2 Meanwhile, heat the oil in a saucepan, add the onion, carrot, garlic, mustard seeds, cumin, asafoetida, and curry leaves and gently cook for 8 minutes to soften the onions. Add the tomatoes, beans, chili powder, and turmeric and simmer for 15 minutes.
3 Transfer the coconut and its soaking water to a blender and blend to a smoothish paste. Mix with the tomato and bean mixture, along with the garam masala and sugar, and heat gently but do not allow to boil. Season to taste with salt and pepper and serve with crusty multigrain bread.

Amount per portion
Energy 320 cals, Protein 9.2g, Fat 22.1g, Saturated fat 15.8g, Carbohydrate 22.6g, Total sugars 11.4g, Fiber 11.0g, Salt 1.01g, Sodium 401mg

Chilled Cucumber and Honeydew Soup with Mint

When people have a craving for chilled soup, they usually turn to a Spanish tomato gazpacho or French potato and leek vichyssoise. I was offered this in Brunei, located on the coast of Borneo; it's lovely and really refreshing on a hot summer's day.

Serves 4
1 honeydew melon, peeled and seeded
1 cucumber
7oz non-fat natural Greek yogurt
12 mint leaves, plus extra shredded leaves
    for garnish
grated zest and juice of 2 limes
½ teaspoon salt
¼ teaspoon ground pepper
½ teaspoon superfine sugar
1 tablespoon toasted sunflower seeds
1 mild red chile, seeded and finely diced
2 teaspoons mint sauce

1 Cut three quarters of the melon and cucumber into large chunks, and the remainder into small dice.
2 In a food processor, blend together the large chunks, the yogurt, whole mint leaves, lime zest and juice, salt and pepper, and sugar. When the mixture is smooth, stir in the small dice of melon, cucumber, and the sunflower seeds. Spoon into individual chilled bowls and garnish with shreds of mint leaves, chile, and a drizzle of mint sauce.

Amount per portion
Energy 106 cals, Protein 7.4g, Fat 1.8g, Saturated fat 0.2g, Carbohydrate 16.0g, Total sugars 14.7g, Fiber 1.7g, Salt 0.89g, Sodium 352mg

Roast Butternut Squash Soup with Crushed Chickpeas

This is a delicious Australian recipe. Butternut squash is one of my favorite vegetables, but its GI rating is not great, so I've compensated by coming up with a delicious garnish.

Serves 4

2 onions, each cut into 6 wedges
8 garlic cloves
1 butternut squash, unpeeled, cut in half lengthwise, seeded, each half cut into 4 wedges
2 teaspoons chopped fresh thyme
salt and freshly ground black pepper
spray olive oil
1½ quarts vegetable stock
1 (14-oz) can chickpeas, drained and rinsed
1 tablespoon extra virgin olive oil
1 cup frozen *petit pois* (small peas), defrosted
1 fresh red chile, seeded and chopped
1 tablespoon chopped fresh parsley

1 Preheat the oven to 400°F. Place the onions in a bowl, add 6 of the garlic cloves, all the squash and thyme, and grind some black pepper over the top. Spray with oil and toss well to coat. Transfer the mixture to a roasting pan, pop in the oven, and roast for about 35 minutes, tossing regularly—keep an eye on the garlic, you don't want it to burn.

2 Remove from the oven. When cool enough to handle, scrape the butternut flesh from the skin and add it to a food processor along with the roast onion and garlic and any juices from the pan. Process until semi-smooth (it's nice to retain a little texture). Transfer the mixture to a saucepan along with the stock and bring to a boil, then check the seasoning and adjust to taste.

3 In another bowl, mash half the chickpeas with a fork and mix with the remaining whole chickpeas. Chop the remaining garlic. Heat the olive oil in a frying pan and cook the garlic along with the mixed chickpeas, the peas, chile, and parsley, for 3 minutes at most.

4 Season to taste and pour the soup into warmed bowls, then spoon the chickpea mix on to the surface.

Variations Where does it end? I could suggest using cilantro instead of parsley, or adding some cumin seeds to the roasting process, or a teaspoon of harissa to the chickpeas—all would go together incredibly well.

Amount per portion
Energy 248 cals, Protein 10.8g, Fat 6.3g, Saturated fat 0.6g, Carbohydrate 39.6g, Total sugars 17.3g, Fiber 10.2g, Salt 1.89g, Sodium 746mg

Quick Sweet-and-Sour Chicken Soup

Whenever I was sick, my mother would give me a bowl of chicken soup to warm me up and make me feel better. This soup has all the benefits, but loads more flavor.

Serves 4

3 shallots, chopped
1 teaspoon crushed black peppercorns
5 garlic cloves, finely chopped
1 tablespoon shrimp paste (*balchan*)
1 tablespoon sunflower oil
1¼ quarts chicken stock
1 tablespoon chopped fresh ginger
1 hot fresh chile, seeded and finely sliced
½ cup tamarind juice (use 1 part tamarind
    paste to 3 parts water)
1 unripe papaya, cut into matchsticks
1lb cooked chicken, thinly shredded
a handful of baby spinach leaves
1 tablespoon honey
juice of 1 lime
1 tablespoon fish sauce (*nam pla*)
4 scallions, finely chopped

To garnish

1 tablespoon fresh cilantro
2 teaspoons shredded fresh mint leaves

1 In a small food processor, blend together the shallots, peppercorns, garlic, and shrimp paste.

2 Heat the oil in a large pan over medium heat, then cook the shallot paste for 1 minute. Add the chicken stock and bring to a boil. Add the ginger, chile, and tamarind juice and cook for 3 minutes.

3 Fold in the papaya, chicken, spinach, honey, lime juice, fish sauce, and scallions. Heat for 2 minutes to warm through. Garnish with cilantro and mint leaves.

Tip Shrimp paste (*balchan*) and fish sauce (*nam pla*) are usually available in Asian food stores.

Amount per portion
Energy 339 cals, Protein 42.4g, Fat 11.9g, Saturated fat 3.2g, Carbohydrate 16.8g, Total sugars 9.8g, Fiber 2.5g, Salt 1.97g, Sodium 778mg

Fava Bean and Pasta Soup

Cans of beans are always a useful pantry ingredient and an excellent way of saving time rather than having to soak beans overnight.

Serves 4
1 tablespoon olive oil
2 onions, finely chopped
1 fennel bulb, finely diced
1 teaspoon fennel seeds
2¼ quarts vegetable stock
2 (14-oz) cans fava, navy, or flageolet
    beans, drained and rinsed
2 cups small macaroni or ditalini
4 tomatoes, seeded and diced
1 tablespoon chopped fresh fennel fronds
    or dill fronds
salt and freshly ground black pepper
crusty multigrain bread, to serve

1 Heat the oil in a large saucepan over low heat. Cook the onions and fennel until softened, about 10 to 12 minutes. Add the fennel seeds and stock, bring to a boil, and simmer for 20 minutes.

2 Add half the beans, return to a boil, then remove from the heat. Leave to cool slightly, then purée in a food processor or blender.

3 Return the smooth soup to the saucepan, then add the pasta and cook for 10 to 12 minutes, stirring regularly, until the pasta is cooked but retains some firmness. Add the remaining beans, along with the tomatoes and fennel fronds, bring back to temperature, and season to taste with salt and pepper. Serve with hot crusty multigrain bread.

Amount per portion
Energy 418 cals, Protein 19.8g, Fat 6.5g, Saturated fat 0.6g, Carbohydrate 74.8g, Total sugars 13.0g, Fiber 12.5g, Salt 2.73g, Sodium 1077mg

Chickpea and Cabbage Soup

A wonderful warming French soup for cold winter days.

Serves 4
1 tablespoon extra virgin olive oil, plus
    extra for drizzling
1 onion, finely chopped
3 garlic cloves, finely chopped
2 bay leaves
1 teaspoon fresh thyme leaves
1 chile, seeded and finely diced
4 tablespoons coarsely chopped fresh
    flat-leaf parsley
1 tablespoon chopped fresh marjoram
1 (14-oz) can chopped tomatoes
1 (14-oz) can chickpeas and their liquid
1 quart vegetable stock
4 cups cabbage (Savoy, cavolo nero, spring
    greens), shredded
salt and freshly ground black pepper
grated Parmesan cheese, to serve

1 In a large saucepan, heat the oil over medium heat, then add the onion, garlic, bay leaves, thyme, and chile and cook for about 10 minutes or until the onions have softened without coloring.

2 Add the parsley, marjoram, and tomatoes and cook for another 3 minutes. Add the chickpeas, their liquid, and the stock and cook for another 30 minutes at a steady simmer.

3 Add the shredded cabbage and cook for another 10 minutes. Season with salt and pepper. To serve, pour into individual bowls, sprinkle with grated Parmesan, and drizzle with olive oil.

Amount per portion
Energy 200 cals, Protein 9.5g, Fat 8.6g, Saturated fat 0.9g, Carbohydrate 22.6g, Total sugars 10.6g, Fiber 9.0g, Salt 1.71g, Sodium 674mg

Pappa al Pomodoro
with Borlotti Beans

The Italians eat a lot of bread, and they like it fresh. Being a creative nation, they created this soup to use up leftovers, and it is very good, too. I, of course, have gone a step further by adding beans for a better GI rating.

Serves 4

1 tablespoon olive oil
3 garlic cloves, finely chopped
2 shallots, finely diced
4 to 5 ripe tomatoes, seeded
   and coarsely chopped
1¾ cups vegetable stock
1¾ cups tomato sauce
¼ teaspoon salt
1 teaspoon freshly ground black pepper
1 teaspoon superfine sugar
8 to 10 slices day-old multigrain bread,
   crusts removed, cut into ½ in cubes
leaves from 1 small bunch of basil, ripped
1 (14-oz) can borlotti beans, drained
   and rinsed
1 tablespoon freshly grated Parmesan
   cheese

1 Heat the oil in a large saucepan over medium heat and cook the garlic and shallots for 4 minutes. Add the tomatoes and cook for another 5 minutes. Add the stock, sauce, salt, and pepper and bring to a boil. Reduce the heat, add the sugar, bread, and basil. Cover, and simmer for 30 minutes, stirring from time to time. Add the borlotti beans and warm through.
2 Adjust the seasoning to taste, spoon into individual bowls, and sprinkle with a little Parmesan.

Amount per portion
Energy 402 cals, Protein 16.3g, Fat 7.5g, Saturated fat 1.4g, Carbohydrate 72.0g, Total sugars 13.4g, Fiber 10.3g, Salt 2.62g, Sodium 1035mg

Pistou

This is a French version of the classic Italian minestrone, finished off with a small dollop of pistou sauce—similar to pesto but without the pine nuts. The good low-GI beans and chunky vegetables make this a great main-course soup.

Serves 4
2 tablespoons olive oil
1 large onion, coarsely chopped
2 leeks, coarsely chopped
4 new potatoes, coarsely diced
2 carrots, sliced
1 celery rib, thinly sliced
1¼ quarts vegetable stock
3 bay leaves
1 (14-oz) can chopped tomatoes
2 teaspoons tomato paste
2 zucchini, thickly sliced
3oz extra fine green beans, cut into
   ½ in pieces
½ cup frozen *petit pois* (small peas)
1 (14-oz) can cannellini beans, rinsed
1 (14-oz) can flageolet beans, rinsed
salt and freshly ground black pepper

For the pistou sauce
4 garlic cloves
¼ cup grated Parmesan cheese
14 fresh basil leaves

1 Heat half the oil in a large saucepan over medium heat. Add the onion and leeks and cook for 8 minutes, stirring occasionally. Add the potatoes, carrots, celery, stock, bay leaves, tomatoes, and tomato paste and stir. Bring to a boil and simmer for 20 minutes.
2 Add the zucchini, green beans, peas, and canned cannellini and flageolet beans. Return to a boil and cook for another 5 minutes. Season to taste with salt and pepper.
3 Meanwhile, make the pistou. With a mortar and pestle or in a small food processor, blend the garlic, Parmesan, and basil together with the remaining oil and a little water if necessary to make a smooth paste. Serve a small dollop on top of each bowl of soup.

Amount per portion
Energy 354 cals, Protein 20.5g, Fat 11.5g, Saturated fat 2.8g, Carbohydrate 45.1g, Total sugars 16.6g, Fiber 13.7g, Salt 2.79g, Sodium 1099mg

Harira

Harira is a chunky North African lamb and chickpea soup that is substantial enough to work as a hearty lunch when served with some crusty multigrain bread. It's got loads of lovely flavors, a few of which I've added to the traditional recipe.

Serves 4

2 tablespoons olive oil
2 onions, chopped
2 garlic cloves, crushed to a paste with a little salt
7oz lamb neck fillet, cut into ½ in cubes
2 tablespoons tomato paste
1 tablespoon harissa paste
2 small sweet potatoes, cut into ½ in dice
1 (14-oz) can chopped tomatoes
1 teaspoon ground ginger
a pinch of saffron
1 (14-oz) can chickpeas, drained
1 quart lamb stock
¾ cup fresh spinach, tough stems removed
2 tablespoons chopped fresh cilantro
juice of 1 lemon
salt and freshly ground black pepper

1 In a large saucepan, heat the olive oil over medium heat, then add the onions and garlic and cook gently until the onion has softened without coloring. Increase the heat and cook the lamb, stirring regularly, until brown all over, about 3 minutes.
2 Stir in the tomato paste and harissa, then add the sweet potatoes, tomatoes, ginger, saffron, chickpeas, and lamb stock. Bring to a boil, reduce the heat, and simmer gently for 1 hour.
3 Add the spinach, cilantro, and lemon juice, and cook until the spinach has wilted. Season with salt and pepper to taste and serve.

Amount per portion
Energy 391 cals, Protein 21.2g, Fat 17.8g, Saturated fat 5.5g, Carbohydrate 39.0g, Total sugars 12.6g, Fiber 7.9g, Salt 2.71g, Sodium 1067mg

Avgolemono Soup

This is one of the first soups Jacinta, my wife, cooked for me—a legacy from her Greek ex-boyfriend. Simple and delicious.

Serves 4

1½ quarts good-quality chicken stock
1 cup quick cook long-grain brown rice
4 large eggs, beaten
juice of 2 large lemons
3 tablespoons chopped fresh parsley
salt and freshly ground pepper

1 Bring the stock to a boil. Pour in the rice and cook over medium heat for 15 minutes or until the rice is tender and cooked. Do not drain.

2 Combine the eggs with the lemon juice. When the rice is cooked, allow the stock to cool slightly then add a little to the egg mixture and whisk well. Pour the mix into the stock, stir, place over low heat, and stir continuously until the liquid has thickened and coats the back of a spoon. Do not allow to boil. Fold in the chopped parsley, season to taste with salt and pepper, and serve.

Tip Wash the rice under the cold running water before cooking to remove some of the starch. If using traditional brown rice, you will need to cook it for about 25 minutes.

Amount per portion
Energy 246 cals, Protein 20.9g, Fat 8.0g, Saturated fat 2.0g, Carbohydrate 24.4g, Total sugars 0.9g, Fiber 1.5g, Salt 1.8g, Sodium 707mg

Fassoulada

Chock-full of vegetables and beans, this Greek soup is a wonderful main-course soup for a really cold day—and as a bonus, you just toss everything in together.

Serves 4

1 large onion, coarsely chopped
2 carrots, sliced
2 leeks, sliced
2 celery ribs, sliced
4 garlic cloves, sliced
1 (14-oz) can chopped tomatoes
2 tablespoons tomato paste
2 bay leaves
1 dried chile, chopped
1 (14-oz) can white butter or lima beans,
    drained and rinsed
1 quart vegetable stock
salt and freshly ground black pepper

To serve
4 slices multigrain bread
2 tablespoons extra virgin olive oil

1 Put all the soup ingredients together in a large saucepan. Stir, bring to a boil, and simmer for 1 hour 15 minutes to 1 hour 30 minutes. Season to taste.

2 Just before the soup is ready, toast the bread, drizzle each slice with a little olive oil, and place in the bottom of individual warmed soup bowls. Pour the soup over the top and enjoy.

Amount per portion
Energy 286 cals, Protein 11g, Fat 8g, Saturated fat 1g, Carbohydrate 44g, Total sugars 14.4g, Fiber 10.7g, Salt 2.56g, Sodium 1008mg

Tuna Salade Niçoise *Oinamul* (Korean Cucumber Salad)
nsalada Mista A Crunchy Pear and Walnut Salad A Lemongr
Cold Chicken and Two Cucumber Salad with Yogurt Dress
ad Spicy Lentil and Salmon Salad Posh Fried Rice Saffron Pe
Onions Charred Cauliflower, Tartare Flavors Spiced Chickp
pice and Rice Dhal with Added Spice Green Vegetables wit
s and Asian Influence Californian Cobb Salad Borlotti and C
p Salad Thai Papaya Salad Rare Tuna Salade Niçoise *Oinam*
Eastern Salad Spanish *Ensalada Mista* A Crunchy Pear and
a Nutty, fruity Tabbouleh Cold Chicken and Two Cucumber

nge, Cumin, and Carrot Salad Spicy Lentil and Salmon Salad
Roasted Carrots and Baby Onions Charred Cauliflower, Tart
ried Beans Fattoush Spice and Rice Dhal with Added Spice
Lima Beans with Chiles and Asian Influence Californian Cob
Mushroom, and Shrimp Salad Thai Papaya Salad Rare Tuna
Beans, and Crunch An Eastern Salad Spanish *Ensalada Mist*
se Dipping Sauce Panzanella Nutty, fruity Tabbouleh Cold C
essing Greek Salad Orange, Cumin, and Carrot Salad Spicy
Beans and Pine Nuts Roasted Carrots and Baby Onions Ch
ese, and Mint Nutty Curried Beans Fattoush Spice and Rice

ckpea and Potato Salad A Salad of Salmon, Beans, and Crun
s, Chicken, and Peanut Salad Vietnamese Dipping Sauce Par
g Tomato Salad with Sumac and Garlic Dressing Greek Sala
Pilaff Smashed Roast Butternut Salad with White Beans and P
s Grilled Zucchini with Chickpeas, Goat Cheese, and Mint N
Almond and Orange Stir-Fried Greens with Mustard Seeds a
tage Cheese Salad French Potato Salad Seafood and Lime S
(Korean Cucumber Salad) Chickpea and Potato Salad A Sal
Walnut Salad A Lemongrass, Chicken, and Peanut Salad Vietn
lad with Yogurt Dressing Tomato Salad with Sumac and Garl

Salads
and Sides

osh Fried Rice Saffron Pea Pilaff Smashed Roast Butternut Sa
e Flavors Spiced Chickpeas Grilled Zucchini with Chickpea
een Vegetables with Almond and Orange Stir-Fried Greens
Salad Borlotti and Cottage Cheese Salad French Potato Sala
alade Niçoise *Oinamul* (Korean Cucumber Salad) Chickpea
A Crunchy Pear and Walnut Salad A Lemongrass, Chicken,
cken and Two Cucumber Salad with Yogurt Dressing Tomato
ntil and Salmon Salad Posh Fried Rice Saffron Pea Pilaff Sma
red Cauliflower, Tartare Flavors Spiced Chickpeas Grilled Z
al with Added Spice Green Vegetables with Almond and O

Californian Cobb Salad

This is a classic salad that is often served in neat lines of different ingredients, but, to be honest, if you want to toss it all together, please feel free to do so.

Serves 4

For the dressing
1 tablespoon red wine vinegar
1 teaspoon sugar or granulated low-calorie
    sweetener
1 teaspoon lemon juice
½ teaspoon ground black pepper
1 teaspoon Worcestershire sauce
1 teaspoon English mustard (such as
    Colman's)
3 garlic cloves, chopped
3 tablespoons olive oil

½ head of iceberg lettuce
½ head of romaine lettuce
½ bunch of watercress
1 small head of chicory, leaves separated
4 medium tomatoes, peeled, seeded
    and diced
2 cooked chicken breasts, diced
6 strips crisp cooked bacon, crumbled
1 avocado, diced
3 eggs, hard-boiled and chopped
2 tablespoons chopped fresh chives
2oz Roquefort blue cheese, crumbled
    into pieces
cornbread, to serve

1 First make the dressing by putting all the dressing ingredients in a clean mason jar, sealing, and shaking to emulsify. Chill until required and shake before serving.

2 Shred the lettuces and place in a salad bowl, then combine them with the watercress and chicory. Scatter the tomatoes over the top, together with the chicken and bacon, then decorate with pieces of avocado. Sprinkle the chopped eggs, chives, and Roquefort over the top. Just before serving, pour over some dressing and mix thoroughly. Serve with some warm cornbread on the side.

Tip If the dressing seems a bit too oily for your taste, you can add in a little water.

Amount per portion (sugar)
Energy 438 cals, Protein 34.1g, Fat 30.2g, Saturated fat 7.9g, Carbohydrate 7.9g, Total sugars 6.3g, Fiber 3.2g, Salt 2.09g, Sodium 823mg

Amount per portion (low-calorie sweetener)
Energy 433 cals, Protein 34.1g, Fat 30.2g, Saturated fat 7.9g, Carbohydrate 6.7g, Total sugars 5.1g, Fiber 3.2g, Salt 2.09g, Sodium 823mg

Borlotti and Cottage Cheese Salad

In this simple Italian salad, it's important that the beans are warm when you add the other ingredients.

Serves 4
1 (14-oz) can borlotti beans, drained
    and rinsed
2 tablespoons extra virgin olive oil
1 tablespoon fresh lemon juice
1 teaspoon dried oregano
¼ teaspoon crushed hot red pepper flakes
½ cup cottage cheese
salt and freshly ground black pepper
3 tablespoons coarsely chopped fresh
    flat-leaf parsley, to garnish

1 Place the beans in a saucepan, add cold water to cover, and heat until warmed through but do not allow to boil.

2 Drain the hot beans well and transfer to a large mixing bowl. Stir in the remaining ingredients except the parsley, being careful to retain some consistency to the cottage cheese.

3 Just before serving, adjust the seasoning to taste. Garnish with parsley and serve immediately.

Amount per portion
Energy 140 cals, Protein 7.9g, Fat 7.3g, Saturated fat 1.5g, Carbohydrate 11.3g, Total sugars 1.2g, Fiber 2.9g, Salt 1.12g, Sodium 444mg

French Potato Salad

Most people associate potato salad with mayonnaise, but actually a vinaigrette-style dressing is excellent.

Serves 4
16 waxy new potatoes (fingerling,
    red-skinned)
2 slices rustic multigrain bread, cut into
    ½ in pieces
1 garlic clove, crushed to a paste
    with a little salt
¼ cup dry white wine
3 tablespoons extra virgin olive oil
2 teaspoons Dijon mustard
1 tablespoon white wine vinegar
salt and freshly ground black pepper
2 shallots, finely chopped
5 cornichons (baby gherkins), finely sliced
1 tablespoon nonpareil capers
    (baby capers)
2 tablespoons chopped fresh parsley

1 Preheat oven to 350°F. Cook the potatoes in boiling salted water until tender, about 20 minutes. Drain and when cool enough to handle, cut into ½ inch slices.

2 Meanwhile, place the bread pieces on a baking sheet and toast in the preheated oven until they have turned into crispy croutons, about 12 minutes.

3 While they are toasting, whisk together the garlic, white wine, olive oil, mustard, and vinegar. Season to taste with salt and pepper, then fold in the shallots, cornichons, capers, and parsley. Pour this flavored vinaigrette over the warm potatoes. Just before serving, fold in the croutons.

Tip Nonpareil is a type of small caper generally considered to be of the finest quality.

Amount per portion
Energy 240 cals, Protein 4.4g, Fat 10.3g, Saturated fat 1.4g, Carbohydrate 31.0g, Total sugars 2.9g, Fiber 2.7g, Salt 1.36g, Sodium 536mg

Seafood and Lime Salad

This Middle Eastern-style salad is just right for a summer lunch or supper. With loads of citrus and fennel flavors, it can be eaten warm or cold. You can vary the choice of seafood, but the balance in this recipe works well for me.

Serves 4

1lb 2oz mussels in their shells, cleaned and any open mussels discarded
¼ cup dry white wine
2 shallots, finely diced
3 garlic cloves, crushed to a paste with a little salt
1 fennel bulb, outside leaves removed, the rest very thinly sliced
1 small red onion, thinly sliced
¼ savoy cabbage, finely shredded
1 carrot, grated
8 new potatoes, cooked and quartered
1 tablespoon chopped fresh dill
1 tablespoon snipped fresh chives
2 tablespoons extra virgin olive oil
12 raw tiger shrimp, shell-off and deveined
½ lb cleaned squid tubes, opened up and cut into ¾ in squares (or clean the tubes of fresh squid tentacles)
salt and freshly ground black pepper
1 tablespoon sumac
grated zest and juice of 2 limes
1 mild red chile, seeded and thinly sliced

1 Pop the mussels into a large saucepan and add the wine, shallots, and a third of the garlic. Cover tightly and cook over high heat, shaking the pan occasionally, for 4 to 5 minutes. With a slotted spoon, transfer the mussels to a bowl, discarding any that have not opened. Return the cooking liquor to the heat and boil until only 2 to 3 tablespoons remain, then strain into a bowl and reserve. When the mussels have cooled enough to handle, scoop the flesh into a bowl and discard the shells.

2 Mix together the fennel, onion, cabbage, carrot, cooked potatoes, and herbs.

3 Heat the oil in a frying pan, then, in batches, cook the shrimp and squid over high heat for about 1 minute on each side. Add them to the vegetables, then cook the mussel flesh briefly (45 seconds) and add them to the salad.

4 Pour the mussel juices into the fish pan to combine with the oil, season to taste with salt and pepper, and heat for 1 minute, then pour this hot liquid over the salad. Add the sumac, lime zest and juice, and the chile, and toss well. Serve immediately, or leave to cool and refrigerate for up to 24 hours.

Amount per portion
Energy 249 cals, Protein 22.8g, Fat 8.3g, Saturated fat 1.0g, Carbohydrate 20.1g, Total sugars 7.0g, Fiber 3.8g, Salt 1.29g, Sodium 512mg

Pea Shoot, Mushroom, and Shrimp Salad

Fresh, delicious pea shoots, harvested from the growing tips of pea plants, are all the rage at the moment and they're becoming commercially more widely available. Of course, you could always get gardening and grow your own . . .

Serves 4
4oz pea shoots
2oz button mushrooms, quartered
¼ lb cooked shrimp, shell-off

For the dressing
2 teaspoons English mustard powder (such as Colman's)
1 teaspoon sugar or granulated low-calorie sweetener
1 tablespoon cider vinegar or white wine vinegar
1 tablespoon chopped fresh mint
1 teaspoon snipped fresh chives
freshly ground black pepper

1 In a large bowl, mix together the pea shoots, mushrooms, and shrimp. Mix together all the dressing ingredients, and thin with a little water if needed. Stir the dressing into the salad.

Tip If you have time, let the dressing rest for 30 minutes to allow the flavors to develop before you mix it into the salad. Serve with bread to mop up the delicious dressing.

Amount per portion (sugar)
Energy 55 cals, Protein 9.1g, Fat 1.3g, Saturated fat 0.1g, Carbohydrate 1.9g, Total sugars 1.6g, Fiber 1.3g, Salt 0.66g, Sodium 259mg

Amount per portion (low-calorie sweetener)
Energy 52 cals, Protein 9.1g, Fat 1.3g, Saturated fat 0.1g, Carbohydrate 1.0g, Total sugars 0.6g, Fiber 1.3g, Salt 0.66g, Sodium 259mg

Thai Papaya Salad

A refreshing salad to which you can add shrimp and crabmeat for a more substantial offering.

Serves 4
2 hard green papayas, peeled, seeded, and grated
2 garlic cloves, finely chopped
2 small red chiles, seeded and finely sliced
4 tomatoes, seeded and diced
2oz peanuts, chopped
4 tablespoons chopped fresh mint
2 tablespoons chopped fresh cilantro
grated zest and juice of 2 limes
1½ tablespoons honey
1 tablespoon dried shrimp powder
crusty bread, to serve

1 Mix together all the ingredients and allow the flavors to develop for 15 minutes before serving. Serve with crusty bread.

Tip Shrimp powder is ground dried shrimp and is often used as a flavoring in Asian soups, salads, and stir-fries.

Amount per portion
Energy 146 cals, Protein 7.0g, Fat 6.3g, Saturated fat 1.1g, Carbohydrate 16.4g, Total sugars 8.2g, Fiber 3.6g, Salt 0.37g, Sodium 149mg

RIGHT Pea Shoot, Mushroom, and Shrimp Salad

Rare Tuna Salade Niçoise

When in the south of France, I love the Niçoise salad served in the beach shacks on the coast.
They use canned tuna, but this version uses fresh.

Serves 4

For the marinade
2 tablespoons extra virgin olive oil
1 tablespoon aged red wine vinegar
1 tablespoon chopped fresh flat-leaf parsley
1 tablespoon snipped fresh chives
1 garlic clove, finely chopped
salt and freshly ground black pepper

4 (4-oz) fresh tuna steaks, each approx 1in thick
16 small new red potatoes
2 eggs, at room temperature
3oz fresh green beans, trimmed
2 little gem lettuce hearts, quartered lengthwise and separated into leaves
2 plum tomatoes, coarsely chopped
½ red onion, finely sliced
2 anchovy fillets, cut lengthwise into thin strips
12 pitted black olives in brine, drained
8 fresh basil leaves, torn

1 First make the marinade. In a bowl, whisk together the olive oil, vinegar, parsley, chives, garlic, and 1 teaspoon each of salt and pepper. Lay the tuna in a shallow non-metallic dish and pour over half the marinade. Cover with plastic wrap and refrigerate for 1 hour to allow the flavors to penetrate the tuna, turning the fish over occasionally. Set the remaining marinade aside.

2 Bring a pan of salted water to a boil, add the potatoes, cover, and simmer for 10 to 12 minutes or until just tender. Drain, then cut into quarters lengthwise.

3 Place the eggs in a small pan and just cover with boiling water, then cook for 8 minutes. Drain and rinse under cold running water, then remove the shells and cut each egg into quarters lengthwise—the yolks should still be slightly soft.

4 Plunge the beans into a pan of boiling salted water and blanch for 3 minutes or so, then drain and refresh under cold running water.

5 Heat a ridged grill pan to very hot. Remove the tuna from the marinade, shaking off any excess. Cook the tuna steaks for about 2 minutes each side, depending on how rare you like your fish.

6 Arrange the lettuce leaves on individual plates or one large platter and add the potatoes, green beans, tomatoes, onion, and anchovies. Place the tuna steaks on top and drizzle over the remaining marinade. Scatter the eggs, olives, and torn basil leaves over the top before serving.

Tip Tuna becomes exceedingly dry when overcooked, so watch it!

Amount per portion
Energy 353 cals, Protein 34.6g, Fat 15.3g, Saturated fat 2.9g, Carbohydrate 20.6g, Total sugars 4.6g, Fiber 2.9g, Salt 1.56g, Sodium 614mg

Oinamul (Korean Cucumber Salad)

A very refreshing salad that is a good accompaniment to grilled or stewed meats.

Serves 4

1 cucumber, peeled and thinly sliced
1 teaspoon salt
3 scallions, chopped
1 fresh red chile, seeded and
    finely chopped
1 tablespoon sesame oil
3 garlic cloves, finely chopped
1 teaspoon sesame seeds
¼ teaspoon chili powder
1 teaspoon roasted unsalted
    peanuts, chopped
multigrain bread, to serve

1 Place the cucumber slices in a colander, sprinkle the salt over the top, and mix well. Set aside for 30 minutes to drain some of the cucumbers' natural liquid. Rinse them in fresh water and squeeze them well to remove as much liquid as possible.

2 Mix together all the remaining ingredients, then add the cucumber and mix well. This will keep, covered and in the fridge, for 3 to 4 days. Serve with multigrain bread.

Tip You could omit the salting stage, but you would then need to eat the salad within an hour or so—otherwise, the flavor will become diluted with the cucumber juices.

Amount per portion
Energy 51 cals, Protein 1.5g, Fat 4.0g, Saturated fat 0.6g, Carbohydrate 2.3g, Total sugars 1.5g, Fiber 0.9g, Salt 0.27g, Sodium 104mg

Chickpea and Potato Salad

A beneficial Indian-influenced salad that has great slow-release qualities; it's excellent as a light lunch, with some crusty multigrain bread and a bowl of soup. You'll probably find it difficult to find one of the ingredients, anardana (dried pomegranate seeds), so omit it if you don't have an Asian or Middle Eastern market nearby.

Serves 4

8 new potatoes, cubed
1 red onion, finely sliced
½ red bell pepper, cut into ½ in dice
1 cup watermelon, cut into ¾ in dice
1 (14-oz) can chickpeas, drained
grated zest and juice of 1 lemon
2 teaspoons chopped fresh mint
1 teaspoon superfine sugar
2 tablespoons fresh pomegranate seeds
1 teaspoon anardana (dried pomegranate
    seeds), coarsely ground
salt and freshly ground black pepper

1 Cook the potatoes in boiling salted water until tender, about 10 minutes, then drain. While the potatoes are still warm, mix them together with the remaining ingredients and season to taste with salt and pepper.

Amount per portion
Energy 147 cals, Protein 6.2g, Fat 2.2g, Saturated fat 0.0g, Carbohydrate 27.3g, Total sugars 8.2g, Fiber 3.8g, Salt 0.98g, Sodium 387mg

LEFT *Oinamul (*Korean Cucumber Salad)

A Salad of Salmon, Beans, and Crunch

Choose wild salmon if it fits your budget, otherwise look for a farmed salmon with a good pedigree. This salad has some lovely elements, and enough going on to keep you from saying, "oh, no, not salmon again!"

Serves 4

1 (1-lb) salmon fillet
1 carrot, sliced
1 onion, halved
2 bay leaves
12 black peppercorns
3 slices multigrain bread, crusts removed, ripped into small pieces
salt and freshly ground black pepper
7oz fresh green beans, ends trimmed and cut into ½ in pieces
7oz fava beans, raw
7oz canned white beans, drained and rinsed
1 tablespoon extra virgin olive oil
juice of ½ lemon
2 tablespoons low-fat mayonnaise
1 teaspoon each snipped fresh chives, chopped fresh parsley, and chopped fresh tarragon

To serve

salad leaves
lemon wedges

1 Preheat the oven to 350°F. Place the salmon fillet in a saucepan along with the carrot, onion, bay leaves, and peppercorns. Cover with water, bring to a boil, and immediately switch off the heat. Leave in the water to cool.

2 Put the bread pieces in a food processor and pulse until you have rustic crumbs. Transfer them to a baking sheet and bake for 15 minutes until crisp and golden. Set aside.

3 Fill a saucepan three-quarters full with water, season with salt, and bring to a boil. Add the green beans and cook for 2 minutes, then add the fava beans and cook for another 2 minutes. Add the white beans and warm through, then drain and stir in the oil and lemon juice and season to taste with salt and pepper.

4 Flake the salmon onto individual plates. Mix together the mayonnaise and herbs and place a dollop on top of the salmon. Scatter with the beans and serve with dressed salad leaves and lemon wedges, topped with crispy crumbs.

Amount per portion
Energy 417 cals, Protein 33g, Fat 18g, Saturated fat 3.1g, Carbohydrate 33g, Total sugars 7.6g, Fiber 9.3g, Salt 1.75g, Sodium 688mg

An Eastern Salad

This is the sort of dish I'll have for lunch on a day off—it's easy to prepare, you can use almost any salad ingredient or vegetable, and when you've finished eating, you'll feel satisfied and a little bit virtuous.

Serves 4

For the dressing
½ cup unsalted roasted peanuts
¼ cup lime juice
2 tablespoons fish sauce (*nam pla*)
2 teaspoons superfine sugar
4 garlic cloves
3 tablespoons coarsely chopped
  fresh cilantro
2 hot Thai chiles, seeded

For the salad
1 head of baby gem lettuce, leaves
  separated
2 tomatoes, coarsely diced
1 carrot, thinly sliced
½ cucumber, peeled, seeded, and cut
  into ½ in half-moons
1 cup small broccoli florets
2 shallots, thinly sliced
½ red bell pepper, seeded and cut into
  small dice
4oz tofu, cubed
1 cup edamame, blanched briefly
  in boiling water
½ bunch of cilantro
10 fresh basil leaves, shredded
8 fresh mint leaves, shredded
2 hard-boiled eggs, cut into wedges

1 To make the dressing, blend together half the peanuts with all the remaining ingredients in a blender or food processor.
2 Mix together all the salad ingredients except the eggs, and toss with the dressing. Arrange on individual plates and garnish with the eggs and the remaining peanuts.

Amount per portion
Energy 295 cals, Protein 18.8g, Fat 17.3g, Saturated fat 3.5g, Carbohydrate 16.9g, Total sugars 10.4g, Fiber 4.9g, Salt 1.62g, Sodium 640mg

Spanish *Ensalada Mista*

Having a house in Spain inevitably means trying out various Spanish dishes, some good, some not so good. Before I tried this salad, I wasn't a fan of jarred asparagus, but it sort of grows on you.

Serves 4

1 head of romaine lettuce
2 tomatoes, each cut into 6 pieces
1 small cucumber, peeled, seeded, and sliced
½ yellow or red onion, thinly sliced
1 red or yellow bell pepper, seeded and sliced into long thin strips
1 (10-oz) jar artichoke hearts, drained
1 carrot, grated
1 (6-oz) can tuna steak, drained
2 eggs, hard-boiled and cut into quarters
1 (15-oz) jar white asparagus, drained
½ cup anchovy-stuffed green olives
2 tablespoons extra virgin olive oil (Spanish for authenticity)
1 tablespoon sherry vinegar
freshly ground black pepper
crusty bread, to serve

1 Break up the lettuce into small pieces, and on a large platter make a bed of lettuce. Top with the tomatoes, cucumber, onions, red or yellow bell pepper, artichoke hearts, and carrot. Break the tuna up into small chunks with a fork then spread it out around the bed of lettuce. Scatter the egg quarters, asparagus, and olives all over the salad.

2 Dress with oil and vinegar, and sprinkle with pepper to taste. Serve with some bread.

Tip Every family in Spain has their own version of *Ensalada Mista*, so it is slightly different in every household—therefore, don't worry if you are missing one of the ingredients.

Amount per portion
Energy 287 cals, Protein 16.0g, Fat 20.4g, Saturated fat 3.1g, Carbohydrate 10.7g, Total sugars 8.6g, Fiber 6.2g, Salt 2.33g, Sodium 917mg

Crunchy Pear and Walnut Salad

In this classic French salad combo, I've added a touch of blue cheese, which is naughty but I'm sure will be forgiven on occasion. You'll enjoy this mix—it's got great textures and flavors.

Serves 4

1 tablespoon walnut oil
2 teaspoons cider vinegar
2 pears, peeled, cored, and thickly sliced
freshly ground black pepper
2 slices rustic multigrain bread, cut in ½ to ¾ in dice
2 tablespoons walnut pieces
1 head of chicory or Belgian endive, leaves separated
2 handfuls of salad leaf mixture
3oz Roquefort or other blue cheese, crumbled

1 Preheat the oven to 350°F. In a bowl, mix together the walnut oil and vinegar. Add the pear slices and some black pepper and mix gently so all the pear slices are coated. Leave to marinate for 20 minutes.

2 Meanwhile, toss the bread and walnuts together and arrange them on a flat baking sheet, then transfer to the oven and cook for 7 minutes.

3 When you are ready to serve the salad, mix together the chicory with the salad leaves in a bowl and add the liquid from the pears. Divide between individual plates. Scatter the pear slices, walnuts, and croutons over the top, then dot with the cheese.

Amount per portion
Energy 228 cals, Protein 7g, Fat 13g, Saturated fat 4.6g, Carbohydrate 22g, Total sugars 12.1g, Fiber 3.6g, Salt 1.01g, Sodium 398mg

Lemongrass, Chicken, and Peanut Salad

I love most Asian salads, and now that so many Asian ingredients are readily available in local supermarkets, they're easy to put together. This one is pretty fiery, but chiles are good for you!

Serves 4

1lb cooked chicken breast, shredded
1 red onion, chopped
½ cucumber, seeded and diced
1 bird's eye chile, seeded and finely diced
1 each red and green mild chile, cut into thin shreds
1 small bunch of fresh cilantro, leaves coarsely chopped
12 fresh mint leaves, shredded
2 gem lettuces, leaves separated
3 tomatoes, seeded and diced
1 tablespoon roasted peanuts, chopped
lime wedges, to serve

For the peanut dressing

2 tablespoons lime juice
1 tablespoon fish sauce (*nam pla*)
2 teaspoons superfine sugar
1 tablespoon crunchy peanut butter

1 In a bowl, mix together the chicken, onion, cucumber, chiles, cilantro, and mint.

2 Make the dressing: In a separate bowl, whisk together the lime juice, fish sauce, sugar, and peanut butter, thinning it down with a little water if too thick. Mix the dressing into the salad.

3 Scatter gem lettuce leaves on to individual plates. Spoon the salad over the lettuce leaves and garnish with diced tomato and chopped peanuts, and serve with lime wedges.

Amount per portion
Energy 272 cals, Protein 41.4g, Fat 8.3g, Saturated fat 2.2g, Carbohydrate 8.6g, Total sugars 7.3g, Fiber 1.9g, Salt 0.98g, Sodium 388mg

Vietnamese Dipping Sauce

This useful Vietnamese condiment will liven up salads and vegetables, and it's also great just to dip grilled food into. It will keep in the fridge for up to a month. I've reduced the usual quantity of sugar.

Serves 4

2 bird's eye chiles, seeded and coarsely chopped
2 garlic cloves, sliced
1 tablespoon superfine sugar
2 tablespoons low-calorie granulated sweetener
½ cup lime juice
¼ cup fish sauce (*nam pla*)
½ cup warm water
1 tablespoon chopped fresh cilantro
1 teaspoon chopped fresh mint

1 In a small food processor, blend together the chiles, garlic, both sugars, and a quarter of the lime juice until smooth; alternatively, use a mortar and pestle. Spoon into a bowl and mix with the remaining ingredients.

Amount per portion
Energy 32 cals, Protein 2.0g, Fat 0.1g, Saturated fat 0g, Carbohydrate 6.2g, Total sugars 5.2g, Fiber 0.1g, Salt 2.45g, Sodium 966mg

LEFT Lemongrass, Chicken, and Peanut Salad

Panzanella

This delicious Tuscan salad traditionally makes use of up to 3-day old bread—soaked in water and squeezed dry before being added to the salad—but I prefer to use fresher bread, rubbed with garlic and grilled for an added crunch.

Serves 4

2 tablespoons extra virgin olive oil
3 (½-in) thick slices ciabatta
3 garlic cloves, 2 of them finely chopped
2 anchovy fillets
1 tablespoon nonpareil capers (baby capers), drained
sea salt
2 tablespoons aged red wine vinegar
2 tablespoons chopped fresh flat-leaf parsley
4 plum tomatoes, seeded and cubed
1 small red onion, finely sliced
½ cucumber, cut lengthwise, seeded and cut into ½ in chunks
2 celery ribs, finely sliced
12 fresh basil leaves, ripped
½ cup pitted black olives, chopped
freshly ground black pepper

1 Drizzle some of the oil on both sides of the ciabatta bread, then toast both sides under the broiler. Rub both sides with the unchopped garlic clove, then rip the bread into ½ inch cubes. Set aside.

2 In a small food processor or with a mortar and pestle, blend together the chopped garlic, anchovies, and capers with about half a teaspoon of sea salt. Add the remaining olive oil, vinegar, and the parsley and pulse the food processor until the ingredients have combined into a dressing.

3 In a bowl, mix together the bread and all the remaining ingredients and toss with the anchovy dressing. Season to taste with black pepper.

Amount per portion
Energy 137 cals, Protein 3.7g, Fat 8.1g, Saturated fat 1.1g, Carbohydrate 13.2g, Total sugars 4.9g, Fiber 2.5g, Salt 2.02g, Sodium 799mg

Nutty, Fruity Tabbouleh

You often see this Middle Eastern salad as a big bowl of white grains with a few flecks of green, when traditionally it's all green with a few flecks of white. This version has a few nice additions too.

Serves 4

¼ cup quick-cook cracked or bulgur wheat
juice of 2 lemons
1 tablespoon extra virgin olive oil
1 bunch fresh flat-leaf parsley, chopped
1 small bunch fresh mint, chopped
1 bunch of scallions, finely sliced
3 tablespoons pistachio nuts, chopped
3 tablespoons brazil nuts, chopped
3 tablespoons golden raisins
2oz dried apricots, chopped
salt and freshly ground black pepper
3 plum tomatoes, seeded and diced

1 Soak the cracked wheat in cold water for 20 minutes, then drain and squeeze dry. Put the wheat in a large glass bowl, season with salt and pepper, and stir in the lemon juice and olive oil. Leave to rest for 30 minutes.

2 Mix in the parsley, mint, scallions, nuts, and fruit. Season with salt and pepper, adjust the seasoning to taste, and top with the plum tomatoes.

Amount per portion
Energy 236 cals, Protein 6.3g, Fat 11.3g, Saturated fat 2.0g, Carbohydrate 29.1g, Total sugars 14.2g, Fiber 3.1g, Salt 0.68g, Sodium 268mg

Cold Chicken and Two Cucumber Salad with Yogurt Dressing

This Scandivanian salad is good and summery and filled with popular flavors.

Serves 4
12 new potatoes, scrubbed and halved
1lb cooked chicken, cut into bite-sized
    pieces
1 cucumber, peeled, seeded, and diced
2 sour gherkins, sliced
salt and freshly ground black pepper

For the dressing
1 tablespoon grain mustard
2 teaspoons honey
½ small bunch of fresh dill, chopped
4⅓ oz non-fat natural Greek yogurt
juice of ½ lemon

1 This one is simple: in one bowl, mix all the dry ingredients together, then in a separate bowl combine all the dressing ingredients. Stir the dressing into the salad, season to taste, and serve.

Variation This works well with many meats or fish, but it works particularly well with cooked salmon.

Amount per portion
Energy 321 cals, Protein 36.8g, Fat 9.3g, Saturated fat 2.8g, Carbohydrate 24.2g, Total sugars 6.0g, Fiber 2.0g, Salt 1.28g, Sodium 503mg

Tomato Salad with Sumac and Garlic Dressing

This ever-so-simple Middle Eastern salad is great as part of a meze buffet or with grilled fish—very garlicky and very delicious, with citrus notes from the sumac. Serve with bread to mop up the juices.

Serves 4
6 garlic cloves
2 tablespoons non-fat natural
    Greek yogurt
1 tablespoon extra virgin olive oil
freshly ground black pepper
3 beefsteak tomatoes, sliced
1 tablespoon sumac
1 teaspoon chopped fresh mint

1 In a small food processor, blend together the garlic, yogurt, and olive oil to a smooth dressing, and season with pepper.
2 Arrange the tomato slices on a flat plate, spread the garlic dressing over the top, and sprinkle with sumac and mint.

Variation If you like your dressing a little tart, add a squeeze of lemon juice.

Amount per portion
Energy 66 cals, Protein 2.3g, Fat 3.5g, Saturated fat 0.5g, Carbohydrate 6.8g, Total sugars 3.8g, Fiber 1.4g, Salt 0.05g, Sodium 19mg

Greek Salad

There is something about a Greek salad that reminds me of sunshine and holidays. You'll never really get the true taste because the Greeks use the dried flower heads of the oregano, but this recipe is still great.

Serves 4
For the dressing
1 tablespoon extra virgin olive oil
1 tablespoon aged red wine vinegar
1 teaspoon dried Greek oregano
1 garlic clove, finely chopped
freshly ground black pepper

4 plum tomatoes, each cut into 6 pieces
½ cucumber, peeled and cut into
    ½ in chunks
2oz Kalamata olives, pitted
1 small red onion, thinly sliced
2 teaspoons fresh oregano leaves
3oz feta cheese

1 Whisk all the dressing ingredients together and set aside for 30 minutes for the flavors to meld.

2 Mix all the salad ingredients except the feta in a large serving bowl. Shake the dressing, pour it over the salad, and toss to coat. Pass the feta through a sieve to create a "snow" effect over the salad.

Tip Delicious served with bread to mop up the fresh juices from the salad.

Amount per portion
Energy 138 cals, Protein 4.9g, Fat 10.8g, Saturated fat 3.6g, Carbohydrate 5.9g, Total sugars 5.0g, Fiber 1.8g, Salt 1.38g, Sodium 547mg

Orange, Cumin, and Carrot Salad

A light, refreshing African salad that is excellent on its own or with some multigrain bread, tossed through some couscous, or as an accompaniment to grilled meat or fish. If you want to impress your guests, serve it in hollowed-out orange halves.

Serves 4
2 teaspoons cumin seeds
4 navel oranges, 1 zested,
   the remainder peeled
2 tablespoons extra virgin olive oil
1 tablespoon harissa paste
2 carrots, grated
½ red onion, thinly sliced
2oz black Kalamata olives, pitted
½ cup toasted almond flakes
salt and freshly ground black pepper
1 tablespoon snipped fresh chives
baby gem or romaine lettuce, to serve

1 Place a small frying pan over medium heat, then add the cumin seeds and toast until fragrant. Crush them with a mortar and pestle or in a small grinder.

2 Using a small sharp knife and working over a bowl to catch the juices, cut out the orange flesh by cutting between the membranes and drop the flesh into the bowl. Squeeze any juice remaining in the membranes into the bowl and discard any seeds. To make the salad dressing, whisk together the olive oil, harissa, and cumin, and set aside.

3 Just before serving, mix the orange segments with the zest, carrots, onion, olives, and almond flakes. Stir in the dressing, season to taste with salt and pepper, and sprinkle with the chives. Serve over baby gem or romaine lettuce leaves.

Amount per portion
Energy 251 cals, Protein 6g, Fat 17g, Saturated fat 1.9g, Carbohydrate 20g,
Total sugars 18.4g, Fiber 5.2g, Salt 1.01g, Sodium 398mg

Spicy Lentil and Salmon Salad

This Middle Eastern-influenced salad is quick to put together and very nutritious, with lovely flavors and a spicy kick. I've used canned lentils here, but feel free to cook your own. Puy lentils are probably the best, as they don't collapse easily. And there's nothing to keep you from poaching your own salmon, but here I am trying to speed things up a little.

Serves 4
4 new potatoes, cut into ½ in dice
1 (14-oz) can brown lentils
4½ oz non-fat natural Greek yogurt
1 tablespoon harissa paste
1 garlic clove, crushed
1 small red onion, thinly sliced
leaves from 1 small bunch of fresh
   flat-leaf parsley
1 fresh red chile, seeded and thinly sliced
freshly ground black pepper
1 (7-oz) can wild red Alaskan salmon, flaked

1 Boil the potatoes in lightly salted water for 10 minutes or until tender, then drain. Meanwhile, gently heat the lentils in a saucepan over low heat.

2 Combine the yogurt with the harissa and garlic. Fold this dressing into the lentils, along with the onion, parsley leaves, chile, and potatoes. Season to taste with pepper. Spoon into a serving bowl, then scatter the salmon flakes over the top.

Amount per portion
Energy 177 cals, Protein 17.0g, Fat 4.7g, Saturated fat 0.9g, Carbohydrate 17.8g, Total sugars 2.7g, Fiber 4.5g, Salt 1.21g, Sodium 475mg

Brown Fried Rice

There's something particularly naughty-but-nice about fried rice, and it is the perfect dish for using up leftovers. Ingredients can be varied to cater for personal taste or according to availability, but here is my suggestion. This is wonderful served alongside salad greens.

Serves 4

2 cups minute brown rice
2 teaspoons sesame oil
3½ oz shell-off shrimp, raw
1 tablespoon sunflower oil
2 eggs, beaten
1 garlic clove, finely chopped
1 hot chile, seeded and finely chopped
3½ oz cooked chicken, shredded
3½ oz green beans, cut into ½ in pieces, blanched briefly in boiling water
3½ oz cooked cabbage or bok choy, shredded
1 carrot, cut into ½ in dice, blanched briefly in boiling water
3 scallions, sliced
¼ teaspoon chili powder
2 teaspoons soy sauce
1 chicken bouillon cube
1 small can of Alaskan crabmeat, drained

To serve
chile, scallions, and cucumber batons

1 Prepare the rice according to the instructions on the package. Set aside.

2 Heat the sesame oil in a wok over high heat and cook the shrimp for 1 minute on each side. Remove and set aside.

3 Add the sunflower oil to the wok then cook the beaten eggs along with the garlic and fresh chile, breaking up the egg mixture with a wooden spoon. Remove and set aside.

4 Add the rice to the wok and cook until starting to crisp. Add the chicken, beans, cabbage, carrot, and scallions and toss to mix well. Mix in the shrimp and eggs, along with the chili powder, soy sauce, and bouillon cube, and heat through briefly.

5 Arrange on individual warmed plates and scatter with crabmeat. Serve with fresh chile, scallions, and cucumber batons.

Amount per portion
Energy 346 cals, Protein 24.6g, Fat 12.5g, Saturated fat 1.9g, Carbohydrate 35.8g, Total sugars 3.6g, Fiber 4.4g, Salt 1.81g, Sodium 714mg

Saffron Pea Pilaf

Dishes mixing rice and peas are popular worldwide, and this one from Kashmir is particularly tasty. It has great color and a lovely blend of spices, nuts, and fruit. Serve it on its own, or as a partner to a stew or tagine.

Serves 4
1¼ cups basmati rice
1 tablespoon olive oil
¼ cup toasted almond flakes
8 walnut halves, coarsely chopped
2 tablespoons raisins
8 dried apricots, diced
4 cloves
2 cardamom pods
1in piece cinnamon stick
12 black peppercorns
2½ cups fresh or frozen peas
½ teaspoon saffron, soaked in
    1 tablespoon hot water
4 scallions, finely sliced
2 cups vegetable or chicken stock
3 tablespoons chopped fresh cilantro
salt and freshly ground pepper

1 Wash the rice and drain it well. Melt the olive oil in a saucepan and sauté the almonds and walnuts until the nuts are golden brown, then sauté the raisins and apricots until they are plumped up. Remove and set aside.

2 Add the cloves, cardamom, cinnamon, and peppercorns to the same pan and cook them over low heat, stirring continuously, until they become aromatic. Stir in the peas, saffron and its soaking liquid, scallions, and rice, and cook for 2 minutes, stirring to ensure the rice is coated with oil.

3 Add the stock and bring to a boil, then reduce the heat, cover with a tightly fitting lid, and simmer for about 20 minutes or until the rice has cooked. Stir in the cilantro, nuts, and fruit, and season to taste with salt and pepper.

Amount per portion
Energy 440 cals, Protein 14.6g, Fat 13.1g, Saturated fat 1.8g, Carbohydrate 70.4g, Total sugars 16.3g, Fiber 8.2g, Salt 1.03g, Sodium 406mg

Smashed Roast Butternut Squash Salad with White Beans and Pine Nuts

I love butternut squash in many guises. This salad with the added GI value of the beans and pine nuts is perfect with some cooked ham, or simply spread on some toasted sesame bread.

Serves 4

1 teaspoon ground fennel
1 teaspoon ground coriander
1 teaspoon dried mint
½ teaspoon hot red pepper flakes
1 butternut squash, unpeeled, halved
   lengthwise, seeded, and each
   half cut into 4 wedges
spray olive oil
¼ teaspoon ground cinnamon
juice of 1 lemon
6 tablespoons non-fat natural
   Greek yogurt
2 teaspoons Dijon mustard
1 (14-oz) can cannellini beans, drained
2 tablespoons toasted pine nuts
salt and freshly ground black pepper
1 tablespoon snipped fresh chives,
   to garnish

1 Preheat the oven to 400°F.

2 Mix together the ground fennel, ground coriander, dried mint, and red pepper flakes. Spread the butternut squash wedges on to a roasting pan and spray them with olive oil. Dust first with the spice/herb mix, and then with the cinnamon. Spray a sheet of parchment paper with olive oil and place oiled-side down over the butternut squash.

3 Roast in the oven for 30 minutes, then remove the parchment paper and roast for another 20 minutes. Remove from the oven and leave to cool, then scrape the flesh off the skin into a bowl.

4 Meanwhile, combine the lemon juice, yogurt, and Dijon mustard, then fold in the cannellini beans and pine nuts. Gently mix with the squash so as not to break up the squash too much. Season to taste with salt and pepper and garnish with chives.

Variation Substitute fresh mint for the chives if you prefer.

Amount per portion
Energy 205 cals, Protein 10.8g, Fat 5.2g, Saturated fat 0.4g, Carbohydrate 30.9g, Total sugars 11.9g, Fiber 6.7g, Salt 1.53g, Sodium 602mg

Roasted Carrots and Baby Onions

A delicious sweet-and-sour carrot dish that goes perfectly with roast chicken.

Serves 4
spray sunflower oil
2 shallots, finely diced
2 garlic cloves, finely chopped
2 tablespoons orange juice
1 tablespoon raisins
1 tablespoon cider vinegar
1 tablespoon sunflower oil
grated zest of ½ orange
grated zest of ½ lemon
1 tablespoon molasses
1 tablespoon ketchup
1 teaspoon Colman's English mustard
1 teaspoon Worcestershire sauce
1 teaspoon Tabasco sauce
salt
1lb carrots
½ lb baby onions

To serve
¼ teaspoon fresh soft thyme leaves
1 tablespoon snipped fresh chives
1 tablespoon chopped fresh flat-leaf parsley
1 tablespoon toasted almond flakes

1 Preheat the oven to 350°F. Spray a heavy-bottomed saucepan with oil and place over medium heat. Add the shallots and garlic and cook for 6 minutes to color and soften.

2 Pour the orange juice into a food processor, add the raisins, vinegar, and oil and blend until smooth. Add this mixture to the shallot mix in the saucepan, along with 1 cup of water, the orange and lemon zests, molasses, ketchup, mustard, Worcestershire sauce, Tabasco, and ¼ teaspoon of salt. Bring to a simmer and simmer for 10 minutes.

3 Place the carrots and onions in a roasting pan and pour over the hot sauce mixture, stirring to coat the vegetables. Roast for about 45 minutes or until the vegetables are tender, basting with the sauce mixture every 10 minutes. Just before serving, toss in the herbs and almonds.

Amount per portion
Energy 128 cals, Protein 2.9g, Fat 5.1g, Saturated fat 0.5g, Carbohydrate 18.8g, Total sugars 17.7g, Fiber 4.0g, Salt 0.98g, Sodium 387mg

Charred Cauliflower with Tartare Flavors

Plain steamed cauliflower is not interesting and cauliflower casserole with cheese is high in fat, so this French recipe dresses it up enough that you'll be glad to add it to your list of vegetable dishes. It also works as a delicious accompaniment to grilled salmon.

Serves 4
1 tablespoon non-pareil capers (baby capers)
3 cornichons (baby gherkins), sliced
1 shallot, diced
1 garlic clove, crushed to a paste with a little sea salt
1 hard-boiled egg, chopped
1 tablespoon chopped fresh parsley
2 teaspoons snipped fresh chives
2 teaspoons chopped fresh tarragon
1 tablespoon whole-grain Dijon mustard
1 tablespoon tarragon vinegar
¼ cup extra virgin olive oil
salt and freshly ground pepper
½ cauliflower, broken into florets, blanched in boiling water for 3 minutes
handful of baby spinach leaves
12 cherry tomatoes, halved

1 In a bowl, mix together the capers, cornichons, shallot, garlic, egg, and herbs. In another bowl, whisk together the mustard and vinegar, then slowly add two thirds of the oil. Mix this dressing with the flavored egg mixture and season to taste with salt and pepper.

2 Heat the remaining oil in a frying pan over high heat and cook the cauliflower florets until charred on all sides—you may need to cook the florets in batches.

3 While the florets are still warm, mix them with the dressing, then fold in the spinach and tomatoes and adjust the seasoning to taste. Serve hot or at room temperature.

Amount per portion
Energy 210 cals, Protein 8.3g, Fat 17.1g, Saturated fat 2.4g, Carbohydrate 6.2g, Total sugars 4.9g, Fiber 3.3g, Salt 1.31g, Sodium 518mg

Spiced Chickpeas

I've prepared this recipe as a vegetable side dish, but it's also excellent at room temperature as a salad. Once puréed and with more chickpeas added, it can be served on toasted multigrain bread as a snack.

Serves 4
2 teaspoons sunflower oil
1 teaspoon anise
1 large onion, coarsely chopped
2 garlic cloves, finely chopped
¼ small savoy cabbage, shredded
1 teaspoon mango powder
1 teaspoon chili powder
½ teaspoon ground turmeric
½ teaspoon salt
1 teaspoon sugar
1 (14-oz) can chickpeas, drained and rinsed

1 Heat the oil in a saucepan over medium heat and cook the anise until it starts to pop. Add the onion and cook gently for 6 minutes. Add the remaining ingredients apart from the chickpeas and stir-fry for 5 minutes. Add the chickpeas and heat through for 2 minutes.

Tip Mango powder, also known as *amchoor*, is an Indian ingredient used in curries, pickles, and chutneys and also used as a souring and tenderizing agent.

Amount per portion
Energy 138 cals, Protein 6.6g, Fat 4.5g, Saturated fat 0.3g, Carbohydrate 19.1g, Total sugars 7.1g, Fiber 5.0g, Salt 0.87g, Sodium 344mg

Grilled Zucchini with Chickpeas, Goat Cheese, and Mint

I file this fresh and vibrant collection of Italy, Greece, and the Middle East under "Australia" because that's where I ate it. It's fantastically easy to make.

Serves 4

3 zucchini, each cut lengthwise into 5 slices
2 tablespoons extra virgin olive oil
salt and freshly ground black pepper
2oz crumbled goat cheese
2 ripe tomatoes, seeded and diced
1 (14-oz) can chickpeas, drained and rinsed
1 tablespoon chopped fresh mint
grated zest and juice of 1 lemon
½ teaspoon hot red pepper flakes

1 Heat a ridged grill pan over medium-high heat, brush the zucchini slices with some olive oil, and cook for 1 to 2 minutes on each side until grill-marked. Season to taste with salt and pepper and arrange as you wish onto a large platter.

2 Scatter the zucchini with the goat cheese, tomatoes, and chickpeas, and drizzle with the remaining olive oil. Sprinkle the mint, lemon zest, and pepper flakes over the top, then drizzle with the lemon juice and adjust the seasoning to taste.

Amount per portion
Energy 176 cals, Protein 9g, Fat 10g, Saturated fat 2.2g, Carbohydrate 14g, Total sugars 4g, Fiber 4g, Salt 1.12g, Sodium 442mg

Nutty Curried Beans

Obviously there are Indian influences here, but it took an Australian to put the package together. This makes a lovely hot dish to go with grilled meat or fish, but it's also great served at room temperature as a salad.

Serves 4

10½ oz fresh green beans, cut in half
1 tablespoon sunflower oil
1 small onion, finely chopped
2 garlic cloves, finely chopped
1 teaspoon brown mustard seeds
6 curry leaves, shredded
2½ oz macadamia nuts, coarsely chopped
1 teaspoon garam masala
¼ teaspoon cayenne pepper
½ teaspoon ground turmeric
½ teaspoon ground cumin
1 (14-oz) can white navy beans, drained and rinsed
½ cup low-fat coconut milk
salt and freshly ground black pepper

1 Cook the beans in boiling salted water for 3 minutes. Drain and plunge into cold water, then drain and set aside.

2 Heat the oil in a frying pan and cook the onions gently until soft, about 6 minutes. Add the garlic, mustard seeds, curry leaves, and macadamias, and cook for another 3 minutes. Add the remaining spices, beans, and coconut milk and simmer for 8 minutes. Add salt and pepper to taste, then fold in the green beans.

Amount per portion
Energy 256 cals, Protein 7.4g, Fat 19.6g, Saturated fat 3.7g, Carbohydrate 13.6g, Total sugars 3.8g, Fiber 6.7g, Salt 0.80g, Sodium 318mg

LEFT Grilled Zucchini with Chickpeas, Goat Cheese, and Mint

Fattoush

This lovely crunchy, herby salad is often served as part of Middle Eastern meze buffets. I've substituted an herby yogurt for the normal olive oil, and oven-cooked the pita bread instead of frying it.

Serves 4

1 whole wheat pita bread, halved horizontally and cut into small squares
1 baby gem lettuce
20 fresh mint leaves
1 small bunch of fresh parsley
1 small bunch of fresh cilantro
2 beefsteak tomatoes, seeded and diced
6 radishes, quartered
6 scallions
1 small green bell pepper, seeded and finely sliced
handful of watercress sprigs
1 small cucumber, seeded and diced
juice and grated zest of 1 lemon
1 teaspoon sumac
salt and freshly ground black pepper
3 tablespoons non-fat natural yogurt

1 Preheat the oven to 350°F. Lay the pita squares on a baking sheet and toast them in the oven for 8 to 10 minutes until crisp. Remove and set aside.

2 Finely chop the lettuce, then finely chop the mint, then the parsley, and then the cilantro. Reserve one teaspoon each of mint, parsley, and cilantro, and mix the remaining herbs with the lettuce in a serving bowl.

3 Add the tomatoes, radishes, scallions, green pepper, watercress, and cucumber. Toss in the lemon juice and zest, sumac, some salt and pepper, and the pita squares. Mix the yogurt with the reserved herbs, drizzle over the salad, and mix.

Variation For a more substantial salad, add a few hard-boiled eggs.

Amount per portion
Energy 73 cals, Protein 4.0g, Fat 1.0g, Saturated fat 0.2g, Carbohydrate 12.7g, Total sugars 5.5g, Fiber 2.8g, Salt 0.87g, Sodium 342mg

Spice and Rice

Let's face it, the word "dull" often springs to mind in relation to brown rice, but not in this case. There are times when I could eat a bowl of this delicious Indian-style rice on its own. It's very filling and contains much of what we need in an all-around balanced diet. Here, I've used a handy quick-cook rice; it's very useful for people in a hurry.

Serves 4

2 teaspoons sunflower oil
½ teaspoon fenugreek seeds
¼ teaspoon asafoetida powder (optional)
2 hot red chiles, seeded and finely diced
1 teaspoon ground coriander
2 teaspoons gram lentils (*channa dal*)
2 teaspoons tamarind paste, diluted
    in a little hot water
1 onion, finely diced
1 garlic clove, finely chopped
1 carrot, cut into ¼ in cubes
1 cup frozen peas, defrosted
1 (14-oz) can navy beans, drained
2 cups minute brown rice
2 tablespoons coarsely chopped
    cashews
2 tablespoons chopped fresh cilantro
salt and freshly ground black pepper
salad, to serve

1 In a frying pan, heat half the oil and stir in the fenugreek, asafoetida, chiles, ground coriander, and lentils. Over medium heat, cook for 3 minutes, stirring continuously. Transfer the mixture to a mini food processor and blend until a smoothish paste, or grind with a mortar and pestle.

2 In a small pan, mix together the diluted tamarind and the spice paste, and cook until the paste is thick, about 2 to 3 minutes.

3 Meanwhile in a separate pan, heat the remaining oil and cook the onions for 8 to 10 minutes until lightly colored. Add the garlic and carrot and continue to cook gently, covered, for about 8 minutes until the carrot is starting to soften but still has a little bite. Add the tamarind paste, peas, and beans and stir well.

4 Prepare the rice according to package instructions and fold it into the vegetable mix, then sprinkle the cashews and cilantro over the top and season to taste with salt and pepper. Serve piping hot, with a salad.

Amount per portion
Energy 303 cals, Protein 11g, Fat 8g, Saturated fat 0.6g, Carbohydrate 50g, Total sugars 6.8g, Fiber 9.1g, Salt 0.73g, Sodium 289mg`

Dhal with Added Spice

Lentils are extremely nutritious, but there is a good reason for spicing them up: they are naturally rich in protein nitrogen compounds, which require much more effort to digest than the protein in meat, fish, and dairy products. So the Indians learned to add certain digestion-friendly spices such as ginger.

Serves 4

9oz red lentils, washed
1 tablespoon sunflower oil
5 garlic cloves, finely chopped
1 onion, finely chopped
1in piece of fresh ginger, peeled and finely chopped
3 green chiles, seeded and finely chopped
1 teaspoon ground coriander
1 teaspoon ground cumin
½ teaspoon chili powder
1 teaspoon black mustard seeds (optional)
1 teaspoon ground turmeric
salt and freshly ground black pepper
3 plum tomatoes, seeded and diced
3 tablespoons chopped fresh cilantro
2 teaspoons lime juice

1 Pour 1½ quarts of water into a saucepan and bring to a boil. Add the lentils and cook for 15 minutes, stirring regularly at the beginning, as the early period of cooking is when the lentils will stick together.

2 Meanwhile, melt the oil in a frying pan and add the garlic, onion, ginger, and chiles, and cook over medium heat for 10 minutes until the onion has softened. Add the spices and cook for another 2 minutes. Fold this mixture into the lentils after they have cooked for 15 minutes.

3 Cook the dhal for another 10 to 15 minutes until the lentils are very tender. Beat with a whisk until completely mashed, season with salt and pepper to taste, then fold in the tomatoes, fresh cilantro, and lime juice.

Amount per portion
Energy 267 cals, Protein 16.8g, Fat 4.4g, Saturated fat 0.4g, Carbohydrate 42.6g, Total sugars 5.7g, Fiber 4.4g, Salt 0.72g, Sodium 284mg

Green Vegetables with Almond and Orange

A pleasant little combo with its roots in Italy that can be served as a salad as here, or hot as an accompaniment to grilled meat or fish.

Serves 4
2 oranges, peeled
⅓ cup toasted almond flakes
1 garlic clove, finely chopped
1 tablespoon snipped fresh chives
1 teaspoon whole-grain mustard
1 shallot, finely diced
1 tablespoon extra virgin olive oil
1 tablespoon walnut or hazelnut oil
salt and freshly ground black pepper
7oz green beans, ends trimmed and cut into
    1¼ in pieces
7oz sugar snap peas
¾ cup edamame, fresh or frozen
a few handfuls of arugula

1 With a small sharp knife and working over a large bowl, cut out the orange segments from their membranes and drop the segments into the bowl. Squeeze the membranes over the bowl to release any juices and discard the membranes and any seeds. Add the almonds, garlic, chives, mustard, shallot, and two oils to the segments. Whisk and season to taste with salt and pepper.
2 Cook the green beans in boiling salted water for 3 minutes, add the peas and edamame, and cook for another 2 minutes. Drain well. While the vegetables are still hot, transfer them into the nutty orange dressing and stir.
3 Scatter some arugula on individual plates and top with the veggies.

Amount per portion
Energy 221 cals, Protein 10.0g, Fat 13.4g, Saturated fat 1.3g, Carbohydrate 16.0g, Total sugars 11.3g, Fiber 5.6g, Salt 0.70g, Sodium 278mg

Stir-Fried Greens with Mustard Seeds and Cashews

A tasty way to dress up your greens. I could eat these on their own without feeling the need for protein.

Serves 2 to 4
1 tablespoon canola oil
¾ in piece of fresh ginger, peeled and
    cut into small matchsticks
2 garlic cloves, thinly sliced
2 teaspoons yellow mustard seeds
1lb greens (spring greens, bok choy, Savoy
    cabbage), cut into bite-sized pieces
1 tablespoon reduced-salt soy sauce
1 tablespoon chopped unsalted
    cashew nuts

1 Heat the oil in a wok and sauté the ginger until it just starts to color, then add the garlic and mustard seeds and continue to sauté until the seeds start to pop.
2 Add the greens, increase the heat, and cook until they start to wilt. Add in the soy sauce, fold in the cashews, and serve immediately.

Tip Serve tossed through some rice noodles.

Amount per portion (for 2)
Energy 163 cals, Protein 7.5g, Fat 10.4g, Saturated fat 0.7g, Carbohydrate 10.7g, Total sugars 6.8g, Fiber 5.9g, Salt 1g, Sodium 395mg

Amount per portion (for 4)
Energy 82 cals, Protein 3.8g, Fat 5.2g, Saturated fat 0.3g, Carbohydrate 5.3g, Total sugars 3.4g, Fiber 3.0g, Salt 0.5g, Sodium 198mg

Lima beans with Chiles and Asian Influence

Lima beans are not often used in Asia, but I had this Asian-influenced dish with a grilled swordfish steak in Adelaide, and it was a good combination. Lima beans have a wonderful silky, creamy texture, but unless you're an expert cook, I wouldn't suggest using dried beans.

Serves 4
For the Asian mix
4 garlic cloves, crushed to a paste
    with a little salt
½ in piece of fresh ginger, peeled and grated
1 hot green chile, seeded and finely
    chopped
2 mild green chiles, seeded and
    thinly sliced
1 red bell pepper, seeded and cut into
    ½ in dice
2 shallots, thinly sliced
2 tablespoons sweet chile sauce
1 tablespoon sesame oil
2 tablespoons reduced-salt soy sauce
2 tablespoons lime juice
3 scallions, sliced

2 (14-oz) cans lima beans, drained
    and rinsed
2 tablespoons chopped fresh cilantro
2 teaspoons chopped fresh mint

1 In a bowl, mix together all the ingredients for the Asian mix and leave for 30 minutes to allow the flavors to develop.
2 Heat the lima beans in boiling water for 2 minutes. Drain, mix them into the Asian mix, and then sprinkle with cilantro and mint. Serve hot or at room temperature.

Amount per portion
Energy 153 cals, Protein 8.2g, Fat 3.6g, Saturated fat 0.4g, Carbohydrate 23.3g, Total sugars 8.7g, Fiber 6.3g, Salt 2.42g, Sodium 956mg

LEFT Stir-Fried Greens with
Mustard Seeds and Cashews

Vegetarian

Stuffed Onions

So, I admit that this recipe requires a little work, but it can be prepared ahead of time. It makes an impressive vegetarian dish, with its mix of creamy and crunchy textures.

Serves 4
4 large onions
1 small sweet potato, cut into ½ in dice
1 (14-oz) can navy beans, drained
    and rinsed
1 garlic clove, crushed to a paste with
    a little salt
pinch of hot red pepper flakes
4½ oz cooked fresh spinach (or defrosted
    frozen spinach), chopped
2 tablespoons non-fat Greek yogurt
1 teaspoon Dijon mustard
¼ teaspoon salt
¼ teaspoon grated nutmeg
2 tablespoons breadcrumbs
salad and new potatoes, to serve

1 Peel the onions without damaging the inner layers, and cut a cross in the root end. Cook, along with the sweet potato, in boiling water for 6 minutes. Drain and set the sweet potato aside.

2 When the onions are cool enough to handle, cut a third off the top. With your fingers or a teaspoon, remove the insides of the onions, leaving the 2 outer layers intact; you will now have four onion containers. Chop a third of the removed onion and place in a bowl with the sweet potato and discard the remaining two thirds of the onions. Add half the beans, the garlic, red pepper flakes, and spinach. Mix well.

3 Mash the remaining beans with the yogurt, mustard, salt, and nutmeg. Mix this with the sweet potato and spinach mix, and spoon the mixture into the onion shells, piling it high. (The recipe can be made ahead to this point.)

4 Preheat the oven to 400°F. Place the onions on a lightly oiled baking sheet, scatter the tops with breadcrumbs, and bake for 25 minutes. Serve with salad and new potatoes.

Amount per portion
Energy 179 cals, Protein 9.7g, Fat 1.4g, Saturated fat 0.2g, Carbohydrate 35.1g, Total sugars 14.6g, Fiber 8.7g, Salt 0.61g, Sodium 242mg

Zucchini Cakes

Great with a poached egg as part of a vegetarian buffet, or served with a spicy tomato sauce or tzatziki.

Serves 4
1 medium zucchini (about ½ lb)
1 teaspoon salt
2 pickled jalapeño chiles, chopped
2 shallots, finely diced
1 garlic clove, finely chopped
1 teaspoon curry powder
2 teaspoons sesame seeds
1 tablespoon extra virgin olive oil
1½ cups whole wheat flour
½ teaspoon baking powder
1 tablespoon sunflower oil, for cooking

1 Grate the zucchini into a colander, sprinkle with the salt, and stir. Leave for 20 minutes to release the liquid, then squeeze out the excess moisture.

2 In a bowl, mix together the grated zucchini, 1 tablespoon of water, and the remaining ingredients except the sunflower oil. With floured hands, shape the mixture into 8 rounds and flatten them slightly.

3 In a large frying pan, heat the sunflower oil then cook the cakes on one side for 1 minute until golden. Gently flip them over, reduce the heat to low, and cook the cakes for 12 to 15 minutes, turning once again halfway through. (Depending on the size of your frying pan, you may need to cook in two batches, in which case keep the first batch warm in a low oven while you cook the next.)

Amount per portion
Energy 214 cals, Protein 7.2g, Fat 8.0g, Saturated fat 1.1g, Carbohydrate 30.2g, Total sugars 2.4g, Fiber 5.0g, Salt 0.83g, Sodium 328mg

Baked Eggs in Spiced Mushrooms

Mushrooms are relatively calorie-free, but the modern mushroom is also free of good flavor, so here's a French recipe that will dress it up. The mushroom mix can be prepared ahead of time and cooked later.

Serves 4
3 tomatoes, coarsely chopped
1 teaspoon coriander seeds, crushed
2 teaspoons tomato paste
½ teaspoon thyme leaves
1 bay leaf
2 tablespoons olive oil
freshly ground black pepper
3 tablespoons golden raisins
3 tablespoons toasted pine nuts
juice of ½ lemon
9oz button mushrooms, quartered
4 eggs
1 tablespoon non-fat Greek yogurt

1 Place the tomatoes, coriander, tomato paste, thyme, and bay leaf in a saucepan. Add the oil and season generously with pepper. Add ½ cup of water and simmer gently for 8 minutes. Increase the heat and add the golden raisins, pine nuts, lemon juice, and mushrooms, and cook for another 5 minutes. (The dish can be prepared ahead up to this point.)

2 Preheat the oven to 350°F. Spoon the mushroom mixture into individual large ramekins and make a well in the center of each one. Break an egg into each indent and top with a dollop of yogurt. Bake for 9 minutes if the mushrooms are hot, or 12 if cold.

Amount per portion
Energy 220 cals, Protein 10.7g, Fat 16.4g, Saturated fat 3.1g, Carbohydrate 7.9g, Total sugars 7.3g, Fiber 1.7g, Salt 0.26g, Sodium 104mg

Slow-Cooked Green Polenta with Vegetables

It's a divided camp when it comes to polenta. Many of us love this creamy cornmeal dish, a staple food throughout much of Northern Italy. If you're one of those who doesn't love it, I'd like you to give this dish a chance—it's packed full of goodness, but best of all it tastes delicious.

Serves 4
1 quart vegetable stock
10½ oz "real" polenta (see Tip below)
2 tablespoons olive oil
4 garlic cloves, sliced
1 onion, coarsely chopped
1 red bell pepper, seeded and cut into
  1in pieces
1 small eggplant, cut into 1in pieces
2 zucchini, cut into 1in pieces
12 cherry tomatoes
salt and freshly ground pepper
2 cups spring greens or dark cabbage,
  coarsely chopped
2 handfuls of spinach, central stems
  removed
1 (14-oz) can chickpeas, drained and rinsed
1½ oz grated Parmesan cheese
warm multigrain bread, to serve

1 In a large saucepan, bring the stock to a boil, then pour in the polenta a little at a time, whisking furiously to prevent lumps. Reduce the heat to low and cook gently, stirring every 3 to 4 minutes to ensure every part of the polenta is moved around to prevent sticking. The polenta will need to cook for about 40 minutes, but follow the instructions on the package.
2 Meanwhile, heat the olive oil in a large frying pan, then add the garlic, onion, red pepper, and eggplant, and cook over low heat until the vegetables are tender. Add the zucchini and tomatoes and cook for another 5 minutes, then season to taste with salt and pepper.
3 At the same time, cook the spring greens or cabbage in boiling water for 3 minutes, then stir in the spinach and cook for another minute. With a slotted spoon, transfer the green vegetables into a food processor, with water clinging. Process to a smooth purée and season again to taste.
4 Just before serving, fold the green purée into the polenta, stir, then fold in the vegetables, chickpeas, and Parmesan, and adjust the seasoning if needed. Serve piping hot, with some warm multigrain bread.

Tip You can use instant or quick-cook polenta; they're not as good, but they are convenient. If you do use either, prepare your vegetables and greens first so you're ready to fold everything together.

Amount per portion
Energy 503 cals, Protein 20.4g, Fat 14.6g, Saturated fat 3.2g, Carbohydrate 77.4g, Total sugars 14.9g, Fiber 10.3g, Salt 1.84g, Sodium 723mg

Texan Spinach and Bean Bake

It's not exactly beans around the campfire, but it's heading in that direction. This is a good, hearty dish that can be prepared ahead of time.

Serves 4
1 tablespoon olive oil
1 onion, chopped
1 garlic clove, finely chopped
1 hot red chile, seeded and
    finely chopped
1 tablespoon smoked paprika
1 tablespoon ketchup
½ teaspoon salt
10½ oz cooked or frozen leaf spinach,
    defrosted, squeezed, and chopped
2 tablespoons golden raisins
2 (14-oz) cans pinto or navy beans,
    drained and rinsed
½ cup grated cheddar cheese
¼ cup vegetable stock
salad, to serve

1 Preheat the oven to 400°F. Heat the olive oil in a saucepan and cook the onion until soft and translucent, about 8 minutes. Add the garlic, chile, paprika, ketchup, salt, spinach, golden raisins, beans, and cheddar. Mix well, then moisten with the stock.

2 Spoon the mixture into a baking dish and cook for 25 minutes in the preheated oven. Serve with salad.

Amount per portion
Energy 302 cals, Protein 17.1g, Fat 9.1g, Saturated fat 3.1g, Carbohydrate 40.6g, Total sugars 9.8g, Fiber 12.6g, Salt 1.08g, Sodium 000mg

One Pot Cauliflower

This Spanish dish makes a lovely vegetarian dinner in its own right, but I've also included chorizo and bacon as optional extras to make it flexible for any occasion.

Serves 4
2 tablespoons extra virgin olive oil
1 cauliflower, broken into florets
1 (14-oz) can chickpeas, drained
1 (8-oz) can chopped tomatoes
6 scallions, sliced
2 garlic cloves, crushed to a paste
    with a little salt
3oz chorizo sausage, diced (optional)
2 to 3 slices thick-cut smoked bacon,
    diced (optional)
3 tablespoons golden raisins
1 tablespoon toasted pine nuts
2 teaspoons smoked paprika
salt and freshly ground black pepper

1 Put all the ingredients in a saucepan, stir, cover, and cook over low heat for 15 to 20 minutes, shaking the pan from time to time— try to resist lifting the lid as you don't want the steam to escape. Season to taste and serve.

Amount per portion
Energy 325 cals, Protein 18.0g, Fat 18.9g, Saturated fat 4.1g, Carbohydrate 22.1g, Total sugars 10.3g, Fiber 6.1g, Salt 2.14g, Sodium 844mg

Herby Green Pilaf Rice

This Middle Eastern rice dish is excellent on its own, or it makes a great accompaniment to grilled meats and fish for non-vegetarians.

Serves 4
1 tablespoon sunflower oil
1 onion, finely chopped
1 garlic clove, finely chopped
4 cardamom pods, crushed
¾ in cinnamon stick
3 cloves
½ teaspoon ground black pepper
½ teaspoon ground turmeric
1¼ cups long-grain rice
1¾ cups hot vegetable stock
2 tablespoons chopped fresh parsley
1 tablespoon chopped fresh cilantro
5 scallions, chopped
2 handfuls of watercress, chopped
2 handfuls of baby spinach leaves
2 tablespoons toasted almond flakes
2 tablespoons raisins
salt

1 Heat the oil in a large lidded saucepan, add the onion, and cook gently until soft, about 6 to 8 minutes. Add the garlic, cardamom, cinnamon stick, cloves, pepper, and turmeric, and cook for 2 minutes. Add the rice, mix well, and cook for 1 minute, then add the hot stock. Bring to a boil and reduce the heat to medium. Cover and cook for 15 minutes.

2 Turn off the heat but leave the rice untouched, covered, for 5 minutes. Fluff up the rice, return to low heat, and add all the herbs and greens, almonds and raisins, and season to taste with salt. Serve hot.

Amount per portion
Energy 317 cals, Protein 7g, Fat 7g, Saturated fat 0.6g, Carbohydrate 60g, Total sugars 8.9g, Fiber 2.6g, Salt 0.93g, Sodium 365mg

Rich but Sinless Vegetable Curry

There's lots going on here, but it's certainly a fantastic way of contributing to your five-a-day. This Indian-influenced dish is very much korma in style, even meat eaters will love it.

Serves 4

2 large onions, coarsely chopped
1 teaspoon chopped garlic
1 tablespoon chopped ginger
1 teaspoon ground turmeric
1 teaspoon chili powder
1 teaspoon ground cumin
1 teaspoon ground coriander
2 tablespoons sunflower oil
1 (14-oz) can chopped tomatoes
1 teaspoon superfine sugar
6oz non-fat Greek yogurt
4 tablespoons ground almonds
2 large carrots, diced
1 (14-oz) can chickpeas, drained and rinsed
8 new potatoes, halved
½ cauliflower, broken into small florets
¼ savoy cabbage, shredded
3½ oz fresh green beans, cut into
    ½ in lengths
2 tablespoons dried cherries, chopped
2 tablespoons sunflower seeds
1 tablespoon chopped fresh cilantro
1 tablespoon garam masala
salt and freshly ground pepper
rice, to serve

1 In a food processor, blend together the onions, garlic, ginger, and spices to a smooth purée.

2 Heat the oil in a saucepan over low heat and cook the spiced onion purée until all the moisture has evaporated. Stir in the tomatoes and cook for another 5 minutes. Add the sugar and yogurt and bring to a simmer. Reduce the heat and add the almonds, carrots, chickpeas, and potatoes, cover and cook for 15 minutes. Add the cauliflower, cabbage, and beans and cook for another 6 minutes.

3 Fold in the cherries, sunflower seeds, fresh cilantro, and garam masala. (If the curry is thicker than you like, add a little water to thin.) Add salt and pepper to taste. Serve with rice.

Tip You can find chopped garlic and ginger in most supermarkets these days—always having a jar of each on hand makes our lives easier.

Amount per portion
Energy 491 cals, Protein 22.5, Fat 21.2g, Saturated fat 1.8g, Carbohydrate 56.0g, Total sugars 27.0g, Fiber 12.2g, Salt 1.39g, Sodium 551mg

A Potato and Lima Bean Curry with Cottage Cheese

In normal circumstances I would use paneer as the cheese in this Indian-influenced dish. Low-fat cottage cheese makes a good replacement, however, acting as a great vehicle for picking up and absorbing all these wonderful curry flavors.

Serves 4
2 tablespoons sunflower oil
2 teaspoons mustard seeds
1 pinch asafoetida powder (optional)
1 onion, coarsely chopped
1 large carrot, cut into ¾ in chunks
1 sweet potato, cut into ¾ in dice
1 teaspoon ground turmeric
1 teaspoon chili powder
1 teaspoon ground coriander
¾ lb new potatoes, halved
salt
3 tablespoons desiccated coconut
1 (14-oz) can lima beans, drained
    and rinsed
3 tablespoons coarsely chopped cilantro
1 teaspoon finely chopped fresh mint leaves
6oz low-fat cottage cheese
brown rice, to serve

1 Heat the oil in a saucepan and cook the mustard seeds over medium-low heat until they start to pop, then add the asafoetida and onion and cook gently for 8 minutes. Add the carrot, sweet potato, turmeric, chili powder, ground coriander, and potatoes. Season with salt, add ¾ cup water, and stir, then cover and cook gently until the vegetables are tender, about 20 minutes.

2 Fold in the coconut, lima beans, cilantro, and mint, adjust the seasoning to taste, and heat until warmed through. Divide between individual warmed bowls and dot with spoonfuls of cottage cheese. Serve with brown rice.

Amount per portion
Energy 316 cals, Protein 13.1g, Fat 12.7g Saturated fat 4.8g, Carbohydrate 40.0g, Total sugars 10.8g, Fiber 6.9g, Salt 1.72g, Sodium 681mg

Broccoli Frittata

This excellent Italian frittata is a useful standby as a simple main course or for fridge snacking. Non-vegetarians could add a little bacon with the onion for extra flavor.

Serves 4
2 tablespoons olive oil
2 onions, finely chopped
2 garlic cloves, finely chopped
1lb small broccoli florets, blanched
    in boiling water for 2 minutes
1 teaspoon thyme leaves
¾ cup cooked brown rice
¼ teaspoon hot red pepper flakes
salt and freshly ground white pepper
6 eggs, beaten
spray oil
1 cup low-fat ricotta or cream cheese
salad and new potatoes, to serve

1 Heat the oil in a frying pan and gently cook the onions until soft and translucent, about 8 minutes. Add the garlic, broccoli, and thyme and stir-fry for 2 minutes. Fold in the rice and red pepper flakes and season to taste with salt and pepper. Transfer the mixture to a bowl and leave to cool. Meanwhile, preheat the oven to 325°F.

2 Fold the cooled rice mixture into the eggs. Spray a non-stick, ovenproof pan with a light coating of oil and place it over medium heat. Pour in the egg mixture and dot the surface with nuggets of ricotta. Cook over low heat for 5 minutes, then transfer to the preheated oven for 15 to 20 minutes, depending on the thickness of the frittata—when ready, the eggs should be set but not dry. Serve with salad and new potatoes.

Amount per portion
Energy 337 cals, Protein 21.0g, Fat 18.8g, Saturated fat 4.7g, Carbohydrate 22.2g, Total sugars 6.0g, Fiber 4.2g, Salt 1.04g, Sodium 412mg

Stuffed Eggplant with Tamarind

I'm an eggplant fan, but it needs to be thoroughly cooked—otherwise it can resemble tasteless shoe leather. That can't be said about this fantastic Indian recipe.

Serves 4

2 large eggplants, cut in half lengthwise
2 tablespoons sunflower oil
salt
1 large onion, finely chopped
2 garlic cloves, finely chopped
4 cloves
2 tablespoons coriander seeds
1 tablespoon cumin seeds
freshly ground pepper
1½ oz desiccated coconut
3 tomatoes, seeded and diced
1 tablespoon toasted pine nuts
2 tablespoons chopped cashew nuts
1 teaspoon chili powder
1 teaspoon ground turmeric
2 teaspoons tamarind paste
6oz frozen spinach, defrosted, squeezed, and chopped
8 cooked new potatoes, diced
1 teaspoon superfine sugar
4 tablespoons non-fat Greek yogurt

1 Preheat the oven to 375°F. When it has come up to temperature, brush the cut surfaces of the eggplant with 1 tablespoon of sunflower oil, sprinkle with a touch of salt, and place cut-side down on a baking sheet. Transfer to the preheated oven and roast for 30 minutes.

2 Meanwhile, heat the remaining oil in a pan, add the onions, and cook over low heat until softening and turning color, about 8 minutes. Remove half and set aside. To the remaining onions, add the garlic, cloves, coriander seeds, cumin seeds, and a dash of pepper, and cook for 1 minute. Add the coconut and continue to cook until the coconut has turned a pale brown color.

3 Process the spicy coconut onion mix in a food processor, adding a little water if necessary. Spoon this mixture into a bowl, then add the reserved softened onions and all the remaining ingredients. Season to taste.

4 When the eggplants are cooked, remove them from the oven but do not turn the oven off. Hollow out the eggplant shells, being careful not to split them. Chop the flesh and add it to the savory mix. Heap the mixture back into the shells, return to the oven, and cook for 20 minutes.

Tip These can be made ahead of time and refrigerated for up to a couple of days until you're ready to heat them through. They'll take 30 to 35 minutes at 375°F to heat through from cold.

Amount per portion
Energy 336 cals, Protein 10.4g, Fat 19.7g, Saturated fat 6.6g, Carbohydrate 31.2g, Total sugars 14.3g, Fiber 8.6g, Salt 0.93g, Sodium 367mg

Stuffed Cabbage Leaves with Tomatoes and Beans

As a child, my mother would regularly make a Polish recipe for stuffed cabbage which usually involved ground pork. Here's an excellent vegetarian version from Greece.

Serves 4

12 leaves savoy cabbage, large rib trimmed
2 tablespoons good-quality olive oil
2 red onions, finely chopped
3 garlic cloves, finely chopped
2 celery ribs, finely sliced
2 cups finely sliced carrots
2 bay leaves
1 cup quick-cook brown rice
1 teaspoon smoked paprika
2 tomatoes, chopped
1 tablespoon each chopped fresh chives,
    parsley, and basil
salt and freshly ground black pepper
1 (14-oz) can chopped tomatoes
1 (14-oz) can borlotti beans, drained
    and rinsed
½ tablespoon dried oregano

1 Cook the cabbage leaves in boiling salted water for 3 minutes, then remove, drain, and refresh under cold running water. Drain and pat dry. Lay the leaves outside-down on a work surface.

2 Using two frying pans, heat half the olive oil in each, then add half the onion and garlic in each. Allow the onions to soften over medium heat, about 5 to 8 minutes. To one pan add the celery, carrots, and bay leaves, and cook gently for 8 minutes.

3 Meanwhile, to the other pan add the rice and paprika and cook for 5 minutes, stirring frequently. Add the fresh chopped tomatoes and half the fresh herbs, season to taste with salt and pepper, and leave to cool.

4 To the vegetable pan add the canned tomatoes, borlotti beans, and dried oregano, then stir in 1 cup of water and simmer gently. Set a heaping teaspoon of the rice stuffing on each cabbage leaf and loosely wrap to allow the rice to expand during cooking. Place the stuffed leaves on the bean and tomato stew, cover, and simmer gently for 20 to 25 minutes.

5 Arrange 3 stuffed leaves on each warmed plate. Add the remaining fresh herbs to the tomato and bean stew and season to taste, then spoon the stew around the stuffed leaves.

Amount per portion
Energy 286 cals, Protein 11g, Fat 8g, Saturated fat 1g, Carbohydrate 46g,
Total sugars 13.4g, Fiber 9.1g, Salt 1.17g, Sodium 459mg

Stuffed Peppers with Braised Potatoes

Peppers make useful containers for some delicious fillings, such as this Greek rice filling. With the potatoes on the side as here, this makes quite a substantial dish, and an excellent vegetarian meal.

Serves 4
4 large red or yellow bell peppers
1 tablespoon olive oil
1 onion, finely chopped
2 garlic cloves, crushed to a paste
    with a little salt
2 tomatoes, chopped
2 tablespoons golden raisins
1 tablespoon toasted pine nuts
1 tablespoon chopped fresh mint
1 cup long-grain brown rice
1lb new potatoes, sliced
½ cup tomato sauce
salad, to serve

1 Preheat the oven to 350°F. Slice one-third off the top of each pepper, then scoop out the seeds and pith and discard, but retain the top.

2 Heat the olive oil in a frying pan, add the onion and garlic, and cook gently for 10 minutes. Add the tomatoes, golden raisins, pine nuts, and mint and cook for another 5 minutes. Stir in the rice.

3 Fill the lower sections of the peppers with the rice mix—do not overfill, as the rice will expand when cooking. Replace the pepper tops and set the peppers on a baking sheet. Scatter the potato slices around the peppers, drizzle with a little olive oil, then pour the sauce over the potatoes.

4 Bake, uncovered, for about 45 minutes, checking toward the end to make sure they are not burning or collapsing. Serve hot or at room temperature, with a salad.

Amount per portion
Energy 318 cals, Protein 7g, Fat 7g, Saturated fat 0.8g, Carbohydrate 61g,
Total sugars 22.1g, Fiber 5.6g, Salt 0.26g, Sodium 102mg

Ratatouille Cakes

Accompanied by a salad, this delicious Australian dish makes a great vegetarian main course, but served as an appetizer, I'm sure it would also appeal to carnivores.

Serves 4

1 medium eggplant
1 tablespoon olive oil
1 small onion, finely chopped
1 garlic clove, finely chopped
½ teaspoon fresh thyme leaves
1 tablespoon tomato paste
½ green bell pepper, seeded and cut into ¼ in dice
1 zucchini, cut into ¼ in dice
1 tomato, seeded and diced
2 tablespoons chopped fresh flat-leaf parsley
1 tablespoon chopped fresh basil
1 egg, beaten
2 tablespoons freshly grated Parmesan cheese
½ teaspoon baking powder
¼ cup fresh multigrain breadcrumbs
spray oil, for frying
salt and freshly ground black pepper
salad or tomato sauce, to serve

1 Preheat the oven to 425°F. Prick the eggplant in several places with a fork, place it on a baking sheet, and roast in the oven for 30 to 40 minutes or until the eggplant is very soft and on the point of collapsing. Remove from the oven and set aside to cool slightly.

2 Meanwhile, heat the oil in a large frying pan. Over medium heat, cook the onion, garlic, and thyme until the onion is softening but without coloring, about 6 minutes. Add the tomato paste, green pepper, and zucchini, increase the heat, and cook for another 5 minutes. Leave to cool slightly.

3 Cut the eggplant in half lengthwise and scoop out the flesh; discard the skin. Mash the eggplant flesh to a purée with a fork, or use a food processor. Mix the purée with the cooked vegetables and all the remaining ingredients except the spray oil, and add salt and pepper to taste. If the mix is very soft, add extra breadcrumbs.

4 Heat a frying pan and spray with a light coating of oil. Take tablespoonfuls of the eggplant mixture and drop on to the frying pan—do not overcrowd the pan. Cook until brown on both sides, about 4 to 5 minutes. Keep the cakes warm in the oven on paper towels while cooking the remaining cakes. Serve with a salad or your favorite tomato sauce.

Amount per portion
Energy 124 cals, Protein 6.3g, Fat 6.7g, Saturated fat 1.7g, Carbohydrate 10.4g, Total sugars 4.8g, Fiber 3.3g, Salt 1.04g, Sodium 411mg

Simple Spaghetti with Fresh Tomato and Cauliflower

I'm sure your initial reaction to the title of this Italian dish will be to give one big yawn, but there will be times when your body demands simplicity, and this quick-and-easy recipe will satisfy that craving.

Serves 4

13oz dried spaghetti
4 garlic cloves
1 bunch of fresh basil leaves
¼ teaspoon salt
¼ teaspoon dried hot red pepper flakes
2 tablespoons extra virgin olive oil
4 tomatoes, coarsely chopped
   (save any juices)
2 tablespoons chopped hazelnuts
¼ cauliflower, finely chopped
¼ cup low-fat ricotta or cottage cheese
freshly ground black pepper
green salad, to serve

1 Cook the spaghetti in boiling salted water for 1 minute less than the package instructions.

2 Meanwhile, in a food processor or with a mortar and pestle, purée the garlic, basil, salt, and hot red pepper flakes together until smooth. Add the oil a little at a time, whisking continuously, then dilute with 2 tablespoons of water. In a bowl, mix together the tomatoes, hazelnuts, and cauliflower, then stir in the garlic and basil sauce.

3 Drain the spaghetti and transfer it into the tomato mixture, toss well, and season with pepper to taste. Spoon into individual bowls and dot the surface with dollops of cheese. Serve with a green salad.

Mediterranean Artichoke Stew

I've cheated a little on your behalf in this Italian dish. I believe artichokes are a vegetable too hazardous for the domestic cook: you get spiked, your hands turn black, the artichoke turns black, and what are you left with—a pile of inedible leaves, leaving you thinking, why did I bother? So, my solution is to buy jars of roasted artichokes; delicious and so simple.

Serves 4

8 new potatoes
12 baby onions
8 baby carrots
3 garlic cloves
grated zest and juice of 1 lemon
4 sage leaves
salt and freshly ground pepper
3 tablespoons olive oil
1 cup vegetable stock
¾ cup frozen peas
2 tomatoes, seeded and diced
1 jar roasted artichokes, drained

1 In a gratin dish, mix together the potatoes, onions, carrots, garlic, lemon zest and juice, sage, and some pepper. Add the olive oil and mix well so that all the ingredients are coated and pour in the stock. Leave to marinate for 30 minutes. Meanwhile, preheat the oven to 350°F.

2 Cover the gratin dish with parchment paper and then some aluminum foil. Transfer the dish to the preheated oven and cook for 35 to 45 minutes. Discard the covering and add the peas, tomatoes, artichokes, and some salt, and cook for another 5 minutes. Serve either hot or at room temperature.

Amount per portion
Energy 216 cals, Protein 4.7g, Fat 14.2g, Saturated fat 1.9g, Carbohydrate 18.4g, Total sugars 7.0g, Fiber 6.9g, Salt 1.62g, Sodium 642mg

Chickpea, Spinach, and Sweet Potato Stew

This Middle Eastern-influenced dish offers a great balance of carbs, protein (the edamame), and wonderful flavors. This is perfect served with Saffron Pea Pilaf (see page 117).

Serves 4

For the sweet potatoes
¾ lb sweet potatoes, cut into ½ in dice
1¾ cups water
1 tablespoon olive oil
2 tablespoons honey
1 teaspoon finely chopped fresh rosemary
½ teaspoon each salt and freshly ground
    black pepper
3½ oz non-fat Greek yogurt
1 garlic clove, crushed to a paste with
    a little salt
grated zest and juice of 1 orange

For the stew
1 tablespoon olive oil
1 large onion, chopped
1 teaspoon ground cumin
1½ teaspoons ground coriander
1 tablespoon harissa paste
1 tablespoon tomato paste
1 (14-oz) can chopped tomatoes
1 cup frozen edamame
1 (14-oz) can chickpeas, drained and rinsed
¾ cup frozen peas
¾ cup baby spinach
2 tablespoons chopped fresh cilantro
salt and freshly ground black pepper

1 Place the sweet potatoes in a saucepan along with the water, oil, honey, and rosemary. Cover and cook gently for 30 to 35 minutes until very little liquid remains and the potatoes have developed a nice sheen. If too much liquid remains, remove the lid and cook until little remains.

2 Meanwhile, prepare the stew: in a separate saucepan heat the oil and cook the onion together with the cumin and coriander until soft, about 8 minutes. Stir in the harissa and tomato paste, then add the tomatoes and cook for another 15 minutes or until thick. Add the edamame, chickpeas, peas, and spinach and cook for another 8 minutes. Fold in the cilantro and season with salt and pepper.

3 To make the sauce for the sweet potatoes, mix together the salt and pepper, yogurt, garlic, and orange zest and juice. Fold in the sweet potatoes. Spoon the chickpea stew into individual warmed bowls, then top with the sweet potato mix.

Amount per portion
Energy 385 cals, Protein 17.3g, Fat 13.2g, Saturated fat 1.8g, Carbohydrate 52.5g, Total sugars 20.6g, Fiber 9.8g, Salt 2.04g, Sodium 803mg

Chickpea and Lentil Curry

This Indian staple is a great curry base for vegetarians, and others, with the option of adding any vegetables you wish.

Serves 4

1 cup yellow lentils (*toor dal*), soaked in water for 30 minutes and drained
2 tablespoons sunflower oil
2 large onions, coarsely chopped
2 small carrots, sliced
1 teaspoon cumin seeds
¼ teaspoon asafoetida powder (optional)
1 teaspoon chopped garlic
1 teaspoon chopped ginger (see Tip on page 144)
2 mild green chiles, seeded and chopped
4 tomatoes, chopped
1 teaspoon chili powder
1 teaspoon ground turmeric
7oz low-fat plain yogurt
1 teaspoon garam masala
1 (14-oz) can chickpeas, drained and rinsed
2 tablespoons chopped fresh cilantro
salt and freshly ground pepper
1 tablespoon fresh pomegranate seeds, to garnish
brown rice, to serve

1 Cook the lentils in fresh water until tender. Drain well and season with salt to taste.

2 Meanwhile, heat the oil in a frying pan, then add the onions and carrots together with the cumin, asafoetida, garlic, ginger, and green chiles, and cook gently until the onions are soft, about 10 minutes.

3 Stir in the tomatoes, chili powder, turmeric, yogurt, and garam masala. Add in the lentils, then add the chickpeas and cilantro and adjust the seasoning to taste with salt and pepper. Spoon into individual bowls and garnish with pomegranate seeds. Serve with brown rice.

Amount per portion
Energy 381 cals, Protein 21.8g, Fat 9.2g, Saturated fat 0.9g, Carbohydrate 56.3g, Total sugars 15.3g, Fiber 8.1g, Salt 1.18g, Sodium 466mg

Three Bean Stew with Grated Feta

No meat, no fish, just beans with flavor, with or without the feta "snow"—your choice. This Greek stew also makes a good partner to roasted or grilled meats.

Serves 4
1 tablespoon olive oil
2 onions, coarsely chopped
2 carrots, coarsely sliced
2 celery ribs, finely sliced
3 garlic cloves, sliced
1 teaspoon dried Greek oregano
1 cup tomato sauce
1 tablespoon tomato paste
1 (14-oz) can red kidney beans, drained
    and rinsed
1 (14-oz) can lima beans, drained
    and rinsed
6oz green beans, de-strung and sliced
3oz feta cheese
freshly ground black pepper

1 Warm the olive oil in a large saucepan over medium heat, then add the onions, carrots, celery, and garlic and cook for 10 minutes. Add the oregano, tomato sauce, and tomato paste. Cover and cook for 45 minutes, topping off with water as necessary.

2 Now add the canned beans and green beans and cook for 20 minutes or until the sauce is thick and the vegetables are cooked. Spoon into warm bowls, then press the feta through a fine sieve over the bowls to create a "snow" effect over the stew.

Variation Want more spice? Then zap the stew with a little chopped fresh chile or season with Tabasco.

Amount per portion
Energy 265 cals, Protein 14.2g, Fat 8.4g, Saturated fat 3.2g, Carbohydrate 35.3g, Total sugars 14.7g, Fiber 9.9g, Salt 2.37g, Sodium 933mg

Watercress and Mushroom Crêpes

Whether you like them thick or thin, big or small, crêpes are a staple for breakfast. For this recipe, though, it is thin crêpes we're aiming for. You can play with the filling if you like, but get used to the crêpe recipe before experimenting.

Serves 4

For the crêpe batter
1 tablespoon sunflower oil
1 shallot, finely diced
8 button mushrooms, sliced
2 tablespoons watercress leaves
¾ cup flour
¼ teaspoon each salt and freshly
    ground black pepper
1 egg, beaten
½ cup skim milk
spray oil, for frying

For the filling
3½ oz button mushrooms, sliced
2 scallions, sliced
2 tomatoes, seeded and diced
1 (14-oz) can cannellini beans, drained
    and rinsed
7oz non-fat Greek yogurt
1 tablespoon lemon juice
¼ teaspoon each salt and freshly ground
    black pepper
3 tablespoons coarsely chopped
    watercress leaves
1 teaspoon chopped fresh oregano leaves

1 To make the crêpe batter, heat the oil in a frying pan, add the shallot and mushrooms, and cook over medium heat for 3 minutes, stirring regularly. Leave to cool slightly.

2 In a food processor, blend together the mushroom mix, the watercress, flour, salt and pepper, egg, milk, and 2 tablespoons of water; blend for about 2 minutes, scraping down the sides from time to time. Pour into a container and leave to rest for 15 minutes.

3 Make the filling by mixing together all the filling ingredients. Set aside.

4 To cook the crêpes, place a non-stick pan over medium heat, spray with oil, remove from the heat, and pour in about 3 tablespoons of batter, tilting the pan in all directions to cover the base thinly. Return the pan to the heat and cook until the edges of the crêpe start to brown, about 1 minute. Flip the crêpe over and cook for 1 to 2 minutes. Transfer to a plate and repeat until all the mixture has been used.

5 Preheat the oven to 350°F. Lightly grease a baking sheet. Set 1 crêpe on a work surface and spoon about 1 tablespoon of the filling down one half, then roll it up, tucking the ends in, and set it on the baking sheet. Repeat with the remaining crêpes.

6 Cover the baking sheet with foil, transfer to the preheated oven, and heat through for 10 to 12 minutes. Serve with a salad.

Amount per portion
Energy 269 cals, Protein 16.7g, Fat 8.8g, Saturated fat 1.3g, Carbohydrate 32.9g, Total sugars 7.0g, Fiber 5.1g, Salt 1.49g, Sodium 589mg

Vegetarian *Nasi Goreng* (Indonesian Fried Rice)

This delicious dish is traditionally served for breakfast and usually includes fish or shrimp. This vegetarian version is just as tasty and very easy to put together

Serves 4

5½ oz mixed fresh mushrooms, such as shiitake, button mushrooms, and oyster mushrooms, chopped
2 garlic cloves, finely chopped
1in piece of fresh ginger, peeled and grated
2 fresh red chiles, seeded and finely chopped
3 shallots, finely chopped
1 tablespoon sunflower oil
salt and freshly ground black pepper
2 cups cold cooked brown rice
1 egg, lightly beaten
1 tablespoon *ketjap manis* (Indonesian sweet soy sauce)
1 tablespoon soy sauce
1 tablespoon soy bean paste
1 cup frozen *petit pois* (small peas)
handful of snow peas, trimmed and shredded
4 scallions, finely chopped
½ small bunch of fresh cilantro, leaves picked
juice of ½ lime
lime wedges, to garnish

1 Preheat the oven to 400°F. Toss the mushrooms with the garlic, ginger, chiles, shallots, and a little of the oil and season with salt and black pepper. Spread the mixture out on a baking sheet, and bake in the oven for 10 minutes until the mushroom and shallots have started to caramelize.

2 Break up the rice with a fork so that the grains are separated. (it is best to use cold leftover rice—if the rice is warm, it absorbs too much oil. If cooking rice just for this dish, cool it as quickly as possible; rice that is kept warm for a long time is prone to dangerous bacteria). Lightly grease a non-stick frying pan with a couple of drops of oil. Cook the beaten egg to make a thin egg pancake, allow to cool, then roll up and cut into thin shreds. Set aside.

3 Heat a wok over high heat. Add the remaining oil and baked mushroom mixture—make sure you get any juices from the bottom of the pan. Add the rice, *ketjap manis*, soy sauce, and soy bean paste, and stir fry for 2 minutes. Add both types of peas. Stir constantly for 4 to 5 minutes until the rice is heated all the way through and the green vegetables are cooked, but still have a bite.

4 Add the scallions, cilantro, and shredded omelet and then add the lime juice. Check the seasoning—it should be sweet, rich, and earthy, hot from the chile, and salty from the soy sauce. Serve with lime wedges.

Amount per portion
Energy 229 cals, Protein 8.6g, Fat 6.2g, Saturated fat 1.2g, Carbohydrate 37.0g, Total sugars 3.6g, Fiber 2.8g, Salt 2.42g, Sodium 953mg

and Cilantro Asian Shrimp Cakes Chermoula Grilled Sea Ba
p Chermoula Grilled Tuna on a Salad of White Beans Pan-Fr
Grilled Sea Bass, Spiced Cabbage Grilled Sardines with W
ette di Sarde (Sardine Cakes) Scallops and Bacon on Sweet
matoes, and Olives Crab and Tomato Linguini Penne with Sa
Cannellini Bean Stew Shrimp Linguini Fragrant Shrimp with
Sour Sauce New Potatoes and Smoked Mackerel with Avoc
Chowder-style Broth Barley Risotto with Greens and Shrimp
Spices Sweet-and-Sour Shrimp Sweet Potato with Crab, Re
Crabcakes with Asian Coleslaw Spicy Stew of Red Lentils, C

Green Salad and Sweet-and-Sour Dressing Omega 3 Plaki (
mbs Seared Tuna with a Sicilian Tomatoey Potato Salad Tunis
Fillets of Sea Bass with Anise-Scented Tomatoes Roast Cod
Tomato Pasta with Anchovies, Pine Nuts, and Golden Raisins
le with Lemon and Basil Stuffing Paella Asian Surf and Turf Ba
sh Dressing Poached Haddock with Eggs and Spinach Cotr
ssels Aromatic Fish Parcels Spicy Goan Fish Curry Sardines
and Cilantro Asian Shrimp Cakes Chermoula Grilled Sea Ba
p Chermoula Grilled Tuna on a Salad of White Beans Pan-Fr
Grilled Sea Bass, Spiced Cabbage Grilled Sardines with W

Fish
and Shellfish

Spicy Asian Mussels

Mussels represent excellent value as a shellfish, but there are times when *moules marinière* has to stand aside for more robust flavors. Serve this Thai-influenced dish with some crusty multigrain bread and a salad . . . but be warned, it's hot!

Serves 4

2 tablespoons sunflower oil
1 stalk lemongrass, bruised
¾ in piece of fresh galangal, bruised
¾ in piece of fresh ginger, peeled and bruised
2 shallots, coarsely chopped
4 bird's-eye chiles, seeded and coarsely chopped
4 garlic cloves
2 tablespoons oyster sauce
1 tablespoon Tabasco sauce
2 teaspoons curry paste
3¼ lb mussels, cleaned, any open ones discarded

To garnish

3 scallions, sliced
1 tablespoon chopped cilantro

1 In a wok, heat half the oil and stir-fry the lemongrass and galangal together for 3 minutes.

2 Meanwhile, in a small food processor, blend together the ginger, shallots, chiles, garlic, and the remaining oil. Add this paste to the wok and cook for 3 minutes over medium heat. Stir in the oyster sauce, Tabasco, and curry paste, then add ½ cup of water, increase the heat, and add the mussels. Cover and boil for 5 minutes, tossing the mix from time to time.

3 Spoon into individual warmed bowls, discarding any mussels that have not opened. Pour over the spicy liquor, then scatter with scallions and cilantro.

Amount per portion

Energy 155 cals, Protein 15g, Fat 8g, Saturated fat 1g, Carbohydrate 6g, Total sugars 1.7g, Fiber 0.3g, Salt 1.87g, Sodium 736mg

Aromatic Fish Parcels

A fantastic Asian dish that is really easy to do for a dinner party and can be prepared well in advance. What sweet flavors ...

Serves 4

5½ oz thick rice noodles
1 teaspoon reduced-salt soy sauce
1 teaspoon fish sauce (*nam pla*)
1 tablespoon sweet chile sauce
juice and zest of 1 lime
2 teaspoons finely chopped lemongrass
2 heads of bok choi, halved lengthwise
4 salmon fillets (about 5½ oz each), skinned
1 cup frozen edamame
1 cup snow peas, thinly sliced lengthwise
1 tablespoon chopped cilantro,
    to garnish

1 Preheat the oven to 425°F. Place the noodles in a large bowl and cover with boiling water. Let sit until tender, about 2 minutes, then drain well.

2 Combine the three sauces, lime juice and zest, and lemongrass, and let stand for 30 minutes to allow the flavors to develop.

3 Set four large pieces of foil on the work surface. Divide the noodles between the sheets, top with bok choi then with the salmon, scatter over the edamame and snow peas, and drizzle with the sauce.

4 Bring up the edges of the foil to seal the parcel, place on a baking sheet, and cook in the oven for 12 minutes. Open the parcels at the table and sprinkle with cilantro.

Amount per portion
Energy 451 cals, Protein 36.9g, Fat 17.6g, Saturated fat 3.5g, Carbohydrate 38.6g, Total sugars 4.4g, Fiber 2.0g, Salt 0.8g, Sodium 316mg

Spicy Goan Fish Curry

This dry curry has airs of vindaloo about it. It packs a punch but has great depth of flavor.

Serves 4

For the spice paste
1 teaspoon ground cumin
1 teaspoon ground coriander
1 teaspoon ground turmeric
3 garlic cloves
1in piece of fresh ginger, peeled
    and grated
4 dried red chiles, seeded and
    soaked in hot water
2 tablespoons lemon juice

For the fish
½ teaspoon salt
½ teaspoon ground turmeric
4 cod or haddock fillets, about 6oz each

For the vegetable curry
2 tablespoons sunflower oil
12 new potatoes, halved
2 large onions, coarsely chopped
1 eggplant, cut into ¾in pieces
3 cloves
1 teaspoon freshly ground black pepper
1 cup button mushrooms, quartered
6 cardamom pods, lightly crushed
4 medium green chiles, split lengthwise and
    seeded
1 teaspoon superfine sugar
brown rice, to serve

1 In a food processor, blend together all the spice paste ingredients to a reasonably smooth paste. Prepare the fish: mix together the salt and turmeric and rub on to the fish, then leave to marinate.

2 Meanwhile, make the vegetable curry. Heat the oil in a large saucepan and cook the potatoes until golden. Remove and set aside. In the same oil, cook the onions and eggplant so that they take on a little color, about 8 minutes. Add the cloves, pepper, mushrooms, and cardamom, and cook for another minute, stirring.

3 Add the potatoes, chiles, and sugar, and cook for another 2 minutes. Add the spice paste, cover, and cook over low heat until the potatoes are half cooked.

4 Place the fish on top of the vegetable curry, cover, and continue to cook over low heat for another 15 minutes. Serve hot, with steaming brown rice.

Variation You can use chicken instead of fish if you like, just add it at the beginning with the onions and eggplant.

Amount per portion
Energy 341 cals, Protein 37.4g, Fat 8.8g, Saturated fat 1.2g, Carbohydrate 29.9g, Total sugars 9.6g, Fiber 4.4g, Salt 0.94g, Sodium 371mg

Sardines filled with Bulgar and Spices

Fresh sardines represent good value, and this oily fish is packed full of all the right omegas. This Middle Eastern recipe will help toward the weekly two portions of oily fish we should all be eating.

Serves 4

For the spiced bulgar mix
6oz quick-cook bulgar wheat
2 scallions, thinly sliced
grated zest and juice of 1 lemon
8 dried apricots, chopped
3 tablespoons pistachio nuts, chopped
2 tablespoons dried cranberries
4 tablespoons chopped fresh parsley
2 teaspoons chopped fresh mint
1 tablespoon chopped cilantro
¼ teaspoon ground cinnamon
½ teaspoon ground allspice
2 tablespoons pomegranate molasses
2 tablespoons extra virgin olive oil
salt and freshly ground black pepper

8 to 12 fresh sardines, scaled, headed, gutted, boned, and butterflied
spray oil, for cooking

To serve
4 lime wedges, to serve
new potatoes
salad

1 To make the bulgar mix, place the bulgar wheat in a bowl, cover with cold water, and soak for 20 minutes. Drain then squeeze dry. Meanwhile, preheat the oven to 400°F.

2 Mix together the bulgar wheat and the remaining mix ingredients. Season with a little salt and lots of black pepper.

3 Lay the sardines skin-side down on a work surface. Spoon a little bulgar mix on to the middle of each fish, bring the head end over the stuffing and then fold the tail end over. Secure with a cocktail stick—some mixture will fall out, but don't worry, because there should be surplus left over to serve with the sardines.

4 Lightly oil a baking sheet and arrange the sardines on it tail-side up. Transfer to the preheated oven and roast for 8 minutes. Serve with lime wedges and the surplus spiced bulgar mix, along with new potatoes and salad.

Tip Pomegranate molasses is a rich, sticky reduction of pomegranate juice often found in Middle Eastern speciality shops. You can make your own, however, by combining 1 quart of pomegranate juice with ½ cup of sugar and ¼ cup lemon juice in a medium saucepan. Bring to a boil over medium heat, stirring to dissolve the sugar. Reduce the heat and simmer, stirring occasionally. The molasses is ready when the liquid has reduced by about three-quarters and is thick and syrupy.

Amount per portion
Energy 536 cals, Protein 33.8g, Fat 22.1g, Saturated fat 3.9g, Carbohydrate 53.9g, Total sugars 17.2g, Fiber 1.8g, Salt 1.06g, Sodium 420mg

Sweet-and-Sour Shrimp

An all-time favorite—this westernized Chinese dish is loved by children and adults alike.

Serves 4

juice of 1 lemon
½ teaspoon salt
24 raw tiger shrimp with tail on, head
    and shells removed
2 scallions, finely sliced at an angle
1 white onion, coarsely chopped
1 carrot, thinly sliced
1 red bell pepper, chopped into 1in pieces
1 green bell pepper, chopped into 1in
    pieces
1 (8-oz) can water chestnuts, drained
    and sliced
1 (8-oz) can pineapple pieces, drained
steamed rice, to serve

For the sauce

2 garlic cloves, finely chopped
1in piece of fresh ginger, peeled
    and grated
1 fresh red chile, seeded and
    finely chopped
½ cup pineapple juice
1 tablespoon soy sauce
2 tablespoons white wine vinegar
1 tablespoon tomato paste
1 tablespoon tomato ketchup
1 tablespoon sugar or low-calorie
    granulated sweetener
1 tablespoon cornstarch mixed to a paste
    with 3 tablespoons cold water

1 In a large bowl, mix together the lemon juice and salt. Add the shrimp and stir well to coat, then set aside to marinate.

2 To make the sauce, cook the garlic, ginger, and chile in a pan, then reduce the heat and cook for 5 minutes. Add the remaining sauce ingredients except for the cornstarch paste, bring to a boil, and cook for 3 minutes.

3 Meanwhile, in a large pan, cook the onions, carrots, and peppers. Stir in the water chestnuts and pineapple pieces and cook just long enough to heat through. Add the shrimp and cook for another minute.

4 Add the cooked sauce and the cornstarch paste, and cook until thickened and glossy, about 2 minutes. Serve with steamed rice on the side.

Amount per portion (low-calorie sweetener)
Energy 174 cals, Protein 18.3g, Fat 1.1g, Saturated fat 0.2g, Carbohydrate 24.4g, Total sugars 18.2g, Fiber 2.5g, Salt 1.99g, Sodium 783mg

Amount per portion (sugar)
Energy 188 cals, Protein 18.3g, Fat 1.1g, Saturated fat 0.2g, Carbohydrate 28.2g, Total sugars 22.0g, Fiber 2.5g, Salt 1.99g, Sodium 784mg

Sweet Potato with Crab, Red Snapper, and Cilantro

To this fantastic rustic West Indian stew brimming with freshness and flavor, I've added some black-eyed peas—not necessarily traditional for this type of dish, but it's good for you. Scotch bonnets are about the hottest chiles, hence the reason West Indians use them whole in cooking: the chiles can be easily removed when the dish has reached the preferred intensity of heat.

Serves 4
1 tablespoon sunflower oil
2 onions, chopped
5 garlic cloves, crushed
2 Scotch bonnet chiles (handle
   with gloves)
2 sweet potatoes, cut into ½ in dice
1¼ quarts reduced-salt fish or
   chicken stock
6oz brown crabmeat
11½ oz red snapper fillets, pin-boned
   and cut into 1in pieces
6oz white crabmeat
juice of 2 limes
2 tablespoons chopped cilantro
1 (14-oz) can black-eyed peas, drained
   and rinsed
warm multigrain bread, to serve

1 Heat the oil in a large saucepan, then add the onion and garlic and cook over low heat for 8 to 10 minutes until the onion has softened. Add the Scotch bonnets whole, the sweet potatoes, and the stock and simmer for 10 minutes.

2 Stir in the brown crabmeat, cook for 2 minutes to create a sauce, then add the snapper and cook for another 3 minutes. Add the remaining ingredients and cook for another for 2 minutes, without allowing the stew to boil. Eat with warm multigrain bread.

Amount per portion
Energy 392 cals, Protein 40.6g, Fat 10.7g, Saturated fat 1.3g, Carbohydrate 35.7g, Total sugars 9.5g, Fiber 4.9g, Salt 2.12g, Sodium 837mg

Asian Shrimp Cakes

This luxurious little number can be served as a canapé, appetizer, or main course, depending on the size of the shrimp cakes. For a main course, serve them with Stir-fried Greens with Mustard Seeds and Cashews (see p.131), rice, and a Vietnamese dipping sauce (see p.107).

Serves 4
¾ lb raw tiger shrimp, shell-off
   and deveined
½ in piece ginger, peeled and
   coarsely chopped
1 garlic clove
2 tablespoons chopped cilantro
3 scallions, sliced
2 teaspoons fish sauce (*nam pla*)
1 egg white
¼ cup chopped water chestnuts
¼ cup sweet corn niblets
1 tablespoon chopped cashew nuts
1 hot red chile, seeded and finely diced
spray oil, for frying

1 In a food processor, blend together the shrimp, ginger, garlic, cilantro, scallions, fish sauce, and egg white to a smooth paste. Transfer a bowl, fold in the remaining ingredients except the oil, and mix well.

2 With wet hands, shape the mixture into 8 small "burgers" or cakes. Refrigerate them to firm up—for about 2 hours if possible.

3 Spray a large frying pan with oil and cook the cakes over medium heat for 2 to 3 minutes on each side.

Amount per portion
Energy 97 cals, Protein 17.5g, Fat 1.1g, Saturated fat 0.2g, Carbohydrate 4.7g, Total sugars 1.2g, Fiber 0.4g, Salt 0.98g, Sodium 389mg

RIGHT Sweet Potato with Crab, Red Snapper, and Cilantro

Chermoula Grilled Sea Bass

In this recipe, I'm using a variation of the North African chermoula marinade as a vegetable flavoring as well as a delicious fish marinade.

Serves 4

For the chermoula marinade
6 garlic cloves
2 bunches cilantro, coarsely chopped
1 tablespoon ground cumin
1 teaspoon hot red pepper flakes
1 tablespoon paprika
2 lemons—grated zest of 1, juice of 2
¼ cup extra virgin olive oil
salt and freshly ground black pepper

4 sea bass fillets, about 6oz each
16 new potatoes, quartered
½ cauliflower, broken into small florets
¾ cup green beans, cut into 1in pieces
¾ cup tomato sauce
1 (14-oz) can chickpeas, drained and rinsed
lime wedges, to serve

1 To make the chermoula, purée together the garlic, cilantro, cumin, red pepper flakes, paprika, and lemon zest and juice in a food processor. When smooth, add the olive oil, running the machine slowly. Season with salt and pepper. Put three-quarters of the chermoula into a saucepan and set aside. Scrape the remaining quarter of chermoula into a bowl, add the sea bass, and stir well to coat both sides of the fillets. Set aside.

2 Cook the potatoes in boiling water for 15 minutes, then add the cauliflower and beans and cook for another 5 minutes. Drain, then transfer the vegetables to the pan containing the chermoula. Fold in the chickpeas and heat gently.

3 When the vegetables are hot, grill the fish for 2 minutes on each side. Spoon the vegetables on to warmed plates, top with the fish fillets, and serve with lime wedges.

Amount per portion
Energy 532 cals, Protein 45.9g, Fat 22.4g, Saturated fat 2.8g, Carbohydrate 39.3g, Total sugars 6.4g, Fiber 5.9g, Salt 1.59g, Sodium 627mg

Tandoori-Style Fish

I've used fish for this Indian classic, but the marinade works well with chicken as well. Serve with brown rice and some spiced chickpeas (see page 121).

Serves 4

4 mackerel or herring fillets, pin bones removed
juice of 1 lime
½ teaspoon salt
4 shallots, coarsely chopped
1 teaspoon ground cumin
½ teaspoon ground turmeric
2 teaspoons chili powder
1 teaspoon garlic powder
4 tablespoons non-fat Greek yogurt
1 tablespoon sunflower oil, plus extra for greasing
1 teaspoon paprika
½ teaspoon ground cardamom
spray oil, to grease

1 Preheat the oven to 425°F. With a small sharp knife, make 3 to 4 shallow incisions on both sides of the fish fillets. Mix together the lime juice and salt, rub into the fish, and leave for 10 minutes to marinate.

2 In a food processor, blend together the shallots, spices, and yogurt. Rub this mixture over the fish on both sides, then leave to marinate for another 20 minutes.

3 Mix together the oil, paprika, and cardamom and set aside. Lightly grease a roasting pan, place the fish skin-side up in the pan, and brush with the flavored oil. Transfer to the oven and roast for 10 minutes.

Amount per portion
Energy 501 cals, Protein 39.9g, Fat 36.5g, Saturated fat 7.1g, Carbohydrate 3.4g, Total sugars 0.9g, Fiber 0.2g, Salt 1.03g, Sodium 406mg

Crabcakes with Asian Coleslaw

There's something very satisfying about crabcakes, and whenever I'm traveling, I always try out different versions. This version from the West Coast owes much to Asian influences.

Serves 4

For the coleslaw
½ lb bok choi, shredded
1 cup carrots, julienned
4 shallots, sliced
½ tablespoon grated fresh ginger
2 tablespoons shredded basil leaves
2 tablespoons cilantro
1 tablespoon mint leaves
1 clove garlic, chopped
1 fresh hot chile, seeded and
    finely chopped
grated zest of 1 orange
juice of 1 orange
juice of 2 limes
1 tablespoon fish sauce (*nam pla*)
½ teaspoon sugar
4 tablespoons peanut oil
salt and freshly ground black
    pepper, to taste

2 scallions, finely chopped
1 fresh red chile, seeded and
    finely chopped
1 tablespoon chopped cilantro
1 tablespoon snipped fresh chives
½ tablespoon chopped fresh mint
1½ tablespoons low-fat mayonnaise
½ teaspoon dry mustard
½ teaspoon wasabi powder
1 egg yolk
1lb fresh white crabmeat
½ cup multigrain breadcrumbs (see Tips)
spray sunflower oil

For the coating
1 cup all-purpose flour, seasoned with salt
    and pepper
2 eggs, beaten
1 cup multigrain breadcrumbs

1 To make the Asian Coleslaw, mix the bok choi in a bowl with the carrots, shallots, ginger, basil, cilantro, mint, garlic, chile, and orange zest. In a small bowl, whisk together the orange juice, lime juice, fish sauce, and sugar. Slowly whisk in the oil until emulsified. Add the dressing to the cabbage and toss well. Season with salt and pepper. Chill, covered, for 2 to 6 hours.

2 In a bowl combine the scallions, chile, and herbs. In another bowl whisk together the mayonnaise, mustard, wasabi, and egg yolk, then add the herb mixture to the mayo. Fold this mixture into the crabmeat, then add enough breadcrumbs to bind efficiently. Shape into 4 patties, then chill to firm up on an oiled plate, uncovered, for an hour but ideally overnight.

3 Preheat the broiler. Lay out 3 plates to prepare the coating: one for the flour, one for the beaten egg, and one for the breadcrumbs. Dip the crab cakes into the flour, then the egg (making sure all floury parts are covered), and then the breadcrumbs.

4 Spray the surface of each crabcake with sunflower oil, slide under the broiler, and cook for 3 to 4 minutes each side, making sure they do not burn. Serve with Asian Coleslaw.

Tip When coating the cakes in breadcrumbs, only coat the surface, not the sides, because you won't be deep-frying. To make multigrain breadcrumbs, dry some multigrain bread slices in a low oven (no higher than 275°F) until brittle enough to snap. Break them up into pieces, pop in a food processor, and pulse into crumbs. Do not pass the bread through a sieve, as you want to retain a little texture.

Amount per portion
Energy 387 cals, Protein 33.0g, Fat 10.2g, Saturated fat 2.1g, Carbohydrate 43.4g, Total sugars 2.3g, Fiber 3.3g, Salt 1.3g, Sodium 911mg

Spicy Stew of Red Lentils, Cod, and Shrimp

Indian food has so much depth of flavor, and it's all about spices, not necessarily about chile. The lentil base here can play host to so many other ingredients. This recipe features lots of ingredients, but most of them should already be in your pantry.

Serves 4

1 tablespoon sunflower oil
1 onion, finely chopped
4 garlic cloves, crushed
1 carrot, coarsely chopped
1 red bell pepper, seeded and cut into
    1in pieces
½ cinnamon stick
1 teaspoon grated ginger
1 teaspoon ground turmeric
2 teaspoons ground cumin
2 teaspoons ground coriander
2 teaspoons yellow mustard seeds
1 teaspoon ground cardamom
2 bay leaves
1 tablespoon chopped cilantro
    stems or roots
¾ cup red lentils, washed
1 (8-oz) can chopped tomatoes
2 cups cold water
½ lb cod fillet, skinned and cut into
    1in pieces
10oz raw tiger shrimp, shell-off
juice of ½ lemon
3 tablespoons chopped cilantro
salt and freshly ground black pepper
brown rice, to serve

1 Heat the oil in a large saucepan, then add the onion, garlic, carrot, red pepper, cinnamon stick, and ginger and cook over medium heat for 10 to 12 minutes until the vegetables have softened.

2 Add all spices, bay leaves and cilantro stems and stir to combine. Cook gently for another 2 minutes. Add the lentils, tomatoes, and water. Bring to a boil, reduce the heat, and simmer gently until the lentils start to break down—this can take from 45 minutes to 1 hour 30 minutes depending on the heat and the lentils.

3 Remove the cinnamon stick, fold in the cod, shrimp, lemon juice, and chopped cilantro and cook for another 6 minutes. Season to taste with salt and pepper and serve, ideally with brown rice.

Variation This works really well as a vegetarian dish. Simply omit the fish and fold in a host of green vegetables.

Amount per portion
Energy 333 cals, Protein 36.0g, Fat 5.9g, Saturated fat 0.5g, Carbohydrate 36.2g, Total sugars 7.8g, Fiber 4.3g, Salt 1.2g, Sodium 471mg

Chermoula Grilled Tuna on a Salad of White Beans

North African chermoula sauce is a great marinade for fish. It requires a certain amount of pantry ingredients, but it's well worth the effort.

Serves 4

For the chermoula marinade
1 bunch cilantro, coarsely chopped
leaves from 1 bunch fresh flat-leaf parsley
4 garlic cloves
1 fresh red chile, seeded
3 scallions, coarsely chopped
2 teaspoons turmeric
2 teaspoons ground cumin
2 teaspoons chili powder
2 teaspoons sweet paprika
juice and grated zest of 1 lemon
1 tablespoon olive oil
salt

For the fish
4 fresh tuna steaks, about 5½ oz each
spray olive oil
2 (14-oz) cans cannellini beans, drained and rinsed
lemon wedges, to serve
green salad, to serve

1 In a food processor, blend all the marinade ingredients together to a paste. Coat the tuna with half the marinade and set aside. Preheat the broiler.

2 Heat a frying pan, spray it lightly with oil, and cook the remaining marinade for 2 minutes. Add the beans and a splash of water, cook for 3 minutes to heat through, and season to taste.

3 Grill the tuna for 2 minutes each side. Serve on the beans, with lemon wedges and a green salad.

Amount per portion
Energy 399 cals, Protein 47.1g, Fat 12.4g, Saturated fat 2.1g, Carbohydrate 26.8g, Total sugars 3.5g, Fiber 7.0g, Salt 2.17g, Sodium 855mg

Pan-fried Sea Bass with Green Salad and Sweet-and-Sour Dressing

There are lots of Asian influences going on here, although their choice of fish would be different. Fresh and tangy, it's the perfect light meal.

Serves 4
½ cup all-purpose flour
½ teaspoon each sea salt and freshly
    ground white pepper
4 firm sea bass fillets
3 tablespoons sunflower oil
lime wedges, to serve

For the zesty vegetable salad
¼ Savoy cabbage, shredded
20 snow peas, finely sliced
2 large fresh red chiles, seeded
    and sliced diagonally.
1 tablespoon cilantro leaves
12 fresh mint leaves
4 shallots, finely sliced
zest of 1 lime

For the sweet-and-sour dressing
1 tablespoon sugar
2 tablespoons water
2 tablespoons fish sauce (*nam pla*)
2 tablespoons lime juice

1 Mix together the flour, salt, and pepper in a bowl and use to coat the skin side of the fish fillets. Heat the oil in a large non-stick frying pan over medium to high heat. Add the fish, skin-side down, and cook for 6 minutes. Turn over, remove the pan from the heat, and allow the fish to cook in the residual heat of the pan for 1 minute until the fish is cooked.

2 Meanwhile, make the salad. In a pan of lightly salted boiling water, cook the cabbage and snow peas together for 2 minutes. Drain and set aside. Into a large bowl, mix the chiles, cilantro, mint, and shallots, then stir in the cabbage and snow peas and the lime zest.

3 To make the dressing, stir the sugar and water in a small pan over low heat until the sugar has dissolved. Remove from the heat, add the fish sauce and lime juice, and stir to combine.

4 Serve the fish on top of the salad, drizzle some sweet-and-sour dressing over the top, and accompany with lime wedges.

Amount per portion
Energy 326 cals, Protein 32.7g, Fat 15.5g, Saturated fat 2.1g, Carbohydrate 14.8g, Total sugars 2.9g, Fiber 1.9g, Salt 2.37g, Sodium 933mg

Omega 3 Plaki (Baked Mackerel)

On average, we eat less than 1 portion of fish per week, but we all know we should be eating at least two portions of oily fish a week. Here's a delicious and nutritious Greek alternative to that same old boring piece of grilled fish.

Serves 4

For the vegetable "sauce"
2 carrots, sliced
2 onions, sliced
1 celery rib, sliced
3 garlic cloves, crushed to a paste
    with a little salt
1 sprig of fresh thyme
2 bay leaves
1 (14-oz) can chopped tomatoes
¼ cup dry white wine
1 (14-oz) canned chickpeas, drained
    and rinsed

8 mackerel or herring fillets, about
    3½ oz each
2 tomatoes, each sliced into quarters
2 tablespoons extra virgin olive oil
salt and freshly ground black pepper
1 tablespoon chopped fresh parsley,
    to garnish
brown rice and salad, to serve

1 Preheat the oven to 350°F. Combine all the "sauce" ingredients and transfer into a lightly oiled deep roasting pan or baking dish. Cover with foil and cook for 20 minutes. Remove the dish from the oven but do not turn the oven off.

2 Season the fish fillets and place them on top of the "sauce." Top each fillet with 2 slices of tomato, drizzle with olive oil. and season to taste with salt and pepper. Return to the oven, uncovered, and bake for 15 minutes. Sprinkle with parsley and serve with brown rice and a salad.

Amount per portion
Energy 636 cals, Protein 44.6g, Fat 40.0g, Saturated fat 7.4g, Carbohydrate 24.0g, Total sugars 11.8g, Fiber 6.2g, Salt 1.46g, Sodium 578mg

Grilled Sea Bass with Spiced Cabbage

Lovely fresh sea bass cooked until the skin is crispy, served with a tamarind relish and spicy cabbage—loads of flavor but pretty quick to prepare.

Serves 4

4 sea bass fillets, about 6oz each, bones removed
¼ teaspoon each salt and ground white pepper
¼ teaspoon ground turmeric
juice of 1 lime
spray cooking oil
rice or new potatoes, to serve

For the salsa relish

2 shallots, finely sliced
1 red bird's eye chile, seeded and finely chopped
1 medium hot chile, seeded and finely sliced
2 tomatoes, seeded and chopped
1 tablespoon shrimp paste (*blachan*)
1 teaspoon grated ginger
¼ cup tamarind juice
1 teaspoon superfine sugar
pinch of salt
1 tablespoon chopped fresh mint leaves

For the cabbage

½ savoy cabbage, shredded
1 medium hot red chile, seeded and coarsely chopped
½ teaspoon shrimp paste (*blachan*)
2 shallots, coarsely chopped
1 teaspoon superfine sugar
¼ teaspoon salt
1 tablespoon sunflower oil
2 sweet potatoes, cut into ½ in dice and cooked

1 In a shallow dish, season the fish with salt, pepper, turmeric, and lime juice, and leave to marinate for 20 minutes. Meanwhile, combine all the ingredients for the salsa relish in a bowl and let stand for at least 15 minutes.

2 Blanch the cabbage in boiling salted water for 3 minutes, then drain well. In a mini food processor, blend together the chile, shrimp paste, shallots, sugar, and salt to a smooth paste. Heat the oil in a frying pan and cook the paste for 3 minutes, stirring regularly. Add the blanched cabbage and sweet potatoes, heat through, and keep warm.

3 Place a large flat griddle or frying pan over high heat, spray with oil, and cook the sea bass skin-side down for 6 minutes. Turn the fish over, remove the pan from the heat, and allow the fish to cook in the residual heat of the pan for 2 minutes until the fish is cooked.

Amount per portion
Energy 354 cals, Protein 39.8g, Fat 8.2g, Saturated fat 1.3g, Carbohydrate 32.3g, Total sugars 15.8g, Fiber 5.4g, Salt 1.79g, Sodium 705mg

Grilled Sardines with Walnut and Chile Crumbs

This dish could have been invented anywhere—it's got a touch of Portugal, a sprinkling of the Middle East, and even a touch of the UK—but I ate it in a restaurant in Sydney, so I must give them the credit. Australian chefs are creative geniuses!

Serves 4

3 slices multigrain bread, crusts removed, shredded
3 garlic cloves
3 scallions, coarsely chopped
1 hot fresh red chile, seeded
1 teaspoon fresh thyme leaves
2 tablespoons fresh curly parsley leaves
2 tablespoons extra virgin olive oil
grated zest of 1 lemon
salt and freshly ground black pepper
¼ cup walnut halves, toasted
12 large fresh sardines, cleaned and gutted
spray olive oil
lemon wedges and salad, to serve

1 Place the bread in a food processor along with the garlic, scallions, chile, thyme, parsley, olive oil, and lemon zest. Process until crumb-like and green. Then, add the walnuts and pulse just enough to break up the walnuts—you need to retain texture. Season to taste with salt and pepper, then transfer the mixture to a dry frying pan and cook the crumbs over low to medium heat, shaking the pan regularly, until golden. This requires careful attention.

2 Meanwhile, heat a ridged grill pan over high heat. Season the sardines with black pepper and spray lightly with olive oil. Cook for 2 to 3 minutes on each side depending on their size. Scatter the crumbs over the sardines and serve with lemon wedges and salad.

Tip This is wonderful when the sardines are cooked on a charcoal grill, adding a lovely smokiness. It's also great served with a tomato and onion salad and some bread to mop up all the juices.

Amount per portion
Energy 478 cals, Protein 38.7g, Fat 28.7g, Saturated fat 4.7g, Carbohydrate 17.2g, Total sugars 1.6g, Fiber 2.5g, Salt 1.48g, Sodium 581mg

Seared Tuna with a Sicilian Tomatoey Potato Salad

A really summery number with lots of Mediterranean flavors, this is a perfect dish for outdoor eating.

Serves 4

1½ lb new potatoes, quartered
2 tablespoons olive oil
2 garlic cloves, sliced
2 onions, finely sliced
1 teaspoon dried oregano
1 fresh chile, seeded and finely chopped
4 anchovy fillets, coarsely chopped
1 (14-oz) can plum tomatoes
juice of ½ lemon
1 teaspoon sugar
salt and freshly ground black pepper
12 cherry tomatoes
4 fresh tuna steaks, about 5½ oz each
1 tablespoon snipped fresh chives, to garnish

1 Cook the potatoes in boiling salted water for 15 to 20 minutes or until tender but still intact. Drain and set aside.

2 Heat 1½ tablespoons of the olive oil in a saucepan, add the garlic, onion, oregano, chile, and anchovies, and cook for 5 minutes. Drain the canned tomatoes into a sieve over a bowl to collect the juices and set the tomatoes aside. Add the juices to the onion mix, then the lemon juice and sugar. Cook until the sauce is thick then season to taste with salt and pepper.

3 Crush the canned tomatoes between your fingers to create small pieces and add to the sauce along with the potatoes and the cherry tomatoes. Cook for 5 minutes.

4 Brush a ridged grill pan with the remaining olive oil and place it over high heat. Season the tuna, then cook for 1 minute on each side. Set the tuna on top of the potato salad and sprinkle with chives.

Tip I urge you not to overcook the tuna, otherwise you might as well open a can. This salad is equally good eaten the next day at room temperature, maybe this time using flakes of canned tuna.

Amount per portion
Energy 427 cals, Protein 41.5g, Fat 13.7g, Saturated fat 2.4g, Carbohydrate 36.7g, Total sugars 10.5g, Fiber 3.6g, Salt 1.36g, Sodium 536mg

Tunisian Fish Stew

North African fisherfolk make this dish with the fish from their catch that is unsuitable for more simple cooking, so traditionally a variety of rock fish would be used. You could also use any non-oily fish, normally a white fish. I've made this dish more GI-friendly by adding new potatoes instead of floury ones, more vegetables than would normally be the case, and white beans.

Serves 4
2 tablespoons olive oil
2 onions, finely diced
1 bird's eye chile, seeded and finely
    chopped
4 garlic cloves, finely chopped
1 tablespoon harissa chile paste
2 teaspoons ground cumin
pinch of saffron
1 bulb fennel, outer leaves removed, diced
12 new potatoes, halved
juice of 2 lemons
1½ quarts reduced-salt fish or vegetable
    stock
1 (14-oz) can chopped tomatoes
1 teaspoon salt
2 zucchini, cut into ¾ in rounds
¼ lb green beans, cut into ¾ in lengths
1 (14-oz) can cannellini beans, drained
    and rinsed
1¼ lb white fish fillets, skinned, cut into
    bite-sized pieces
½ bunch cilantro, coarsely chopped
1 lemon, cut into wedges, to serve

1 Heat the olive oil in a large saucepan, then add the onions, chile, and garlic and cook gently for 8 to 10 minutes. Add the harissa, cumin, saffron, fennel, potatoes, lemon juice, and stock. Bring to a boil, then cover, reduce the heat, and simmer for 15 minutes.

2 Add the tomatoes and salt and simmer for another 10 minutes. Add the vegetables, beans, and fish and simmer for 10 minutes more. Stir in the cilantro and serve with lemon wedges on the side for a citrus kick.

Amount per portion
Energy 700 cals, Protein 47.6g, Fat 32.6g, Saturated fat 1.1g, Carbohydrate 57.6g, Total sugars 13.5g, Fiber 15.9g, Salt 4.36g, Sodium 1718mg

Polpette di Sarde (Sardine Cakes)

A great Italian dish from the pantry, full of omega 3 and perfect with a summery bean salad.

Serves 4

3 (4-oz) cans sardines in brine, drained
1 cup multigrain breadcrumbs
   (see page 173)
¼ cup skim milk
2 tablespoons currants, soaked in hot water
   for 5 minutes and drained
5 brazil nuts, chopped
1 tablespoon grated Parmesan cheese
1 tablespoon chopped fresh parsley
1 teaspoon snipped fresh chives
1 egg, beaten
salt and freshly ground black pepper
whole wheat flour, for dusting
spray olive oil, for cooking
bean salad and tomato sauce, to serve

1 In a bowl, mash the sardines, bones and all. Soak the breadcrumbs in the milk for 5 minutes, then squeeze out and discard any excess fluid.

2 Add the bread to the sardines, along with the currants, nuts, Parmesan, parsley, chives, and egg. Mix the ingredients thoroughly with your hands, season to taste with salt and pepper, then shape them into small fishcakes about ¾ inch in diameter; if the mixture is too wet, add more breadcrumbs. Dust the fishcakes with flour.

3 Heat a frying pan and spray with oil, then cook the fishcakes over medium heat for 5 minutes on each side until golden and hot. Serve with a bean salad and a cooked tomato sauce.

Amount per portion
Energy 297 cals, Protein 23.0g, Fat 13.3g, Saturated fat 3.1g, Carbohydrate 22.8g, Total sugars 6.9g, Fiber 2.4g, Salt 2.03g, Sodium 803mg

Scallops and Bacon on Sweet-and-Sour Cabbage

Scallops, bacon, and cabbage—I'm in heaven! It's the perfect threesome and so easy for such a treat. Serve with new potatoes.

Serves 4

1 Savoy cabbage, shredded
1 egg yolk
½ onion, finely diced
3 teaspoons sugar or low-calorie
   granulated sweetener
¼ cup cider vinegar
5½ oz non-fat natural Greek yogurt
2 teaspoons Dijon mustard
1 bunch fresh dill, finely chopped
salt and freshly ground black pepper
12 large scallops
4 slices bacon

1 Preheat the broiler to high. Cook the cabbage in boiling salted water for about 8 minutes.

2 Meanwhile, in a large saucepan over low heat, whisk together the egg yolk, onion, sugar or sweetener, and vinegar until the mixture thickens; do not allow the mixture to boil. Remove from the heat and fold in the yogurt, mustard, and dill. Drain the cabbage thoroughly and fold into the sauce. Season to taste with salt and pepper.

3 Broil the scallops and bacon together for 2 minutes each side, or until cooked. Serve the scallops and bacon on top of the cabbage.

Tip If you prefer your scallops a little underdone in the center, cook them for a little less than 2 minutes each side.

Amount per portion (low-calorie sweetener)
Energy 273 cals, Protein 40.4g, Fat 8.5g, Saturated fat 2.5g, Carbohydrate 9.5g, Total sugars 8.4g, Fiber 4.9g, Salt 2.4g, Sodium 945mg

Amount per portion (sugar)
Energy 286 cals, Protein 40.4g, Fat 8.5g, Saturated fat 2.5g, Carbohydrate 13.0g, Total sugars 11.9g, Fiber 4.9g, Salt 2.4g, Sodium 945mg

Fillets of Sea Bass with Anise-Scented Tomatoes

This is the sort of dish you would die for when sitting in a Greek tavern overlooking the sea. Unfortunately, it's usually just roasted or barbecued sea bass with a wedge of lemon, but this is what I dream of.

Serves 4

2 tablespoons extra virgin olive oil
3 garlic cloves, thinly sliced
pinch of hot red pepper flakes
2¼ lb spinach, tough stems removed, shredded
pinch of grated nutmeg
salt and freshly ground black pepper
4 fillets of sea bass, about 6oz each, skin on, each fillet cut in 3 crosswise
3 tablespoons anise-flavored liqueur (ouzo, sambuca, Pernod)
3 tablespoons dry white wine
1 (14-oz) can chopped tomatoes
1 tablespoon flaked almonds
1 teaspoon chopped fresh tarragon
new potatoes or brown rice, to serve

1 Heat half the oil in a large saucepan, add the garlic, and cook over low heat until the garlic turns golden. Add the hot red pepper flakes, then the spinach, and cook until wilted, about 5 minutes. Sprinkle some nutmeg over the top and season to taste with salt and pepper.

2 Set a colander over a bowl and drain the spinach well, pressing to remove as much liquid as possible. Retain the liquid, set aside, and keep the spinach warm.

3 Meanwhile, place a frying pan over medium heat and add the remaining oil. Cook the fish skin-side down for 4 minutes until the skin is golden and the flesh has nearly cooked through. Turn the fish over, then add the anise liqueur and white wine and cook until the liquid has almost evaporated, about 2 minutes. Remove the fish and keep warm.

4 Add the spinach liquid to the fish pan and boil vigorously to reduce, then add the tomatoes, flaked almonds, and tarragon and cook for 15 minutes until slightly thickened. Return the fish to the pan briefly to warm through.

5 Divide the spinach between individual warmed plates and top each with 3 pieces of fish, then spoon over the sauce. Serve with new potatoes or brown rice.

Amount per portion
Energy 361 cals, Protein 43g, Fat 13g, Saturated fat 2.1g, Carbohydrate 11g, Total sugars 9.2g, Fiber 6.6g, Salt 1.95g, Sodium 768mg

Roast Cod with Lemon, Tomatoes, and Olives

Italian cooks would use whole red mullet for this simple, delicious dish—tasty, but hard to come by (plus, home cooks tend not to like bony, head-on fish). I've used cod fillets, but use whatever fish you prefer, adjusting the cooking time accordingly.

Serves 4

1lb new potatoes, left unpeeled
12 garlic cloves
spray olive oil
freshly ground black pepper
4 thick cod fillets, about 6oz each
1 tablespoon smoked or sweet paprika
1 lemon, zested and finely sliced
¾lb cherry tomatoes
1 yellow bell pepper, seeded and cut into
 1in pieces
handful of pitted black olives
6 anchovy fillets, chopped
handful of ripped fresh basil leaves,
 to garnish
green salad, to serve

1 Preheat the oven to 450°F. Add the potatoes and garlic to a pan of boiling water and cook for 15 minutes until tender. Drain and transfer to a roasting pan, spray with oil, and season with black pepper. Slide the pan into the oven and cook for 15 minutes.

2 Meanwhile, spray the fish fillets with olive oil, dust with paprika and lemon zest, then set aside.

3 Remove the roasting pan from the oven and add the lemon slices, tomatoes, yellow pepper, olives, and anchovies, and stir to combine. Place the cod on top and return to the oven for 15 minutes. Arrange on to individual warmed plates, scatter with basil, and serve with a green salad.

Variation If you prefer crispier potatoes, ignore the boiling stage in Step 1 and roast the potatoes for 40 minutes before adding the other ingredients.

Amount per portion
Energy 296 cals, Protein 38.4g, Fat 4.7g, Saturated fat 0.6g, Carbohydrate 26.7g, Total sugars 7.3g, Fiber 3.5g, Salt 1.07g, Sodium 422mg

Crab and Tomato Linguini

I love crab—fresh, ideally, but rarely can I be bothered with the hassle of boiling and cleaning a whole crab. Decent crabmeat is offered in many supermarkets, but failing that, you could try Alaskan canned crab; it's certainly much better than the frozen stuff. In this Italian-influenced dish, it makes a great partner to pasta.

Serves 4
1 tablespoon olive oil
3 garlic cloves, sliced
1 small onion, finely chopped
2 mild fresh chiles, seeded
    and chopped
1 bay leaf
1 cup tomato sauce
20 cherry tomatoes, halved
¾ lb dried linguini
¾ lb fresh or canned white crabmeat
3½ oz brown crabmeat (optional)
salt and freshly ground black pepper

1 Heat the oil in a large frying pan over medium heat and cook the garlic, onion, chiles, and bay leaf until the onion has softened. Add the tomato sauce and cook for 8 to 10 minutes until thickened. Add the cherry tomatoes and cook for another 5 minutes.
2 Meanwhile, cook the linguini in boiling salted water for 1 minute less than the package instructions. Drain.
3 Fold the crabmeat into the sauce, then fold in the pasta with a little cooking water still clinging to it. Stir to combine, season with salt and pepper to taste, and serve.

Variations There's a lot of room to play around with this recipe. Try it with shrimp or cubes of white fish or salmon, and add a few peas or chopped beans when you add the cherry tomatoes.

Amount per portion
Energy 412 cals, Protein 27.4g, Fat 5.8g, Saturated fat 0.8g, Carbohydrate 66.9g, Total sugars 7.4g, Fiber 3.0g, Salt 1.6g, Sodium 628mg

Penne with Salmon, Beans, Mint, and Tomato

Italian recipes don't normally mix cheese and fish, but this Sicilian recipe is an exception that usually uses mozzarella. I'm not a fan of low-fat mozzarella, though, so I've substituted low-fat cottage cheese, which is added at the end of the recipe.

Serves 4
2 tablespoons olive oil
2 garlic cloves
1 (7-oz) can chopped tomatoes
1 bunch of fresh mint leaves, chopped
1 red chile, seeded and sliced
½ cup dry white wine
11½ oz salmon fillet, skinned and cut into
  ½ in dice
1 (14-oz) can borlotti beans, drained
  and rinsed
¾lb dried penne
salt and freshly ground black pepper
3oz low-fat cottage cheese
green salad, to serve

1 Heat the oil in a frying pan, add the garlic cloves, and cook over medium heat until pale golden. Add the tomatoes, half the mint, all the chile, and white wine and simmer for 5 minutes. Remove the garlic and discard.

2 Add the salmon and beans to the tomato sauce and return to a boil, then reduce the heat and cook for another 3 minutes.

3 Meanwhile, cook the penne in boiling salted water for 1 minute less than the package instructions. Drain the pasta briefly and add it, along with a little of its cooking water and the remaining mint, to the sauce. Toss to combine and season to taste with salt and pepper.

4 Divide between individual warmed bowls, then dot the surface with cottage cheese. Serve with a green salad.

Amount per portion
Energy 580 cals, Protein 34.1g, Fat 16.8g, Saturated fat 2.8g, Carbohydrate 75.4g, Total sugars 5.2g, Fiber 5.8g, Salt 1.25g, Sodium 496mg

Pasta with Anchovies, Pine Nuts, and Golden Raisins

Simplicity is often best, as in this energy-giving Sicilian dish. It's got lovely flavors, as long as you enjoy anchovies, and lots of different textures.

Serves 4
1lb dried spaghetti
2 tablespoons olive oil
1 fennel bulb, very finely sliced
2 garlic cloves, finely sliced
⅓ cup golden raisins, soaked in 2 tablespoons
  of Pernod or ouzo
⅓ cup pine nuts
8 anchovies in oil, drained and coarsely
  chopped
1 tablespoon chopped fresh oregano
  or marjoram
1 cup toasted multigrain breadcrumbs
  (see page 173)

1 Cook the spaghetti in plenty of boiling salted water for 1 minute less than specified on the package instructions, then drain, retaining a little of its cooking water, and keep warm.

2 Meanwhile, heat the oil in a pan, add the fennel and garlic, and cook gently for 8 to 10 minutes until softened without coloring. Add the golden raisins with their liquid, pine nuts, anchovies, and oregano and cook until the anchovies break down.

3 Add the pasta with a little of its cooking water and toss to mix well. Divide between individual plates and scatter with crunchy multigrain breadcrumbs.

Amount per portion
Energy 668 cals, Protein 20.5g, Fat 17.8g, Saturated fat 00g, Carbohydrate 109.0g, Total sugars 16.2g, Fiber 6.3g, Salt 1.11g, Sodium 440mg

Roast Cod on a Cannellini Bean Stew

Inspired by Italy but created by Australians—they're great at flavors and this marriage of ingredients shows off this talent to the full.

Serves 4

1 tablespoon olive oil
4oz chorizo, sliced and diced
1 large onion, finely diced
2 carrots, cut into ½ in dice
2 celery ribs, cut into ½ in dice
3 garlic cloves, crushed to a paste
   with a little salt
1 teaspoon fresh thyme leaves
1 bay leaf
4 jarred artichoke hearts in oil, drained
   and quartered
pinch of saffron
1 medium red chile, seeded and diced
1 cup reduced-salt chicken stock
1 (14-oz) can cannellini beans, drained
   and rinsed
1 tablespoon freshly grated Parmesan
   cheese
1 tablespoon chopped fresh parsley
4 fillets of cod, about 6oz each, skin on
salt and freshly ground black pepper
spray oil, for cooking

1 Preheat the oven to 425°F. Heat the oil in a saucepan or frying pan and cook the chorizo for 2 to 3 minutes to release fats and crispen the sausage. Remove and set aside.

2 In the chorizo fat, cook the onion, carrots, celery, garlic, thyme, and bay leaf for 8 minutes. Add the artichokes, saffron, chile, stock, and cannellini beans and continue cooking gently until most of the liquid has evaporated. Fold in the Parmesan, parsley, and the cooked chorizo. Adjust the seasoning to taste.

3 Meanwhile, season the cod fillets with salt and pepper, spray with oil, and place them in a lightly sprayed roasting pan. Transfer to the preheated oven and cook for 12 to 15 minutes. Spoon the bean mixture on to individual plates, then top with the oven-roasted cod.

Amount per portion

Energy 411 cals, Protein 45.7g, Fat 16.2g, Saturated fat 4.3g, Carbohydrate 21.9g, Total sugars 8.8g, Fiber 5.9g, Salt 3.09g, Sodium 1217mg

Shrimp Linguini

Pasta with a touch of class, a bestseller in Italian restaurants—and it's quick and easy to make. Feel free to substitute a firm white fish for the shrimp.

Serves 4
¾ lb dried linguini
spray olive oil
1 tablespoon non-pareille capers
    (baby capers), rinsed and drained
4 anchovy fillets, sliced
4 garlic cloves, sliced
½ teaspoon hot red pepper flakes
24 raw shrimp, shell-off
¼ cup dry white wine (optional)
½ cup fish or chicken stock
½ cup tomato sauce
4 scallions, coarsely sliced
12 cherry tomatoes, halved
handful of arugula
handful of baby spinach
1 teaspoon chopped fresh oregano
salt and freshly ground black pepper

1 In a large pan of boiling salted water, cook the pasta for a minute less than the package instructions. Drain and keep warm.

2 Meanwhile, spray a saucepan with a little oil. Over low heat, gently cook the capers, anchovies, garlic, and hot red pepper flakes until the anchovies start to break down. Add the shrimp, increase the temperature, and cook for another 3 minutes. Remove the shrimp and keep warm.

3 Add the wine (if using), stock, and tomato sauce to the pan and boil until reduced by half. Add the scallions and tomatoes and cook for 3 minutes. Add the arugula, baby spinach, oregano, and shrimp and continue cooking until the greens have wilted. Add the pasta, toss to combine, and season to taste with salt and pepper.

Variation For a more intense sauce, buy shell-on raw shrimp and peel them before you start cooking. Add the shells to the capers and anchovies in Step 2. After you have reduced the sauce in Step 3, remove the shells and blend them, then pass them through a sieve, return to the pan, and continue as in the recipe.

Amount per portion
Energy 373 cals, Protein 26.4g, Fat 2.9g, Saturated fat 0.5g, Carbohydrate 64.4g, Total sugars 5.3g, Fiber 3.2g, Salt 2.32g, Sodium 915mg

Fragrant Shrimp with Hints of Fire

I love this Malaysian street food, cooked in an instant and yet packing a flavor punch. If shrimp isn't your thing, then try the same recipe with a white fish, but treat it a bit more delicately.

Serves 4

2 tablespoons sunflower oil
14oz raw tiger shrimp, shell off
    and deveined
¾ cup all-purpose flour, seasoned with salt
    and pepper
2 tablespoons ketchup
3 tablespoons sweet chile sauce
2 tablespoons hot chile sauce
1 tablespoon hot bean paste
1 tablespoon light soy sauce
1 teaspoon reduced-salt chicken
    bouillon cube
4 garlic cloves, chopped
1in piece of fresh ginger, peeled
    and grated
1 bird's eye chile, seeded and
    finely chopped
1 mild green chile, coarsely chopped
½ green bell pepper, seeded and diced
4 scallions, sliced
salt and freshly ground black pepper
brown rice, to serve

1 Heat the oil in a wok, toss the shrimp in the seasoned flour, then cook them in the oil until pink all over, about 2 to 3 minutes. Remove them from the wok and set aside to keep warm.

2 Drain the wok of most of the oil, then add the ketchup, chile sauces, bean paste, soy sauce, and bouillon cube. Heat until boiling then add the remaining ingredients except the shrimp, and cook for 3 minutes. Fold in the shrimp and warm through, then season to taste. Serve with a nutty brown rice.

Amount per portion

Energy 267 cals, Protein 21.7g, Fat 7.1g, Saturated fat 0.9g, Carbohydrate 31.0g, Total sugars 9.8g, Fiber 1.6g, Salt 3.34g, Sodium 1318mg

Lemon Sole with Lemon and Basil Stuffing

Let's be honest: it's quite hard to find indigenous American cuisine, because it's usually been influenced by one country or another. This, however, is a dish I had in Boston, albeit made with another fish. It has wonderful flavors and can be prepared in advance and cooked just before serving.

Serves 4

1 tablespoon canola oil
1 celery rib, finely diced
1 garlic clove, chopped
½ onion, finely chopped
juice and zest of 1 lemon
1 teaspoon smoked paprika
1¼ cups cooked brown rice
4 tablespoons low-fat Greek natural yogurt
2 tablespoons chopped fresh basil
oil, for greasing
8 lemon sole fillets

1 In a medium saucepan, heat the oil over medium heat and cook the celery, garlic, and onion, stirring frequently, until softened without coloring—about 8 minutes. Add the lemon juice and zest, paprika, and a couple of tablespoons of water, and bring to a boil. Add the rice, stir to combine, remove from the heat, and set aside to cool for 10 minutes. Add the yogurt and basil.

2 If you are preparing the dish for eating immediately, preheat the oven to 350°F. Lightly oil a baking sheet. Roll each fillet, head to tail, slightly overlapping to form a hollow tube, secure with cocktail sticks, then place on their ends on the baking sheet. With a tablespoon, fill each cavity with the rice mix, slightly mounded. (At this point the dish can be set aside, lightly covered, ready to cook later.)

3 Pop the fish into the oven for 12 to 15 minutes from room temperature or 20 minutes from refrigerated. Serve with greens.

Amount per portion
Energy 332 cals, Protein 39.2g, Fat 9.4g, Saturated fat 1.9g, Carbohydrate 24.1g, Total sugars 1.8g, Fiber 0.8g, Salt 0.54g, Sodium 212mg

Paella

Paella is a wonderful one-pot dish, but traditionally the shellfish has the texture of rubber, so I am abusing tradition by cooking and adding the shellfish toward the end.

Serves 4

2 cups chicken stock
pinch of saffron, soaked in
 a little warm water
2 tablespoons olive oil
2oz chorizo sausage, cut into thin slices
2oz pancetta, cut into small dice
4 skinless, boneless chicken thighs,
 each cut in half
2 garlic cloves, finely chopped, plus
 4 garlic cloves, unpeeled
1 Spanish onion, finely diced
1 small red bell pepper, seeded and diced
1 teaspoon fresh thyme leaves
good pinch of hot red pepper flakes
1½ cups Spanish short-grain rice
 (calasparra)
½ teaspoon paprika
¼ cup dry white wine
⅓ cup fresh or frozen peas
2 large tomatoes, peeled, seeded
 and diced
salt and freshly ground black pepper
¾ lb small raw clams or mussels, cleaned
12 raw jumbo shrimp, shell-on
½ lb squid, cleaned and chopped into
 bite-sized pieces
sprigs of flat-leaf parsley, to garnish

1 Heat the stock and saffron together in a pan to boiling point and keep it hot. Heat half the olive oil in a *paellera*,* add the chorizo and pancetta, and cook for a few minutes until crisp and lightly golden. Transfer to a plate and set aside. Add the chicken pieces to the pan and cook for a few minutes on each side until golden, then remove and set aside with the chorizo and pancetta.
2 Add the chopped garlic, onion, and red bell pepper to the pan and cook for a few minutes until the vegetables have softened but not colored, stirring occasionally. Add the thyme, hot red pepper flakes, and rice and stir for about 2 minutes or until all the rice grains are nicely coated and glossy. Stir in the paprika, then pour in the wine and allow it to simmer down a little, stirring. Pour in the hot chicken stock, add the cooked chorizo, pancetta, and chicken, and cook for another 5 minutes or so, stirring occasionally. Fold in the peas and tomatoes and season to taste with salt and pepper.
3 Add the clams to the paella, with the edges that will open facing upward, and continue to cook gently for another 10 to 15 minutes or until the rice is just tender. Remove from the burner and leave to rest in a warm place for 10 minutes.
4 Meanwhile, heat the remaining oil in a separate large frying pan. Add the unpeeled garlic cloves and then quickly add in the shrimp. Stir-fry for a minute or two, then scatter the shrimp over the paella, leaving the garlic in the pan. Add the squid to the pan and stir-fry for 1 minute or so until just tender, then scatter the squid over the paella; discard the garlic. Garnish with the parsley sprigs and serve immediately, straight from the pan, with a salad on the side.

*****Tip** If you don't have a *paellera*, or a traditional paella dish, use a large heavy-bottomed frying pan.

Amount per portion
Energy 678 cals, Protein 62.2g, Fat 17.2g, Saturated fat 4.6g, Carbohydrate 72.0g, Total sugars 8.5g, Fiber 4.2g, Salt 2.97g, Sodium 1171mg

Asian Surf and Turf Balls in Sweet and Sour Sauce

A lovely Asian combination of shrimp and pork: sophisticated yet simple, and a perfect supper for hungry children.

Serves 4

For the balls
½ lb raw shrimp, shell-off and finely chopped
½ lb ground pork
1 fresh red chile, seeded and finely diced
½ in piece of fresh ginger, peeled and grated
2 scallions, finely chopped
1 tablespoon light soy sauce
1 tablespoon sesame oil
1 tablespoon chopped cilantro
½ tablespoon cornstarch
2 tablespoons chopped water chestnuts
1 teaspoon sunflower oil

For the sauce
2 garlic cloves, finely chopped
1 in piece of fresh ginger, peeled and grated
1 fresh red chile, seeded and finely chopped
⅓ cup pineapple juice
1 tablespoon light soy sauce
1 tablespoon white wine vinegar
1 tablespoon tomato paste
2 tablespoons dark brown sugar or low-calorie granulated sweetener
1 tablespoon cornstarch, mixed to a paste with 2 tablespoons cold water

1 To make the balls, mix together all the ingredients except the water chestnuts and the oil. Combine well, then take about 2 tablespoons of the mixture and roll into a ball. Repeat. Make an indentation in each ball and insert a little chopped water chestnut in the center, then enclose within the balls.

2 Heat the oil in a wok and cook the balls until brown all over. Add the garlic, ginger, and chile from the sauce ingredients, reduce the heat, and cook for 5 minutes. Add the remaining ingredients, except for the cornstarch paste, bring to a boil, and cook for 3 minutes. Add the cornstarch paste and cook until thickened and glossy, about 2 minutes. To serve, place some steaming rice in individual warm bowls and top with the meatballs.

Tip If you find soy sauce too strong and salty, you can either dilute it with a little water or try a light soy sauce instead, as I have in this recipe; this is now widely available in larger supermarkets.

Amount per portion (sugar)
Energy 237 cals, Protein 21.9g, Fat 9.7g, Saturated fat 2.6g, Carbohydrate 16.7g, Total sugars 11.6g, Fiber 0.3g, Salt 1.78g, Sodium 700mg

Amount per portion (low-calorie sweetener)
Energy 211 cals, Protein 21.9g, Fat 9.7g, Saturated fat 2.6g, Carbohydrate 9.5g, Total sugars 4.5g, Fiber 0.3g, Salt 1.78g, Sodium 700mg

New Potatoes and Smoked Mackerel with Avocado Horseradish Dressing

Smoked mackerel is a wonderfully nutritious standby, plus it's plentiful. The addition of new potatoes (good G.I.) and avocado (all the right fats), make this recipe a veritable superfood—so much goodness and tastiness in one plate!

Serves 4

1lb new potatoes
1 tablespoon olive oil
4 bay leaves, broken
4 garlic cloves, smashed
juice and grated zest of 2 lemons
salt and freshly ground black pepper
2in piece of fresh horseradish, grated,
    or 2 tablespoons from a jar
1 avocado, diced
4 tablespoons non-fat natural
    Greek yogurt
3 smoked peppered mackerel fillets,
    skin removed, flaked
handful of arugula

1 Preheat the oven to 400°F.

2 Place the potatoes in a bowl and toss with the olive oil, broken bay, garlic, and half of the lemon juice and zest. Season with a little salt and a few grindings of pepper. Transfer to a roasting pan and cook in the oven for about 40 minutes, tossing from time to time. When cooked, the potatoes will be tender, wrinkly, and golden. Discard the bay leaves.

3 Combine the remaining lemon zest with the horseradish, avocado, and yogurt. Mash with the back of a fork, retaining some texture. Gently fold in the mackerel flakes, leaving them as chunky as possible. If the mixture is very stiff, add a little of the remaining lemon juice. Season to taste.

4 Arrange the potatoes onto individual plates, top with the mackerel mix, scatter with arugula, and serve.

Amount per portion
Energy 595 cals, Protein 27g, Fat 45g, Saturated fat 9.7g, Carbohydrate 23g, Total sugars 3.1g, Fiber 3.1g, Salt 2.84g, Sodium 1118mg

Poached Haddock with Eggs and Spinach

This classic combination is wonderfully comforting. You could use smoked haddock, but beware of its salt content. You do need a certain amount of precise timing for this dish. Serve with some toasted multigrain bread.

Serves 4

2 cups skim milk
2 bay leaves
1 onion, quartered
1 teaspoon black peppercorns
2¼ lb fresh spinach, washed and tough
   stems removed
freshly ground black pepper
4 (6-oz) haddock fillets
2 tablespoons white wine vinegar
4 eggs
2 tablespoons white wine vinegar

1 In a frying pan over low heat, heat the milk with the bay, onion, and peppercorns, and simmer gently for 10 minutes.

2 Meanwhile, heat about 1 inch of water in a large saucepan, add the spinach with a little pinch of salt, and allow the heat to wilt and cook the leaves. Drain the spinach well, pressing down to release the water, return to the pan, loosen the leaves, and keep warm. Season with pepper.

3 Place the haddock fillets in the simmering milk skin-side down and poach for 6 minutes, turning carefully once.

4 Meanwhile, bring about 4 inches of water to a boil in a small pan, then add the vinegar. Break the eggs into separate coffee cups, then, one after the other, pour them into the roll of the boil and immediately reduce the heat slightly. Cook for 2 minutes 30 seconds and drain.

5 Arrange the spinach in the center of a warmed plate and top with the haddock and then a poached egg. Grind over some pepper and, if you like, spoon a little of the poaching milk around the spinach.

Tip For the best poached eggs with the best shape, you'll need ultra-fresh eggs—if they are very fresh you won't even need any vinegar, which with older eggs helps coagulate the white so you don't get ugly strands. I'm lucky my chickens lay daily.

Amount per portion
Energy 312 cals, Protein 48.6g, Fat 9.9g, Saturated fat 2.4g, Carbohydrate 7.5g, Total sugars 6.1g, Fiber 5.7g, Salt 2.78g, Sodium 804mg

Cotriade

Normally this fish and potato stew uses floury potatoes, but here I use new; it would also be served with a saffron mayonnaise or an aioli but you'll have to make do with a delicious saffron yogurt, unless, of course, you can be good and use only a scant amount of aioli.

Serves 4

For the saffron yogurt
small pinch of saffron, soaked in about
    2 tablespoons hot fish stock
4oz non-fat natural Greek yogurt
¼ cup leftover mashed potato
juice and zest of 1 lemon
2 garlic cloves, crushed
1 tablespoon extra virgin olive oil
freshly ground white pepper

For the stew
spray olive oil
4 shallots, thinly sliced
3 garlic cloves, thinly sliced
sprig of thyme
1 bay leaf
½ cup dry white wine
2 cups fish stock or dashi stock
½ lb new potatoes, halved
1lb mixed fish fillets (cod, monkfish, mullet)
    cut into 1in pieces
1lb mussels, cleaned
¾ cup peas, frozen or fresh
½ lb leeks, chopped

1 Whisk together all the saffron yogurt ingredients.

2 Heat a large saucepan and spray it with oil, add the shallots, garlic, thyme, and bay leaf and cook for 5 minutes over medium heat. Add the wine, stock, and potatoes and cook gently until the potatoes are tender.

3 Add the fish, mussels, peas, and leeks and cook vigorously for 5 minutes until the mussels have fully opened (discard any that have not). Serve, topping each individual bowl with a dollop of the saffron yogurt.

Variations Normally the solids are removed just before serving and kept warm while mayonnaise is whisked into the liquid to thicken it. For a healthier way to thicken your stew, make a cornstarch paste and stir it in just before serving.

Amount per portion
Energy 282 cals, Protein 32.5g, Fat 7.0g, Saturated fat 1.4g, Carbohydrate 21.1g, Total sugars 5.9g, Fiber 4.2g, Salt 1.72g, Sodium 675mg

Roast Hake in a Chowder-style Broth

The broth that accompanies the hake could be served as a light soup, but it goes very well with the roast fish. I've included more vegetables than there would be in a traditional North American chowder but, in essence, anything goes.

Serves 4
1 cup dry white wine
2¼ lb raw baby clams, washed
1lb raw mussels, washed
1 tablespoon sunflower oil, plus sunflower oil spray
3 slices smoked bacon, diced
1 large onion, finely chopped
2 garlic cloves, sliced
12 new potatoes, halved
2 bay leaves
sprig of thyme
1 cup good-quality fish stock
1 cup skim milk
¾ cup canned corn
¾ cup frozen peas
2 ripe tomatoes, seeded and diced
salt and freshly ground white pepper
4 (6-oz) hake steaks, skin and bone retained
1 tablespoon snipped fresh chives, to garnish

1 Pour the wine into a large saucepan and bring to a boil. Add the clams, cover, and cook for 2 minutes, then add the mussels, cover, and cook for about 3 minutes or until the shellfish has opened, shaking the pan from time to time. Strain the shellfish in a colander, retaining the liquor, and discard any that have not opened. Set the shellfish aside.

2 Preheat the oven to 400°F. Heat the sunflower oil in a large saucepan and cook the bacon until crispy. Drain any excess fat and discard. Add the onion and garlic to the bacon and cook for 6 minutes to soften them without coloring. Add the potatoes, bay leaves, thyme, stock, and the shellfish cooking juices. Cook until the potatoes are tender, about 15 to 20 minutes. Add the milk, return to a boil, and add the corn, peas, and tomatoes. Cook for 5 minutes and season with salt to taste.

3 Spray the fish with sunflower oil, season with pepper, and place on a baking sheet. Transfer to the oven and cook for 12 minutes.

4 While the broth is cooking and the hake roasting, get shucking—remove the clams and mussels from their shells. When the broth is ready, add the shellfish to heat through but do not re-boil. Spoon the broth with its contents into individual warmed bowls, top with the hake, and sprinkle with chives.

Variation If desired, the broth can be thickened with a paste of cornstarch and water.

Amount per portion
Energy 511 cals, Protein 53.3g, Fat 12.5g, Saturated fat 2.7g, Carbohydrate 43.2g, Total sugars 15.9g, Fiber 4.5g, Salt 2.73g, Sodium 1073mg

Barley Risotto with Greens and Shrimp

Barley makes an interesting change to traditional Italian risotto rice—it produces a lovely nutty texture and taste and has a low GI. Give risotto your full attention, as it needs regular stirring and additions of stock. Once you've mastered the basic technique, you can add all sorts of flavorings.

Serves 4
1 tablespoon olive oil
2 shallots, finely chopped
2 garlic cloves, finely chopped
1 bay leaf
sprig of thyme
1½ cups pearl barley
½ cup dry white wine
1 quart fish or chicken stock, heated
    almost to boiling point
¾ cup fava beans, frozen or fresh and
    podded, blanched
1 cup green beans, blanched
¾ cup petit pois, (small peas) frozen
handful of pea shoots
handful of baby spinach
½ lb raw shell-off tiger shrimp
freshly ground black pepper

1 Melt the olive oil in a large saucepan, add the shallots and garlic, and cook gently for 5 minutes. Add the herbs and barley and stir to combine. Add the wine and boil vigorously until the liquid has all but disappeared.

2 Add the hot stock one ladle at a time, and, just like with the wine, wait until the liquid has nearly disappeared before adding the next ladle. About 20 minutes or so into this process, test the barley to see whether it is cooked; it should be soft but still slightly nutty.

3 Add the vegetables and shrimp, stir to combine, and cook for 3 minutes (you may need a little extra stock). Season to taste with pepper and serve.

Tip Be sure the stock is almost boiling before you start the risotto process.

Amount per portion
Energy 427 cals, Protein 23.0g, Fat 6.0g, Saturated fat 0.8g, Carbohydrate 72.0g, Total sugars 4.3g, Fiber 5.2g, Salt 2.26g, Sodium 892mg

Meat and Poultry

Casserole of Lamb with Spring Vegetables

The French have a dish called navarin of lamb on which this dish is loosely based. Spring offers lots of new vegetables, but this casserole can be made any time of the year, just buy vegetables that are in season. Serve with some crusty French bread to mop up all the juices.

Serves 4

1 tablespoon olive oil
1½ lb lamb neck fillets, cut into 1in pieces
salt and freshly ground black pepper
4 garlic cloves, crushed
2 onions, coarsely chopped
2 sprigs of fresh rosemary
½ cup dry white wine
1 bay leaf
1 (14-oz) can chopped tomatoes
1¼ quarts lamb or chicken stock
8 carrots, trimmed
8 new potatoes, halved
¾ cup fresh green beans
¾ cup fava beans, frozen or fresh and podded
½ spring cabbage, shredded
¾ cup peas, frozen or fresh and podded

1 Heat the oil in a deep flameproof casserole or Dutch oven. Season the lamb pieces with salt and pepper, then brown them all over on a fairly high heat. Remove and set aside, then discard any excess fat from the dish before adding the garlic, onion, and rosemary. Reduce the heat and cook for 8 minutes, stirring occasionally, allowing the onions to turn golden brown.

2 Add the wine, bay leaf, tomatoes, and stock and bring to a boil. Return the meat to the dish, cover with a lid, reduce the heat, and simmer gently for 1 hour 30 minutes.

3 Time now to stagger the introduction of the vegetables to the casserole: first add the carrots and potatoes and cook for 15 minutes. Add the green beans and fava beans and cook for another 4 minutes. Add the cabbage and peas and cook for a final 3 minutes. Taste and adjust the seasoning, and serve.

Tip Diced shoulder of lamb tends to have more flavor, but it's fairly fatty so would need thorough trimming.

Amount per portion
Energy 623 cals, Protein 43.7g, Fat 34.8g, Saturated fat 15.6g, Carbohydrate 32.5g, Total sugars 13.8g, Fiber 9.1g, Salt 2.67g, Sodium 1051mg

Chicken Tagine with Prunes, Almonds, and Chickpeas

North African tagines always have a wonderful contrast of flavors and textures, and in this one there's a lovely balance of sweet and savory.

Serves 4
3 tablespoons olive oil
6 boneless, skinless chicken thighs, each cut in 2
2 onions, 1 grated, 1 finely sliced
3 garlic cloves, crushed to a paste with a little salt
2 teaspoons ground coriander
1 teaspoon ground cinnamon
pinch of saffron
½ teaspoon each salt and freshly ground black pepper
2 cups chicken stock
1 teaspoon orange flower water (optional)
1 tablespoon superfine sugar
8 prunes, pitted and coarsely chopped
⅓ cup raisins
1 (14-oz) can chickpeas, drained and rinsed
½ cup toasted almond flakes
1 bunch of cilantro, leaves coarsely chopped
1 tablespoon toasted sesame seeds
jeweled couscous, to serve

1 In a large, heavy saucepan heat 2 tablespoons of the oil then gently brown the chicken all over. Add the grated onion and cook over medium heat for 10 minutes. Add the garlic, ground coriander, cinnamon, saffron, and the salt and pepper, and cook for another minute. Pour in enough stock to just cover the chicken and bring to a boil, then reduce the heat, cover, and simmer for about 1 hour.

2 Meanwhile, heat the remaining oil in a frying pan. Add the sliced onion, orange flower water, and sugar, then cover and cook over low heat, stirring from time to time, until the onions have collapsed and are becoming brown. Remove from the heat.

3 About 10 minutes before the chicken is cooked, add the prunes, raisins, chickpeas, almond flakes, cilantro, and the caramelized onions. At the end of the cooking time, transfer the solids to a serving dish and keep warm. Taste the sauce and adjust the seasoning to taste, and reduce by boiling if you like. Pour the sauce over the chicken and sprinkle with toasted sesame seeds. Serve with Jeweled Couscous.

Amount per portion
Energy 510 cals, Protein 40.0g, Fat 23.1g, Saturated fat 3.4g, Carbohydrate 38.0g, Total sugars 24.8g, Fiber 5.1g, Salt 1.60g, Sodium 634mg

Turkey and Ham Meatballs with a Roasted Red Pepper and Bean Sauce

This has a very loose association with Italy as I don't think the Italians would ever have dreamed up a dish like this. Still, that's their loss and your gain.

Serves 4

For the sauce
1 tablespoon olive oil
1 onion, coarsely chopped
2 garlic cloves, coarsely chopped
1 hot red chile, seeded and
    coarsely chopped
5 roasted red peppers from a jar, drained
    and coarsely chopped
2 tablespoons sweet chile sauce
1 (14-oz) can chopped tomatoes
1 (14-oz) can cannellini beans, drained
    and rinsed
juice of 1 lemon
salt and freshly ground black pepper

For the meatballs
1 tablespoon olive oil
½ cup fresh or frozen corn niblets
3 slices multigrain bread, crusts removed
1oz prosciutto, Parma or serrano ham,
    chopped
1 small red onion, finely chopped
1 garlic clove, crushed to a paste with
    a little sea salt
1 teaspoon dried oregano
1 teaspoon ground cumin
1 tablespoon grated Parmesan cheese
1 egg, beaten
½ teaspoon each salt and freshly ground
    black pepper
14oz ground turkey or chicken
spray oil, for frying
pasta and a leaf salad, to serve

1 To make the sauce, heat the olive oil in a saucepan and cook the onion over low heat until soft but not browned, about 8 to 10 minutes. Add the garlic, chile, and roasted peppers, and cook for another 3 minutes. Blend in a food processor or with a hand-held blender.

2 Return the sauce to the pan and add the chile sauce, tomatoes, and beans, and cook gently until thick. Season with lemon juice, a pinch of salt, and some pepper.

3 To make the meatballs, heat the oil in a small pan and cook the corn until lightly charred. Remove and set aside.

4 Soak the bread in a little cold water for a couple of minutes. Remove, squeeze dry, and place in a bowl with the corn and the remaining meatball ingredients. With your hands, mix the mixture for 2 to 3 minutes, making sure all the ingredients are evenly distributed. With wet hands, shape the mix into balls about ½ inch in diameter.

5 Lightly coat a frying pan with spray oil and brown the meatballs all over—you'll need to do this in batches. As they're ready, pop them in the red pepper and bean sauce and cook for 15 minutes. Serve with pasta and a leaf salad.

Amount per portion
Energy 498 cals, Protein 40.0g, Fat 23.1g, Saturated fat 3.4g, Carbohydrate 34.6g, Total sugars 21.5g, Fiber 5.1g, Salt 1.60g, Sodium 633mg

Couscous Royal

This is the giant of North African cooking: a meat and vegetable stew served with a big bowl of steaming couscous, which traditionally is cooked above the simmering stew. The stew would normally include *merguez*, a grilled spicy sausage, but in the interest of your health I've made it optional. To serve, present the broth, meat, and vegetables together in one central serving dish and the couscous in another dish, and let everyone help themselves.

Serves 4

7oz lean lamb, diced
3 boneless, skinless chicken thighs,
    each cut into 3 pieces
2 onions, cut in chunks
4 garlic cloves, crushed
2 quarts chicken or lamb stock
2 *Merguez* sausages (optional)
pinch of salt
1 teaspoon freshly ground black pepper
pinch of saffron
1 teaspoon ground cinnamon
1 teaspoon ground coriander
½ teaspoon ground ginger
1 (14-oz) can chopped tomatoes
12 new potatoes, halved
2 carrots, halved lengthwise
2 turnips, quartered
1 (14-oz) can chickpeas, drained
3 zucchini, each cut into 4 pieces
2 celery ribs, cut into ¾in pieces
¼ cup golden raisins
1 tablespoon harissa chile paste
plain couscous, to serve

1 Place the lamb and chicken in a large saucepan and add the onions, garlic, stock, salt, pepper, saffron, cinnamon, coriander, and ginger. Bring to a boil, cover, reduce the heat, and simmer for 1 hour.

2 Add the tomatoes, potatoes, carrots, turnips, and chickpeas, then cover and simmer for 30 minutes.

3 Preheat the oven to 360°F, then roast the sausages for 15 minutes, turning regularly until golden.

4 Add the zucchini, celery, and golden raisins to the stew and cook for another 20 minutes.

5 With a ladle, remove a little of the broth and combine with the harissa to make a hot liquid condiment, which should be served separately. Check the seasoning of the stew and serve with plain couscous and the sausages cut into bite-sized pieces.

Amount per portion
Energy 574 cals, Protein 54.7g, Fat 17.3g, Saturated fat 5.8g, Carbohydrate 53.7g, Total sugars 21.1g, Fiber 10.6g, Salt 2.97g, Sodium 1172mg

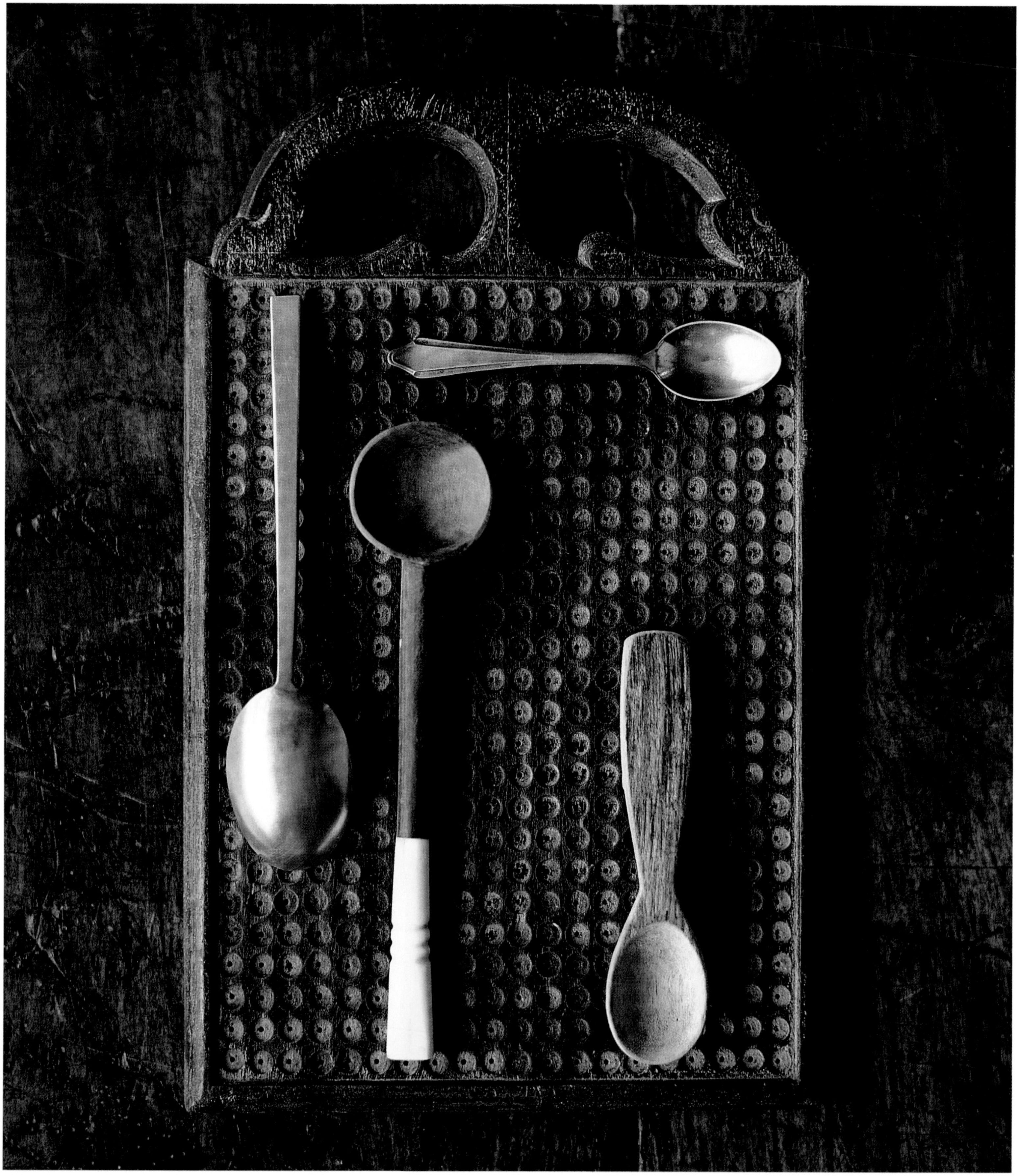

Quick Chicken and Eggplant Salad

I'm sure this fast and furious warm salad, loosely based on Middle Eastern and North African dishes, is the sort of thing they'd eat there if they'd thought of it first!

Serves 4

1 tablespoon olive oil
1 onion, chopped
2 garlic cloves, chopped
1 small eggplant, cut into ½ in dice
1 teaspoon ground coriander
½ teaspoon ground cumin
½ tablespoon tomato paste
½ tablespoon harissa chile paste
1 (14-oz) can chickpeas, drained with
a tablespoon of the water retained
¾ lb cooked chicken, cut into strips
2 teaspoons chopped fresh mint
2 tablespoons pomegranate seeds

1 Heat the oil in a frying pan and cook the onion and garlic over medium heat until golden, about 10 minutes. Add the eggplant, ground coriander, and ground cumin, stir, and cook for 6 to 7 minutes until the eggplant is well colored.

2 Stir in the tomato paste and harissa, then the chickpeas with a little of their water to loosen the mixture. Add the chicken and warm through, then adjust the seasoning to taste. Transfer to a bowl and scatter with mint and pomegranate seeds.

Amount per portion

Energy 293 cals, Protein 31.4g, Fat 12.3g, Saturated fat 2.7g, Carbohydrate 15.1g, Total sugars 4.0g, Fiber 4.3g, Salt 0.58g, Sodium 227mg

Paprika Goulash

Paprika and caraway give this deliciously rich casserole a spicy sweetness. Serve it with rice noodles and a green vegetable such as cabbage, green beans, or broccoli or with a dollop of yogurt sprinkled with paprika, and some rice or new potatoes.

Serves 4

2 tablespoons cornstarch
1lb chuck steak or brisket,
cut into 1½ in pieces
1 tablespoon sunflower oil
2 to 3 slices bacon, chopped
3 garlic cloves, finely chopped
1lb onions, grated
2 red bell peppers, cut into ½ in dice
1 tablespoon caraway seeds
1 tablespoon hot-smoked paprika, plus
extra to garnish
2 cups beef stock
2 tablespoons tomato paste
6 cornichons (baby gherkins), sliced
freshly ground black pepper
non-fat Greek yogurt, to serve

1 Add the cornstarch and beef to a plastic bag, seal the top, and shake well until all the beef pieces are lightly dusted.

2 Heat the oil in a flameproof casserole or Dutch oven, add the bacon, garlic, onions, red bell peppers, caraway, and paprika and cook for 3 minutes. Add the beef, followed by the stock and tomato paste and cornichons, and season with black pepper. Bring to a simmer, then cover and cook very gently for 2 hours, stirring occasionally, until the meat is tender and the sauce is reduced to a rich consistency.

Amount per portion

Energy 360 cals, Protein 32.2g, Fat 16.2g, Saturated fat 5.4g, Carbohydrate 22.7g, Total sugars 12.1g, Fiber 3.2g, Salt 1.32g, Sodium 522mg

Peruvian Chicken Kebabs with Garlic and Orange Salsa

Inspired by a recipe I found in a Peruvian cookbook. Simple, quick, tasty—what more do you need? Oh, and it's pretty good value for money, too, and perfect for the grill.

Serves 4
6 garlic cloves
¼ teaspoon salt
1 teaspoon ground cumin
1 teaspoon ground coriander
1 teaspoon sweet paprika
4 tablespoons cilantro leaves, half of them chopped
juice and grated zest of 3 limes
2 large chicken breasts, skinned and cut into 1in cubes
5 juicy oranges
1 red onion, thinly sliced
1 tablespoon toasted almond flakes
spray olive oil
green salad and tortillas, to serve

1 In a mini food processor, blend the garlic and salt to a smooth paste. Remove half and set aside. To the remaining half in the food processor add the ground cumin, ground coriander, paprika, the whole cilantro leaves, and half the lime zest and juice, and blend to a paste.

2 Mix the chicken with the spicy garlic paste and allow to marinate for a couple of hours, or at least 30 minutes.

3 Meanwhile, grate the zest of 2½ oranges and juice 2 of them. Combine the orange zest and juice with the remaining lime zest and juice, the onion, the remaining chopped cilantro leaves, and the remaining garlic paste to make a salsa. Then remove the peel and pith from the remaining oranges, slice the flesh, and combine with the garlic salsa.

4 Heat a ridged grill pan or outdoor grill. Thread the marinated chicken on to four wooden skewers. Spray the kebabs with olive oil then cook for 12 to 15 minutes, turning from time to time. Serve with the garlic and orange salsa and a green salad, and maybe some kind of tortilla/flatbread.

Variations If you're a leg person, try this recipe with boneless chicken thighs; you could also try pork, lamb, salmon, tuna, or halloumi cheese.

Amount per portion
Energy 154 cals, Protein 20.5g, Fat 3.1g, Saturated fat 0.4g, Carbohydrate 11.8g, Total sugars 9.3g, Fiber 0.9g, Salt 0.44g, Sodium 175mg

Barley-stuffed Quail with Indian Spices

These little game birds' sweet-flavored flesh has more depth than chicken and they represent good value for money. And with these lovely Indian flavors, it's a knockout recipe.

Serves 4

For the marinade
2 teaspoons ground coriander
½ teaspoon ground black pepper
½ teaspoon ground cardamom
½ teaspoon ground clove
½ teaspoon ground cumin
1 teaspoon curry powder
¼ teaspoon chili powder
½ teaspoon ground turmeric
1 teaspoon grated fresh ginger
1 tablespoon sunflower oil

4 quails
Nutty Curried Beans, to serve
    (see page 123)

For the stuffing
1 tablespoon unsalted butter
1 onion, finely chopped
1 teaspoon cumin seeds
grated zest and juice of 1 orange
½ cup golden raisins
2 tablespoons toasted pine nuts
1¼ cups quick-cook pearl barley, cooked
½ teaspoon salt
¼ teaspoon ground black pepper

1 Mix together all the marinade ingredients to form a paste. Gently lift the skin of each quail, trying not to puncture the skin, and work a little of the paste under the skin. Rub some paste inside the cavity of each bird and over the outside. Leave to marinate for as long as possible (ideally overnight or for at least 1 hour).

2 Meanwhile, preheat the oven to 350°F, and make the stuffing. Heat the butter in a pan and gently cook the onion until soft and translucent, about 8 minutes. Add the cumin seeds, orange zest and juice, golden raisins, and pine nuts and mix well. Stir in the pearl barley and season to taste with salt and pepper. Use the mixture to stuff the cavity of each marinated quail.

3 Place the birds in a roasting pan and cook in the preheated oven for 20 to 25 minutes. Serve with Nutty Curried Beans (see page 123).

Amount per portion
Energy 550 cals, Protein 28g, Fat 25g, Saturated fat 6.3g, Carbohydrate 57g, Total sugars 17.6g, Fiber 1.1g, Salt 0.82g, Sodium 324mg

Involtini in Ragu

In Italian *involtini* means "little birds." These stuffed meat parcels are usually served with pasta, but here I've used cannellini beans to boost the slow-release carbohydrates.

Serves 4

4 very thin sirloin steaks, about 3 to 4oz each, fat removed
freshly ground black pepper
2 tablespoons drained cannellini beans (from the sauce ingredients, see below)
3 tablespoons grated Parmesan cheese
2 garlic cloves, coarsely chopped
1 tablespoon chopped fresh parsley
½ tablespoon snipped fresh chives

For the sauce

spray olive oil
1 onion, finely chopped
3 garlic cloves, crushed to a paste with a little salt
1 teaspoon chopped fresh oregano
1 carrot, diced
1 celery rib, finely sliced
2 fresh red chiles, seeded and finely chopped
6 tablespoons red wine
¾ cup tomato sauce
¾ cup chicken stock
2 teaspoons sugar or low-calorie granulated sweetener
1 (14-oz) can chopped tomatoes
1 (14-oz) can cannellini beans, drained and rinsed
handful of fresh basil leaves, ripped
salt and freshly ground black pepper

1 Beat the steaks flat with a meat mallet or a rolling pin, being careful not to tear the meat. Season with black pepper. In a mini food processor blend the beans with the Parmesan, garlic, parsley, and chives and season again with pepper. Spread this mixture over the steaks, then roll each slice tightly, securing each involtini with a cocktail stick.

2 Spray a little oil in the bottom of a large ovenproof lidded pan or flameproof casserole, then over medium heat cook the involtini all over to brown. Remove from the pan and set aside, then add the onion, garlic, oregano, carrot, celery, and chiles to the same pan. Cook over medium heat until the onions have softened and are starting to brown, about 12 to 15 minutes.

3 Meanwhile, preheat the oven to 325°F. When the onions in the pan have softened, pour in the wine and boil vigorously until the liquid has all but disappeared. Add the tomato sauce, chicken stock, sugar or sweetener, and chopped tomatoes. Return the involtini to the sauce and bring to a boil, cover, and place in the preheated oven. Cook for 2 hours, stirring from time to time.

4 Remove the involtini from the sauce and keep them warm, then add the beans and basil to the pan and cook over medium heat for 5 minutes. Season to taste with salt and pepper, then return the involtini to the dish. Serve hot.

Variation Italians will often eat the sauce with pasta first, and then serve the involtini with a salad or a green vegetable such as broccoli or spinach.

Amount per portion (low-calorie sweetener)
Energy 274 cals, Protein 30.7g, Fat 6.2g, Saturated fat 2.3g, Carbohydrate 23.7g, Total sugars 10.0g, Fiber 5.9g, Salt 2.04g, Sodium 804mg

Amount per portion (Ssugar)
Energy 283 cals, Protein 30.7g, Fat 6.2g, Saturated fat 2.3g, Carbohydrate 26.1g, Total sugars 12.4g, Fiber 5.9g, Salt 2.04g, Sodium 804mg

Chicken in a Nutty Sauce with Cauliflower

I love chicken in creamy Indian curries. In this dish, butter and cream are replaced by yogurt to make it much healthier, but equally delicious.

Serves 4
grated zest and juice of 1 lemon
1 teaspoon salt
8 boneless and skinless chicken thighs
5½ oz non-fat Greek yogurt
1 teaspoon superfine sugar
2 tablespoons sunflower oil
⅓ cup unsalted cashews, soaked in
    a little hot water for 10 minutes
⅓ cup whole peeled almonds, soaked in
    a little hot water for 10 minutes
2 onions, coarsely chopped
2 teaspoons chopped garlic (see page 144)
1 teaspoon chopped ginger (see page 144)
1 teaspoon ground cumin
1 teaspoon ground coriander
4 tablespoons tomato paste
1 (14-oz) can chopped tomatoes
2 teaspoons chili powder
1 teaspoon ground turmeric
½ cauliflower, cut into florets
¾ cup frozen peas
2 handfuls of baby spinach
brown rice, to serve

1 In a large bowl, mix together the lemon zest and juice with the salt. Roll the chicken in this mixture then leave for 10 minutes. Massage in the yogurt.

2 Heat the sugar in a saucepan until it starts to caramelize. Stir in 1 tablespoon of the oil, add the chicken pieces, and brown them all over. Remove and set aside.

3 While the chicken is browning, grind together the cashews and almonds to a coarse paste in a mini food-processor and set aside.

4 To the pan the chicken was cooked in, add the remaining oil, the onions, garlic, ginger, cumin, and coriander and cook over medium heat until the onions start to brown. Add the tomato paste, canned tomatoes, and nut paste and cook for 10 minutes.

5 Return the chicken to the pan, add the chili powder and turmeric, cover, and cook for 20 minutes. Add the cauliflower and cook for another 8 minutes. Add the peas and spinach and cook for another 5 minutes. Adjust the seasoning to taste and serve with brown rice.

Amount per portion
Energy 517 cals, Protein 53.8g, Fat 24.3g, Saturated fat 3.9g, Carbohydrate 22.2g, Total sugars 13.8g, Fiber 6.5g, Salt 1.48g, Sodium 584mg

Dhansak-style Lamb Curry

If you want to be a serious cook, it's important to have a pantry full of useful spices, but buy small amounts because they lose their flavor—you really should replace them every year. Spices are very useful to people with diabetes—they contain little or no calories but are massive flavor converters and enhancers, as you'll see in this Indian dish.

Serves 4

10½ oz cubed leg of lamb, most fat removed, soaked in warm water
2 sweet potatoes, cut into ¾ in pieces
½ butternut squash, peeled, seeded, and cut into chunks
2 large onions, coarsely chopped
3 garlic cloves, coarsely chopped
1 (14-oz) can chopped tomatoes
1 cup split yellow lentils (*toor dal*), washed and drained
1 hot red chile, seeded and finely chopped
2 teaspoons fenugreek seeds
1 teaspoon ground turmeric
1 teaspoon chili powder
1 bunch of cilantro, coarsely chopped
1 small bunch of fresh mint leaves, coarsely chopped
½ teaspoon salt
1 teaspoon sugar
2 cups lamb or chicken stock
2 tablespoons lemon juice
2 teaspoons garam masala
10½ oz fresh spinach
brown rice, to serve

1 Add all the ingredients except the lemon juice, garam masala, and spinach to a large pan and bring to a boil. Reduce the heat, cover, and cook gently for 1 hour 30 minutes.

2 Remove the lid, stir in the lemon juice, garam masala, and spinach, and cook for another 5 minutes. Serve with brown rice.

Amount per portion
Energy 482 cals, Protein 36.0g, Fat 9.3g, Saturated fat 3.3g, Carbohydrate 67.9g, Total sugars 20.9g, Fiber 12.4g, Salt 2.08g, Sodium 821mg

Slow-cooked Pork Chops with Lentils and Cider

Pork, sage, and apple are a great partnership. I use old British breeds, such as a Gloucester Old Spot. This may be hard to find in America, so go with your local's oldest breed: old breeds, more flavor.

Serves 4

1 tablespoon olive oil
4 pork chops, about 6oz each, rind and most of the fat removed
1 onion, chopped
1 carrot, sliced
2 crunchy eating apples, unpeeled and grated
2 sprigs of fresh sage
1 cup puy lentils
1 cup good-quality dry cider
1½ cups chicken stock
1 tablespoon Dijon mustard
splash of Worcestershire sauce
¾ cup + 3 tablespoons non-fat natural Greek yogurt
freshly ground black pepper

1 Heat the oil in a large flameproof casserole or Dutch oven, add the pork chops, and brown them all over. Remove the meat from the dish and set aside, discarding any excess fat in the bottom of the pan. Add the onion, carrot, grated apple, and sage and cook over medium heat for 8 minutes.

2 Add the lentils, stir to combine, then add the cider and stock and bring to a boil. Return the chops to the dish, reduce the heat, cover, and cook gently for 1 hour. Remove the chops, cover with foil, and set aside to rest.

3 Increase the heat under the casserole and boil the sauce to reduce it. Meanwhile, whisk together the mustard, Worcestershire sauce, and yogurt, and season with pepper. When the sauce has reduced by half, fold in the flavored yogurt, return the chops to the pan, and turn off the heat. Taste and adjust the seasoning before serving.

Variation This works really well with whole pheasant, if you can find it; reduce the cooking time from 1 hour to 30 minutes.

Amount per portion
Energy 491 cals, Protein 54.3g, Fat 14.2g, Saturated fat 4.1g, Carbohydrate 36.4g, Total sugars 14.1g, Fiber 6.1g, Salt 0.87g, Sodium 344mg

Roast Pork with Potatoes in Retsina Wine

Called *hirino yiouvetsi* in Greece, this delicious roast pork dish is simple to make.

Serves 4 to 6

spray olive oil
2¼ lb loin of pork, rind and most of the fat
    removed, boned and rolled
1lb potatoes, halved
2 onions, sliced
2 teaspoons chopped fresh oregano
1¼ cups fava beans, frozen or fresh and
    podded
2 celery ribs, sliced
1 (14-oz) can chopped tomatoes
¾ cup retsina white wine
leaf salad, to serve

1 Preheat the oven to 350°F. Spray some oil over the base of a heavy-bottomed pan and cook the pork until brown all over.

2 Toss together the potatoes, onions, oregano, fava beans, and celery. Oil a flameproof casserole or Dutch oven and spread the potato mix at the bottom, then spoon over the canned tomatoes and their juice. Set the pork on top, transfer to the preheated oven, and cook for 1 hour 20 minutes.

3 Remove the casserole from the oven, set the pork aside, cover the meat with foil, and allow to rest. Meanwhile, add the wine to the potatoes in the casserole and boil on the stove, without stirring, until the liquid has reduced by half. Slice the pork and serve with the potatoes and sauce. A leaf salad is the only extra you will need.

Tip If you can't find retsina or another resinated white wine, use a gewürztraminer-style white.

Amount per portion
Energy 495 cals, Protein 58.9g, Fat 12.8g, Saturated fat 4.2g, Carbohydrate 33.6g, Total sugars 9.7g, Fiber 7.0g, Salt 0.45g, Sodium 178mg

Garbure

This hearty French soup is a meal in itself, made with a profusion of vegetables and several meats, including the fabulous duck confit.

Serves 4

3oz lean smoked bacon, cut into lardons
2 leeks, coarsely chopped
½ lb new potatoes, halved
3 celery ribs, thinly sliced
4 baby turnips
4oz cooked ham, coarsely chopped
4 garlic cloves, finely chopped
2 sprigs of thyme
1 onion, thinly sliced
2 carrots, sliced
2 bay leaves
2 quarts reduced-salt chicken stock
1 (14-oz) can navy beans, drained and
    rinsed
½ Savoy cabbage, shredded
2 legs duck confit, store-bought, skin
    removed, picked off the bone
salt and freshly ground black pepper
chopped flat-leaf parsley, to garnish

1 Put the bacon in a large saucepan, add the leeks, potatoes, celery, turnips, ham, garlic, thyme, onion, carrots, bay leaves, and stock, and cook gently for 45 minutes.

2 Add the beans, cabbage, and duck confit and cook for another 15 minutes. Remove the bacon and ham, blend them in a food processor until smooth, and add back to the soup. Season to taste with salt and pepper and garnish with parsley.

Amount per portion
Energy 629 cals, Protein 34.0g, Fat 40.0g, Saturated fat 10.3g, Carbohydrate 35.5g, Total sugars 13.8g, Fiber 11.7g, Salt 3.35g, Sodium 1322mg

Venison with Blackcurrants, Kale, and Barley

Venison takes to red fruits perfectly. I've often seen it cooked with redcurrants but when I had it with blackcurrants, I thought, yes, this is really good.

Serves 4

1lb blackcurrants
½ cup robust red wine
4 venison loin or haunch steaks, about 5½ oz each
1 tablespoon olive oil
3 garlic cloves, sliced
1 onion, finely chopped
2 carrots, finely sliced
¾ cup pearl barley
3 cups game or beef stock
2½ cups curly kale, coarse stems removed, shredded
salt and freshly ground black pepper

1 In a food processor, blend half the blackcurrants with the wine until smooth, then pass through a sieve. Transfer to a large non-metallic dish and add the remaining blackcurrants and the venison steaks, cover, and leave to marinate overnight in the refrigerator, or for a minimum of two hours.

2 Before cooking the venison, heat half the olive oil in a saucepan and cook half the garlic, three quarters of the onion, and all the carrot for about 10 minutes until the vegetables start to color. Add the barley and stir well to mix in, then pour in just over three quarters of the stock, setting aside the remainder for the sauce. Bring to a boil, then reduce the heat and simmer for 20 minutes. Add the kale and cook for another 10 minutes. Season to taste with salt and pepper.

3 Meanwhile, remove the venison from the marinade, wipe dry with paper towels, and reserve the marinade. Heat the remaining oil in a frying pan over high heat, sear the venison on both sides, then reduce the heat and cook for another 2 minutes on each side. Remove, cover to keep warm, and set aside.

4 In the pan used for cooking the venison, cook the remaining onion and garlic gently until soft, about 6 minutes. Add the marinade with the blackcurrants and boil over high heat until reduced by half, then add the remaining stock and continue boiling until reduced by a third. Check the seasoning and adjust to taste.

5 Spoon the barley and kale mix on to individual warmed plates, top with the venison, and spoon the sauce over the meat.

Variation This recipe works very well with pork chops, turning them slightly gamey.

Amount per portion
Energy 467 cals, Protein 45.7g, Fat 7.6g, Saturated fat 1.0g, Carbohydrate 53.8g, Total sugars 15.6g, Fiber 8.1g, Salt 1.54g, Sodium 606mg

Chicken Pot in the style of Cacciatore

One pot that goes in the middle of the table, everyone happy, very little clean-up, and an Italian-influenced dish that explodes with flavor.

Serves 4

2 (14-oz) cans chopped tomatoes
¼ cup red wine
8 chicken thighs, skin off, bone in
4 sprigs of fresh rosemary
2 bay leaves
2 onions, finely chopped
6 garlic cloves, crushed to
    a paste with a little salt
1 teaspoon dried oregano
6 anchovy fillets, coarsely chopped
2 tablespoons capers
½ lb new potatoes, thinly sliced
20 kalamata olives, pitted
salt and freshly ground black pepper
2 handfuls of baby spinach
leaf salad or green vegetables, to serve

1 Preheat the oven to 350°F. Place all the ingredients except the spinach and salt and pepper in a large bowl and stir to blend well. If possible, leave for a couple of hours for the flavors to develop—but don't worry if not. Transfer everything into a large baking dish, pop on the lid, and cook for 1 hour 15 minutes, checking after 45 minutes to see whether it is drying out—if so add a little water.

2 At the end of the cooking time, remove the chicken pieces and keep warm. Season with salt and pepper to taste, then fold in the spinach and stir until wilted. Return the chicken to the pot. Serve with a leaf salad or steamed green vegetables.

Amount per portion
Energy 392 cals, Protein 44.4g, Fat 13.5g, Saturated fat 3.1g, Carbohydrate 22.8g, Total sugars 10.7g, Fiber 4.9g, Salt 3.83g, Sodium 1511mg

Pot Roast Rabbit with Tomato and White Beans

The Northern Italians love a good stew, and this one is really gutsy, with strong flavors. Ask your butcher to joint the rabbit for you. If bunny is not your thing, then use skinless chicken thighs instead.

Serves 4

1 rabbit, jointed (legs, shoulders, belly flaps cut into strips, the saddle and neck cut into 4)
freshly ground black pepper
1 tablespoon olive oil
1 bunch baby carrots, about 12
4 shallots, cut in half through the root
2oz thick-cut bacon, cut into lardons
8 garlic cloves
¼ cup dry white wine
2 cups chicken stock
2 bay leaves
4 sprigs of fresh thyme
grated zest and juice of 1 orange
2 cups cherry tomatoes, halved
1 (14-oz) can cannellini beans, drained and rinsed
1 tablespoon anchovy extract
2 tablespoons chopped fresh parsley

1 Preheat the oven to 350°F. Season the rabbit pieces with ground black pepper. In a flameproof casserole or Dutch oven, heat the olive oil over medium heat and brown the rabbit pieces all over. Remove the meat and set aside.

2 Put the carrots into the casserole, add the shallots, bacon, and whole garlic cloves, and cook for about 10 minutes, stirring occasionally, until everything has a golden color.

3 Pour in the wine, scrape the bottom of the casserole to remove any residue, then add the stock, bay leaves, thyme, and orange juice. Return the rabbit to the dish and stir. Cover, transfer to the preheated oven, and cook for 40 minutes, stirring from time to time.

4 With a slotted spoon, transfer the meat and vegetables to a serving platter and keep warm. To the juices in the pan add the cherry tomatoes, cannellini beans, and anchovy extract. Bring to a boil and reduce the juices by one third. Meanwhile, combine the orange zest with the parsley.

5 Spoon the tomato and bean sauce over the rabbit and vegetables, and sprinkle with the orange parsley.

Amount per portion
Energy 356 cals, Protein 38.1g, Fat 13.0g, Saturated fat 4.0g, Carbohydrate 21.1g, Total sugars 9.3g, Fiber 6.1g, Salt 2.43g, Sodium 955mg

Lamb Tagine

A lovely dish packed full of flavor, perfect for cold winter nights, plus it's full of good GI foods too.

Serves 4

1 tablespoon ground ginger
1 tablespoon paprika
2 teaspoons ground turmeric
1 teaspoon ground cinnamon
1 teaspoon cayenne pepper
1 teaspoon freshly ground black pepper
1lb lean lamb, cut into 1in pieces
1 tablespoon olive oil
½ head of garlic, peeled and crushed
    with ¼ teaspoon salt
1 onion, grated
½ cup dried apricots, halved and soaked
    in a little water
½ cup almond flakes
¼ cup golden raisins
½ teaspoon saffron, soaked in
    1 teaspoon cold water
½ cup lamb stock
½ cup tomato juice
1 (14-oz) can tomatoes, coarsely chopped
1 (14-oz) can chickpeas, drained and rinsed
cilantro, to garnish
couscous, to serve

1 Combine all the spices. Put half the mix into a bowl and stir in the lamb, ensuring all the pieces are well coated. Leave for a few hours, or overnight if possible.

2 Preheat the oven to 325°F. Heat half the oil in a large heavy-bottomed ovenproof lidded pan over high heat and brown the lamb pieces, then remove the meat and set aside. In the same pan, cook the remaining spices, crushed garlic, and grated onion using the remaining oil, over low to medium heat. Allow the onion to soften without browning.

3 Add the apricots and their soaking water, the almonds, golden raisins, saffron, stock, tomato juice, canned tomatoes, chickpeas, and the browned meat. Bring to a boil, cover, place in the preheated oven, and cook for 1 hour 30 minutes to 2 hours.

4 Remove from the oven. If you like, remove the meat pieces and boil the sauce over high heat until reduced and thickened, then return the meat to the pan. Garnish the tagine with cilantro, and serve with couscous.

Tip The cilantro leaves scattered over the cooked dish are vital to a truly authentic tagine.

Amount per portion
Energy 439 cals, Protein 33.6g, Fat 18.4g, Saturated fat 5.3g, Carbohydrate 37.2g, Total sugars 19.4g, Fiber 6.7g, Salt 1.43g, Sodium 562mg

Barley with Greens, Sausage, and Ham

A bowl of this Australian-inspired dish will nourish you in every way.

Serves 4

1 tablespoon sunflower oil
2 onions, finely chopped
2 garlic cloves, finely chopped
½ teaspoon fresh thyme leaves
2 handfuls of mixed spinach and
    arugula, coarsely chopped
1 cup pearl barley
2oz prosciutto, chopped
½ teaspoon cayenne pepper
3 cups chicken stock
¼ lb chorizo sausage, diced
2 tablespoons freshly grated Parmesan
    cheese
4 tablespoons chopped fresh flat-leaf
    parsley
2 tablespoons snipped fresh chives
2 tablespoons toasted pine nuts

1 Melt the butter in a saucepan over medium heat, then add the onions, garlic, and thyme and cook for 8 minutes until the onions have started to soften.

2 Stir in the chopped greens, then the barley, prosciutto, cayenne, and stock. Bring to a boil, then cover, reduce the heat, and simmer until the liquid has been absorbed and the barley is tender.

3 Add the chorizo, Parmesan, parsley, chives, and pine nuts. Mix well and heat through.

Amount per portion
Energy 448 cals, Protein 24.2g, Fat 16.4g, Saturated fat 4.7g, Carbohydrate 54.4g, Total sugars 4.6g, Fiber 2.2g, Salt 2.30g, Sodium 909mg

Chickpeas with Chicken and Blood Sausage

This is the sort of dish you might get as a tapa when visiting Spain. Chicken wouldn't necessarily be featured, but I've added it to reduce the potency of the blood sausage.

Serves 4
spray olive oil
1 onion, finely chopped
2 garlic cloves, finely chopped
1 chicken breast, skinned and cut into
    ½ in cubes
2oz good-quality blood sausage,
    skinned and cut into ½ in cubes
3 tablespoons hazelnuts, coarsely chopped
3 tablespoons toasted pine nuts
2 tablespoons golden raisins
1 teaspoon ground coriander
½ teaspoon hot red pepper flakes
1 (14-oz) can chickpeas, rinsed
1 tablespoon chopped fresh parsley
1 tablespoon sherry or red wine vinegar
freshly ground black pepper
leaf salad, to serve

1 Spray a large frying pan with olive oil and warm over medium heat. Add the onion and garlic and cook for 10 minutes until the onions have softened and slightly browned.
2 Add the chicken pieces, increase the heat, and cook for 5 minutes, then add the sausage and cook for another 2 minutes. Fold in the hazelnuts and pine nuts, golden raisins, coriander, pepper flakes, and chickpeas. Cook for about 5 minutes more until the chickpeas have heated through. Fold in the parsley, stir in the vinegar, and add pepper to taste. Serve with a leaf salad.

Variation If blood sausage is not to your liking, then omit it and use a small amount of your favorite sausage, skin removed.

Amount per portion
Energy 265 cals, Protein 17.3g, Fat 13.5g, Saturated fat 1.0g, Carbohydrate 19.8g, Total sugars 6.9g, Fiber 3.7g, Salt 0.67g, Sodium 263mg

Pot Roast Pheasant with Chestnuts, New Potatoes, and Cabbage

It's a shame that game birds tend to be under-utilized, despite being readily available in season. They are raised in the wild, are good value, and are lower in fat and thus healthier to eat than most other meats. There are lots of flavors going on here, perfect for autumn and winter.

Serves 4
1 tablespoon olive oil
2 pheasants
2 onions, coarsely chopped
1 bay leaf
sprig of thyme
6 juniper berries
12 new potatoes, halved
1¼ cups chestnuts, cooked and peeled
1½ cups game or beef stock
½ cup robust red wine
1 cup cranberries
2½ Savoy cabbage, shredded
grated rind and juice of 1 orange
salt and freshly grated black pepper

1 Preheat the oven to 400°F. Heat the olive oil in a flameproof casserole or Dutch oven, then add the pheasants and brown them all over. Remove and set aside. Put the onions in the casserole and cook until softened and golden, about 8 minutes.

2 Add the bay leaf, thyme, juniper berries, new potatoes, and chestnuts, and stir to combine. Return the pheasants to the dish, breast side up. Pour the stock and wine around the pheasants, cover the casserole, and bring to a boil. Transfer to the preheated oven and cook for 25 minutes.

3 Remove the pheasants and set aside to rest. Transfer the casserole to the stove. Add the cranberries, cabbage and orange zest and juice. Cook over medium heat for 10 minutes.

4 Carve the pheasants and return the meat to the casserole. Season to taste with salt and pepper and serve in warmed bowls.

Tip The pheasant carcasses and drumsticks are excellent for soup. If you prefer a thicker sauce, add a little cornstarch thinned with cold water and simmer gently for a few minutes to thicken.

Amount per portion
Energy 570 cals, Protein 46.8g, Fat 21.1g, Saturated fat 6.0g, Carbohydrate 45.0g, Total sugars 12.4g, Fiber 6.1g, Salt 1.15g, Sodium 454mg

Pot Roast Chicken with Leeks, Green Beans, and Peas

You see this delicious simple stew on many menus of unpretentious restaurants in France. It's just what you want on a winter's evening.

Serves 4
8 new potatoes, halved
spray olive oil
2oz pancetta or smoked
    bacon lardons
6 boneless and skinless chicken
    thighs, halved
1lb 10oz leeks, cut in 1in pieces
8 garlic cloves, crushed
sprig of fresh rosemary
2 bay leaves
2 tablespoons soy sauce
6 tablespoons dry white wine
4 anchovy fillets
1 cup fresh green beans,
    trimmed and cut into 1in pieces
1 cup petit pois (small peas), frozen
12 cherry tomatoes
juice of ½ lemon
freshly ground black pepper
warm multigrain bread, to serve

1 Add the new potatoes to a pan of lightly salted water, bring to a boil, and cook for 10 minutes. Drain and set aside.

2 Lightly spray a large saucepan with olive oil and place over medium heat. Add the lardons and cook for 5 to 6 minutes, stirring occasionally until golden. Discard excess fat, then add the chicken and brown all over.

3 Add the leeks and garlic and cook for another 3 minutes, stirring regularly, then add the rosemary, bay leaves, soy sauce, white wine, anchovies, and partly cooked potatoes. Cover and cook gently for 15 minutes.

4 Add the beans, peas, and cherry tomatoes and cook, uncovered, for 8 minutes. Stir in the lemon juice and pepper to taste. Spoon into warmed bowls and serve with warm multigrain bread.

Variation I'm a leg man, but feel free to use chicken breasts if you prefer them, although I don't believe they will be as juicy.

Amount per portion
Energy 345 cals, Protein 38.2g, Fat 9.4g, Saturated fat 2.9g, Carbohydrate 26.4g, Total sugars 10.0g, Fiber 7.5g, Salt 2.77g, Sodium 1090mg

Duck Breast with a Nutty Filling

This is a dish for a dinner party—it's got lots of ingredients, as you'd expect with Indian food, but it's relatively simple to make. Serve it with some dhal and rice.

Serves 4

1 quart chicken stock, or duck stock
 if you can find it
4 duck breasts, skin removed
1 tablespoon each almond flakes
 and chopped cashews
rice and dhal, to serve

For the stuffing

½ cup low-fat ricotta or cream cheese
1 tablespoon ground almonds
1 tablespoon chopped pistachios
½ cup cooked spinach, squeezed dry
 and chopped
1 tablespoon dried cherries
¼ teaspoon ground cardamom
1 teaspoon chopped fresh mint
¼ teaspoon chili powder
¼ teaspoon salt

For the sauce

1 teaspoon sunflower oil
2 onions, finely sliced
2 teaspoons chopped garlic
1 teaspoon grated ginger
½ teaspoon ground turmeric
½ teaspoon ground cumin
½ teaspoon ground coriander
1 teaspoon garam masala
1¼ in piece of cinnamon stick
3 cardamom pods
5 curry leaves
½ cup ground almonds
1 cup chicken stock, or duck stock from
 poaching the duck
1 tablespoon chopped cashews
2 tablespoons chopped cilantro
salt and freshly ground pepper

1 In a saucepan, gently heat the stock. Meanwhile, with a sharp knife make a horizontal slice through the duck breasts, leaving each joined at the side so you can open it up like a book—this is called butterflying. Cover each open breast with plastic wrap and beat flat with a mallet or rolling pin.

2 Mix together all the stuffing ingredients, then spread a quarter of the mix over each breast, leaving a small border all around. Roll up the breasts then wrap in plastic wrap to create tight sausages. Place them in the hot stock and poach gently for 20 minutes. Leave them in the stock to keep warm until ready to serve.

3 Meanwhile, make the sauce. Heat the oil in a frying pan and cook the onions gently until soft, about 8 minutes. Add the garlic, ginger, spices, and ground almonds and cook for another 5 minutes, stirring frequently. Add the sauce stock and simmer gently for 15 minutes. Discard the cinnamon stick and allow the sauce to cool slightly. Liquidize or purée the sauce, return it to the heat, and stir in the cashews and cilantro. Season to taste with salt and pepper.

4 Remove the plastic wrap from the duck and slice each "sausage" into 6 pieces, arrange on to individual plates, and spoon over the sauce. Sprinkle with slivered almonds and chopped cashews and serve with rice and dhal.

Amount per portion
Energy 510 cals, Protein 51.1g, Fat 28.2g, Saturated fat 5.2g, Carbohydrate 14.2g, Total sugars 8.2g, Fiber 3.7g, Salt 2.43g, Sodium 959mg

Souvlakia

This brings back memories of being in a Greek port snacking on this delicious lamb stuffed in pita with salad and a yogurt dressing.

Serves 4
2 tablespoons extra virgin olive oil
1 tablespoon lemon juice
1 tablespoon grated onion and juice
1 tablespoon finely chopped fresh oregano
1lb lamb (from leg), fat removed and cut
    into ½ in cubes
salt and freshly ground black pepper
salad and pita bread, to serve

1 In a large bowl, mix together the oil, lemon juice, onion, and oregano to make a marinade. Stir in the meat and let it stand at room temperature for 1 hour, or preferably overnight.
2 Preheat the broiler or a grill. Drain the marinade off the lamb and thread the meat pieces on to metal skewers. Cook for 5 to 10 minutes, depending on how rare you like your lamb. Season and serve with salad and warm pita bread.

Tip The meat is best when nicely brown on the outside but still pink on the inside.

Amount per portion
Energy 225 cals, Protein 22.8g, Fat 14.5g, Saturated fat 5.2g, Carbohydrate 0.6g, Total sugars 0.3g, Fiber 0.1g, Salt 0.82g, Sodium 325mg

Lamb and Lentil Burgers

We know that meat burgers can often be high in fat, but the lentils make these a healthier choice and the Indian flavorings will certainly make them enjoyable.

Serves 4

2 tablespoons sunflower oil
2 onions, finely chopped
1 teaspoon chopped garlic (see Tip on page 144)
1 teaspoon chopped ginger (see Tip on page 144)
1 medium-heat green chile, seeded
    and finely chopped
1 teaspoon ground turmeric
1 teaspoon hot curry paste
10½ oz ground lamb
1 cup split red lentils, washed and drained
2 tablespoons brown breadcrumbs
1 tablespoon chopped fresh mint
1 tablespoon chopped pine nuts
3 eggs, beaten
spray oil, for frying
salad and multigrain bread, to serve

1 Heat the oil in a large frying pan and cook the onions over low heat for 6 to 8 minutes. Add the garlic, ginger, and chile and cook for another 2 minutes, then add the lamb and cook until brown.

2 Add the lentils, turmeric, and curry paste and cook this mixture until the lamb and lentils are cooked (about 20 minutes), making sure the mixture is completely dry. Drain off any liquid fat and leave the mixture to cool. (The burger mixture can be made in advance up to this point.)

3 Mix together the cooled burger mixture with the breadcrumbs, mint, and pine nuts, then add a third of the beaten egg and mix well to bind. Divide the mixture into 4 patties and refrigerate for about an hour, or as long as possible, to firm up.

4 Spray a frying pan with oil, then dip the burgers into the remaining egg and cook for 3 minutes each side until golden. Serve with salad and multigrain bread.

Amount per portion
Energy 464 cals, Protein 32.1g, Fat 23.7g, Saturated fat 7.3g, Carbohydrate 32.6g, Total sugars 4.9g, Fiber 3.3g, Salt 0.43g, Sodium 172mg

Bulgogi (Marinated Beef and Lettuce Parcels)

One of Korea's best-known dishes, this combination of salty and sweet has great depth of flavor and a lovely crunch from the iceberg lettuce. It's not difficult to make, but allow plenty of time before cooking for all the flavors to develop. In this adaptation, I've substituted brown rice for the usual sticky white rice.

Serves 4

For the marinade
1½ tablespoons *ketjap manis* (Indonesian sweet soy sauce)
1 tablespoon sesame oil
2 tablespoons low-calorie sweetener
4 garlic cloves, crushed to a paste with a little salt
2 tablespoons sesame seeds

13oz beef (sirloin or rump), fat removed, frozen for 1hr 30mins to firm up
1 medium Bramley or Granny Smith apple, cored and peeled
1 large dessert pear, cored and peeled
1 onion, grated
2 garlic cloves, grated
2 large carrots, cut into matchsticks
4 scallions, thinly sliced
2 green chiles, seeded and thinly sliced
½ head of iceberg lettuce, leaves separated
2 cups cooked and cooled brown rice
1½ tablespoons soybean paste
2 teaspoons garlic purée

1 Mix together all the marinade ingredients in a bowl. Set aside for the flavors to develop.

2 Meanwhile, slice the frozen piece of beef into very thin strips, then put them into a large bowl. Grate the apple and pear on to the meat and mix, along with the onion and garlic. Set aside for 20 minutes for the beef to take in the different flavors.

3 Pour the marinade over the beef and mix well, then mix in the carrots, scallions, and chiles. Leave to marinate, ideally overnight but at least for 1 hour.

4 When ready to cook, heat a wok over high heat and add the beef mix with its marinade. Stir-fry for 3 minutes. To eat, take a lettuce leaf, place some rice in it, then add a touch of soybean paste and a dab of garlic purée. Top with hot beef, then enjoy the contrast of hot and cold, silky and crunchy.

Amount per portion
Energy 428 cals, Protein 28.8g, Fat 12.3g, Saturated fat 2.7g, Carbohydrate 54.0g, Total sugars 20.2g, Fiber 5.6g, Salt 1.93g, Sodium 764mg

Malaysian Roast Chicken

Most meat eaters love a roast chicken, and this recipe gives Sunday lunch a new dimension. Roast the chicken with the skin on, but tempting as it is, forgo that little fatty treat and remove the skin before eating.

Serves 4
For the marinating paste
2 onions, coarsely chopped
3 garlic cloves
3 scallions, sliced
4 medium-hot red chiles, coarsely chopped
½ in piece of fresh ginger, peeled
1 in piece of galangal (optional)
1 stalk lemongrass, outer leaves discarded,
    coarsely chopped
1 teaspoon ground turmeric
½ bunch of cilantro, coarsely chopped
4 kaffir lime leaves
1 tablespoon honey
1 teaspoon shrimp paste (*blachan*)
juice of 1 lime
3 tablespoons thick coconut milk,
    from the top of the can
½ teaspoon salt

1 chicken, about 3¼ lb
brown rice and stir-fried bok choy, to serve

1 In a food processor, blend together all the marinating paste ingredients until smooth. Rub the paste under the chicken skin, over the skin, and inside the cavity. Leave to marinate for a few hours, and overnight if possible.

2 When ready to cook, preheat the oven to 350°F. Roast the chicken for about 1 hour 15 minutes. Serve with brown rice and stir-fried bok choy.

Amount per portion
Energy 458 cals, Protein 49.5g, Fat 24.7g, Saturated fat 9.0g, Carbohydrate 10.1g, Total sugars 7.2g, Fiber 1.1g, Salt 1.16g, Sodium 459mg

Tofu, Pork, and Shellfish Hot Pot

And you thought healthy food had to be boring . . . not so! This Korean winter warmer smacks you in the mouth, rolls you over, and challenges you to have more.

Serves 4
1 teaspoon sunflower oil
4 garlic cloves, crushed to a paste
1 teaspoon grated ginger
3 teaspoons chili powder
2 teaspoons sesame oil
4oz pork fillet or tenderloin, cut into strips
1 tablespoon *ketjap manis* (Indonesian
    sweet soy sauce)
1 quart reduced-salt fish or chicken stock
½ lb fresh mussels, cleaned and any open
    mussels discarded
4 scallions, sliced
¼ lb sugar snap peas
8oz silken tofu, cut into bite-sized pieces
4oz raw tiger shrimp, shell-on
1 tablespoon chopped cilantro
salt and freshly ground black pepper
lime wedges and brown rice, to serve

1 Heat the oil in a frying pan and cook the garlic, ginger, and chili powder for 1 to 2 minutes. Add the sesame oil and increase the heat, then add the pork and cook for 4 minutes until browned. Stir in the ketjap manis and set aside.

2 In a separate deep pan, bring the stock to a boil. Add in the mussels, cover, and cook for 3 minutes until all the shells have opened—discard any that have not. Add the pork mix, the scallions, peas, tofu, and shrimp, bring back to a boil, and cook for 1 minute. Season to taste with salt and pepper and stir in the cilantro. Serve with lime wedges and some brown rice.

Amount per portion
Energy 189 cals, Protein 19.9g, Fat 8.8g, Saturated fat 1.5g, Carbohydrate 8.2g, Total sugars 2.0g, Fiber 0.8g, Salt 2.12g, Sodium 837mg

Malaysian Lamb Biryani

One-pot dining at its best. I've given the classic Asian flavors little twists such as adding puy lentils to make the meal much more beneficial.

Serves 4

2 tablespoons sunflower oil
10½ oz diced leg of lamb, cut into
  ½ in pieces
1 large onion, finely diced
2 garlic cloves, finely chopped
¾ in piece of cinnamon stick
1 teaspoon ground turmeric
1 teaspoon ground cardamom
1 star anise, broken
2 tablespoons curry paste
1 cup brown rice, rinsed
½ cup puy lentils
8 new potatoes, cut into ½ in dice
¼ cup raisins
1 carrot, cut into ½ in dice
1 quart lamb stock
⅓ cup frozen peas
½ red bell pepper, seeded and cut into
  ½ in dice
2 tomatoes, seeded and diced
⅓ cup chopped cashews, to garnish
1 tablespoon chopped cilantro,
  to garnish

1 Preheat the oven to 350°F. Heat the oil in a flameproof casserole or Dutch oven and, when very hot, add the lamb and cook briefly (maximum 2 minutes) to seal the meat. Remove and set aside.

2 Cook the onion in the same casserole for 6 minutes. Add the garlic, cinnamon, turmeric, cardamom, star anise, and curry paste, and cook gently for another 3 minutes. Add the rice and lentils and stir to coat. Add the potatoes, raisins, and carrots, return the meat to the casserole, pour in the stock, and stir. Cover, transfer to the preheated oven, and cook for 30 minutes.

3 Check that the rice is cooked. Add the peas, red bell pepper, and tomatoes, and return to the oven for 3 minutes. Divide the biryani between individual warmed bowls and scatter with the chopped cashews and cilantro.

Amount per portion
Energy 669 cals, Protein 32.8g, Fat 24.5g, Saturated fat 6.4g, Carbohydrate 84.6g, Total sugars 17.7g, Fiber 8.0g, Salt 1.75g, Sodium 690mg

Braised Lamb Stew with Barley

This rustic dish is heart-warming, perfect for winter, with loads of flavor. Here I've used pot barley (also known as Scotch barley or milled barley), which still contains the bran—a good source of fiber. You may have to go to an organic or health food store to obtain it.

Serves 4

1 tablespoon sunflower oil
2¼ lb lamb shanks or neck chops
 (flavorwise, mutton would be even better
 but can be too fatty)
2 onions, coarsely chopped
2 celery ribs, thinly sliced
2 carrots, thickly sliced
2 bay leaves
2 sprigs of thyme
1 tablespoon tomato paste
1 quart lamb or chicken stock
8 tablespoons pot barley
1 small sweet potato, cut into ½ in dice
¼ Savoy cabbage, shredded
1 cup peas, frozen or fresh and podded
salt and freshly ground black pepper
multigrain bread, to serve

1 Heat the oil in a large flameproof casserole or Dutch oven and brown the meat all over, then remove and set aside. Add the onions to the casserole, then the celery, carrots, bay leaves, and thyme, and cook for 6 minutes until the onions have browned slightly.

2 Stir in the tomato paste, then add the stock, cover, and simmer gently for 2 hours. Remove the meat and allow it to cool enough for you to pick the meat off the bone.

3 While the meat is cooling, add the barley and sweet potato to the casserole and simmer for another 20 minutes. Add the cabbage and peas, cook for another 3 minutes, then mix the meat back in and continue cooking just long enough to heat through. Season with a touch of salt and plenty of black pepper. Serve piping hot, with chunks of multigrain bread.

Tip If you're worried about the dish containing too much fat, make it the day before you want to eat it, allow to cool, then refrigerate. When cold, the fat will have solidified on the surface and can be skimmed off.

Amount per portion
Energy 571 cals, Protein 48.3g, Fat 26.0g, Saturated fat 11.1g, Carbohydrate 38.3g, Total sugars 11.5g, Fiber 6.4g, Salt 2.34g, Sodium 922mg

Bo Bun (Vietnamese Beef and Noodles)

Really this is like a warm salad, with classic Asian flavors, offering both protein and carbs. Serve it with a few extra vegetables, as I've suggested here, for a more complete meal.

Serves 4

1lb rump or sirloin steak, fat removed and cut into 2in-wide strips, then sliced very thinly crosswise
2 garlic cloves, crushed to a paste with a little salt
4 scallions, sliced
1 stick of lemongrass, outer leaves removed, very finely chopped
2 tablespoons fish sauce (*nuoc mam, nam pla*)
½ teaspoon granulated low-calorie sweetener
6oz rice vermicelli
2 tablespoons sunflower oil
¼ teaspoon hot red pepper flakes
1 onion, thinly sliced
1 carrot, finely sliced
2 tablespoons diced water chestnuts
2 heads of bok choy, coarsely chopped
salt and freshly ground black pepper

To serve

mung bean sprouts
shredded lettuce
cucumber sticks
carrot strips
cilantro leaves
crushed peanuts

1 In a bowl, mix together the beef, garlic, scallions, lemongrass, fish sauce, and sugar, and leave to marinate for at least 30 minutes.

2 Bring a large pot of salted water to a boil, add the rice vermicelli, and cook for approximately 2 minutes until the noodles are white but still firm. Drain and rinse in cold water. (This can be done ahead of time.)

3 Just before serving, drain the beef and reserve the marinade. Heat a wok, add the oil, and when nearly smoking, add the beef and stir-fry for about 1 minute until brown. Remove and set aside.

4 Add the hot red pepper flakes and the onion to the wok and cook for about 5 minutes, then add the carrot and stir-fry for 3 minutes. Add the water chestnuts and bok choy along with a splash of water, and cook until the bok choy starts to wilt, about 2 minutes.

5 Add the beef, reserved marinade, and noodles and stir-fry for 1 minute, and season to taste with salt and pepper. Serve with the accompaniments suggested.

Amount per portion

Energy 373 cals, Protein 31g, Fat 11g, Saturated fat 2.5g, Carbohydrate 41g, Total sugars 5.3g, Fiber 1.5g, Salt 1.74g, Sodium 684mg

Singapore Fried Noodles

A good bowl of noodles makes an excellent lunch or light supper. As you would expect from an Asian dish, this has lots of flavor.

Serves 4

14oz rice noodles
2 tablespoons sunflower oil
3½ oz raw tiger shrimp, shells removed and deveined
3½ oz chicken breast, skin removed, thinly sliced
2 eggs, well beaten
1 large onion, sliced
2 carrots, sliced
1 cup sugar snap peas, thinly sliced
2 teaspoons chopped garlic
1 cup bean sprouts
1 cup water chestnuts, chopped
½ red bell pepper, seeded and thinly sliced
2 teaspoons fish sauce (*nam pla*)
1 tablespoon light soy sauce
1 tablespoon *ketjap manis* (Indonesian sweet soy sauce)
1 tablespoon Worcestershire sauce
3 red chiles, seeded and thinly sliced
handful of watercress sprigs, large stems removed
handful of baby spinach leaves

1 Bring a pan of lightly salted water to a boil, add in the noodles, and cook for 1 to 3 minutes depending on their thickness. Drain and leave in a colander.

2 Heat half the oil in a wok, add the shrimp and chicken, and cook for 2 minutes, stirring regularly. Remove and set aside. Pour the beaten eggs into the wok and stir-fry for 1 minute, then remove and set aside.

3 Heat the remaining oil in the wok, then add the onion and carrots and stir-fry for 5 minutes. Add the sugar snaps, garlic, bean sprouts, water chestnuts, and red pepper, and cook for 2 minutes.

4 Return the noodles, shrimp, chicken, and eggs to the wok, then add the fish sauce, soy sauce, *ketjap manis,* and Worcestershire sauce. Stir well, then add the chiles, watercress, and spinach, and stir until wilted. Serve hot.

Amount per portion
Energy 544 cals, Protein 23g, Fat 10g, Saturated fat 1.8g, Carbohydrate 96g, Total sugars 10.9g, Fiber 3.1g, Salt 2.36g, Sodium 928mg

Chicken with Lentils, Dried Fruits, and Spices

This dish might have its roots in India, but I had it in a restaurant in Sydney.

Serves 4

1 cup yellow lentils (*toor dal*) soaked in
    water for 30 minutes
¾ cup dried apricots, soaked in water
    for 30 minutes and then chopped
¼ cup dried cherries
¼ cup dried blueberries
2 tablespoons sunflower oil
1½ in piece of cinnamon stick
2 onions, finely chopped
½ teaspoon hot red pepper flakes
1 teaspoon ground cumin
1 teaspoon ground coriander
4 cardamom pods, lightly crushed
¼ teaspoon ground cloves
1 tablespoon finely chopped garlic
2 teaspoons grated ginger
6 boneless, skinless chicken thighs,
    each cut into 3 pieces
4 tomatoes, coarsely chopped
2 green chiles, seeded and finely sliced
2 tablespoons chopped cilantro
salad, to serve

1 Drain the lentils, then cook them in fresh water until they are very soft. Drain well, then add the soaked, chopped apricots and other dried fruits.

2 Heat the oil in a saucepan, add the cinnamon stick, and cook for 2 minutes. Add the onions and cook for 8 minutes over medium heat. Add the hot red pepper flakes, cumin, coriander, cardamom, cloves, garlic, and ginger, and cook for another 5 minutes.

3 Add the chicken pieces and cook for 10 minutes. Spoon in the lentil mixture and cook gently for another 5 minutes. Add the tomatoes, chiles, and cilantro and cook for another 5 minutes. Serve with salad.

Amount per portion
Energy 508 cals, Protein 43.9g, Fat 11.8g, Saturated fat 2.5g, Carbohydrate 60.3g, Total sugars 29.8g, Fiber 9.1g, Salt 0.40g, Sodium 159mg

Dukkah-coated Chicken Liver Kebabs with Lemon Mint Yogurt

Dukkah is a fragrant nutty mix found in Egypt and the Middle East, usually served for dunking bread that has been coated in olive oil (the amount per person isn't going to have significant GI input). It makes a great coating for these livers.

Serves 4

For the yogurt sauce
½ cup + 3 tablespoons non-fat natural yogurt
juice and grated zest of 1 lemon
1 tablespoon chopped fresh mint
¼ teaspoon chili powder or cayenne pepper
¼ teaspoon salt

For the dukkah
⅓ cup shelled hazelnuts
1½ tablespoons sesame seeds
1½ tablespoons coriander seeds
1½ tablespoons cumin seeds

For the kebabs
¾ cup multigrain breadcrumbs (see Tip on page 173)
⅓ cup dukkah (see above)
grated zest of 1 lemon
1 cup whole wheat flour
2 eggs, lightly beaten in a shallow dish
1lb chicken livers or duck livers, cleaned, cut in half, and soaked in milk for 1 hour
spray olive oil

1 To make the yogurt sauce, combine all the ingredients and allow the flavors to develop for up to 1 hour.

2 To make the dukkah, toast the nuts and seeds in a dry frying pan over low heat, shaking the pan from time to time, until you smell a delicious fragrance—about 2 to 3 minutes depending on the heat of the pan. Grind to a coarse powder. You have several options for this: use a pulse action in a mini food processor, or a coffee grinder with a coarse grind, or a hard surface and a rolling action with the bottom of a clean pan; alternatively, wrap the seeds in a clean, non-favorite kitchen towel and lightly crush with a rolling pin or mallet. Whichever method you use, you need to retain some texture.

3 If using wooden skewers for the kebabs, soak four medium skewers in water for 30 minutes. Preheat the broiler to high. Now get yourself organized to prepare the kebabs. First combine the breadcrumbs with the dukkah mix and the lemon zest on a flat plate. Put the flour on another plate next to the dukkah mix, and next to that set the dish with the beaten egg.

4 Drain the livers and pat dry with paper towels, then thread on to the skewers. Roll them in flour and shake off any excess, then dip them in egg, making sure no dry flour patches remain, and then roll them in the dukkah crumbs. Spray the kebabs with oil and pop them under the broiler; cook them to medium rare (5 to 6 minutes), turning regularly. Serve with the yogurt sauce.

Tip An accompanying salad of white beans, red onion, and cilantro would be delicious.

Variation Cubes of calf's liver can be substituted if you prefer.

Amount per portion
Energy 361 cals, Protein 32.8g, Fat 12.1g, Saturated fat 2.4g, Carbohydrate 32.2g, Total sugars 3.8g, Fiber 4.2g, Salt 0.94g, Sodium 372mg

Desserts and Drinks

Crumble in a Flash

What could be more comforting than a homemade crumble? This version using sunflower seeds and sesame seeds is much healthier for you than traditional recipes.

Serves 4

2 (8-oz) cans pineapple, drained and
    lightly crushed
1 dessert pear, diced
1 dessert apple (Pippin, Granny Smith),
    diced
1 cup unsweetened muesli or granola
2 tablespoons sunflower seeds
2 teaspoons sesame seeds
3½ oz low-fat Greek yogurt
2 tablespoons honey

1 Preheat the oven to 350°F.

2 Mix together the pineapple, pear, and apple then spoon the mixture into four medium-sized ramekins. Crumble the muesli or granola into a bowl, stir in the seeds, then mix in the yogurt and honey. Spoon on to the fruit.

3 Bake, uncovered, for 20 to 25 minutes or until golden brown. Serve with a little extra yogurt if you like.

Amount per portion (granola)
Energy 261 cals, Protein 5.9g, Fat 7.8g, Saturated fat 1.6g, Carbohydrate g 44.5g, Total sugars g 30.5g, Fiber 3.6g, Sodium 35mg

Amount per portion (muesli, no added sugar)
Energy 254 cals, Protein 6.4g, Fat 7.5g, Saturated fat 1.6g, Carbohydrate 42.9g, Total sugars 27.7g, Fiber 4.3g, Sodium 35mg

Another Crumble

Fruity, nutty, loved by all, this crumble has a Christmassy touch to it. Within reason, you can invent your own combo for the filling, but this is my suggestion. However, it is an indulgence, so save it for the right occasion.

Serves 4

For the filling
½ lb Granny Smith apples, peeled, cored
    and sliced
4 plums, halved and stoned
¾ cup dried cranberries
2 tablespoons dried cherries
2 tablespoons superfine sugar
    or low-calorie sweetener
¼ cup toasted almond flakes
½ teaspoon ground cinnamon
¼ teaspoon grated nutmeg

For the topping
1 cup all-purpose flour
8 tablespoons soy spread
1¼ cups unsweetened muesli
¼ cup brazil nuts, chopped
¼ cup hazelnuts, chopped
½ cup dark brown sugar

1 Preheat the oven to 350°F. Mix together all the filling ingredients and transfer to an ovenproof pie dish, ensuring the plums are evenly distributed.

2 To make the topping, place the flour in a bowl and rub in the soy spread with your fingers until the mixture resembles coarse breadcrumbs. Mix in the remaining topping ingredients.

3 Scatter the topping over the fruit and bake for about 50 minutes or until the topping has firmed and is golden. Serve piping hot.

Amount per portion (sugar)
Energy 770 cals, Protein 10.7g, Fat 36.9g, Saturated fat 6.3g, Carbohydrate 105.3g, Total sugars 65.3g, Fiber 7.6g, Salt 0.28g, Sodium 110mg

Amount per portion (low-calorie sweetener)
Energy 745 cals, Protein 10.7g, Fat 36.9g, Saturated fat 6.3g, Carbohydrate 98.7g, Total sugars 58.7g, Fiber 7.6g, Salt 0.27g, Sodium 110mg

Citrus and Honey Cheesecake with Plum Compote

Come on, spoil yourself. Maybe not every day, but as they say, a little of what you enjoy does you good.

Serves 10

For the crust

2¾ cups walnut pieces, toasted and cooled to room temperature
2 tablespoons sugar
½ teaspoon ground cinnamon

For the filling

2lb low-fat cream cheese
¼ cup + 1 tablespoon non-fat natural yogurt
2 tablespoons acacia honey
1 tablespoon sugar
4 large eggs
grated zest of 1 lemon
grated zest of 1 orange
1 teaspoon vanilla extract

For the plum compote

½ cup red wine
¼ cup superfine sugar
sprig of fresh rosemary
1 bay leaf
1 strip each lemon and orange zest
2 cloves
2in piece of cinnamon stick
1¼ lb red plums, halved and pitted

butter, for greasing

1 Preheat the oven to 350°F. Grease an 8-inch flan dish or loose-bottomed cake pan and line with parchment paper. Make the crust by placing the toasted walnut pieces, sugar, and ground cinnamon in a food processor and pulsing until finely ground. Spread the mixture into the bottom of the prepared dish and press well to compact it.

2 Ensure all the filling ingredients are at room temperature. In the bowl of an electric mixer, combine the cream cheese and yogurt. Beat at a medium speed with the paddle attachment, scraping the sides of the bowl and the paddle often, until smooth. Add the honey and sugar and continue beating until there are no lumps. Add the eggs one at a time, beating between each addition. Then add the lemon and orange zest and the vanilla, and mix well. Pour the mixture over the crust in the prepared pan—do not scrape the sides of the bowl as this will add lumps to the mixture.

3 Set the flan dish or cake pan in a large roasting pan and add enough water to come halfway up the side of the cheesecake dish. Bake for about 25 minutes until just barely set. Turn off the oven, leave the cake in it with the door ajar, and leave to cool gently for 1 to 2 hours; this will prevent the cake from splitting on the top. When cold, cover in plastic wrap and refrigerate overnight.

4 To make the compote, bring all the ingredients except the plums to a boil and simmer until the sugar has dissolved. Add the plums, cover, and cook gently until the plums are just tender, about 10 minutes. Remove the plums and set aside. If you like, boil the juices to reduce slightly, and discard the rosemary sprig, bay leaf, zests, clove, and cinnamon stick. Set aside to cool before using.

5 To serve, remove the cheesecake from its dish: first line a baking sheet with plastic wrap then dip the cheesecake dish in a hot-water bath and turn the cake out on to the prepared baking sheet. Then invert the cake on to a serving dish—the cake should be just barely set in the center. Serve at room temperature, topped with juicy plum compote.

Amount per portion

Energy 435 cals, Protein 18.4g, Fat 29.6g, Saturated fat 5.8g, Carbohydrate 23.1g, Total sugars 21.8g, Fiber 2.0g, Salt 1.02g, Sodium 403mg

Apricot Fool

This is a dessert for those in need of a little sweetness.
Dried apricots have a more intense flavor than fresh.

Serves 4
½ lb dried apricots, soaked in 2 cups water
    for 1 hour
2 teaspoons superfine sugar or low-calorie
    granulated sweetener
½ teaspoon vanilla extract
6 tablespoons non-fat Greek yogurt
4 tablespoons fresh pomegranate seeds
1 teaspoon chopped fresh mint leaves

1 In a covered saucepan, cook the apricots and their soaking
liquid together with the sugar or sweetener until the fruit is
soft, about 30 minutes. Toward the end of cooking, remove the
lid and boil until you are left with about 3 tablespoons of liquid.
2 Set aside a quarter of the apricots. Blend together the remaining
apricots, all the poaching liquid, the vanilla extract, and the yogurt
in a food processor. Spoon into glasses and refrigerate until chilled.
3 Just before serving, chop the remaining apricots, then mix
together with the pomegranate and the mint. Scatter the mixture
over the chilled fools and serve.

Amount per portion (low-calorie sweetener)
Energy 126 cals, Protein 5.1g, Fat 0.4g, Saturated fat 0.3g, Carbohydrate 27.1g,
Total sugars 26.8g, Fiber 4.7g, Salt 0.12g, Sodium 48mg

Amount per portion (sugar)
Energy 135 cals, Protein 5.1g, Fat 0.4g, Saturated fat 0.3g, Carbohydrate 29.5g,
Total sugars 29.2g, Fiber 4.7g, Salt 0.12g, Sodium 48mg

Gooseberry Fool Crunch

Along with rhubarb, I love gooseberries when they are available, with their short seasons of fabulous tart fruit that demand you do something with them. A fool may be a slight cop-out, but it's delicious, so go for it.

Serves 4

14oz gooseberries, stalks removed

⅓ cup superfine sugar, plus 3 tablespoons sugar or low calorie granulated sweetener

3 vanilla beans, split lengthwise or 2 teaspoons vanilla extract

1¾ cups non-fat natural Greek yogurt

4 tablespoons unsweetened muesli

1 Put the gooseberries and ⅓ cup of sugar in a saucepan and cook over low heat for about 10 minutes until the gooseberries have softened. Scrape out the seeds from the vanilla beans and stir them into the gooseberries, retaining the beans for another use. Stir to combine. Leave the gooseberries to cool and put 4 empty glasses (wine or tumbler) to chill.

2 Set aside half the stewed gooseberries. To the remaining half, add the additional sweetener and yogurt and mix well to blend.

3 In each of the four glasses, spoon in a layer of stewed gooseberries followed by some gooseberry yogurt and then the crunchy muesli, then add a layer of gooseberry yogurt and finish off with some stewed gooseberries. Chill until ready to eat.

Amount per portion (sugar)

Energy 265 cals, Protein 15 g, Fat 1 g, Saturated fat 0.2 g, Carbohydrate 52g, Total sugars 44.1g, Fiber 3.3g, Salt 0.25g, Sodium 100mg

Amount per portion (low-calorie sweetener)

Energy 225 cals, Protein 15g, Fat 1g, Saturated fat 0.2g, Carbohydrate 41g, Total sugars 33.4g, Fiber 3.3g, Salt 0.25g, Sodium 99mg

Peaches and Cream Ice Cream

A little treat is essential from time to time and this luscious ice cream fits the bill perfectly. If you're freezing ahead, ensure you remove it from the freezer well in advance to allow it to soften.

Serves 4
¾ cup superfine sugar
4 ripe peaches, cut into ½ in cubes
3 tablespoons peach schnapps, brandy, or orange-flavored liqueur
4 tablespoons heavy cream
¾ cup + 2 tablespoons natural Greek yogurt
2 tablespoons chopped toasted hazelnuts

1 Put 1 cup of water into a saucepan, add the sugar, and bring to a boil, stirring occasionally, and continue to boil to a clear syrup. Pour the syrup over the peaches while hot, stir in the alcohol, and leave to cool.

2 Set aside half the fruit. In a blender or food processor, blend together the remaining peaches with all of the syrup liquor, the cream, and the yogurt.

3 If using an ice-cream maker, pour the mixture into the machine and follow the manufacturer's instructions; alternatively, pour the mixture into containers and chill in the freezer, whisking every 30 minutes as it freezes. Toward the end of the freezing process, fold in the remaining diced fruit and the hazelnuts. Enjoy immediately or freeze until needed.

Amount per portion
Energy 355 cals, Protein 7g, Fat 12g, Saturated fat 4.8g, Carbohydrate 54g, Total sugars 53.4g, Fiber 2g, Salt 0.11g, Sodium 43mg

Pomegranate and Red Berry Jello

I always think of jellies as quintessentially British, but I'm sure a whole host of countries have their own versions, so I've experimented with a Middle Eastern ingredient. There's no added sugar in this recipe, and it is a low-calorie dessert, so no need to go easy.

Serves 6
12 gelatin sheets
1½ quarts unsweetened pomegranate juice
3 tablespoons pomegranate seeds
¼ lb blueberries
¼ lb raspberries

1 Put a jello mold in the freezer to chill. Soak the gelatin in a small bowl of cold water for 8 to 10 minutes. Heat 1¾ cups of the pomegranate juice in a saucepan over low heat. Squeeze any excess water from the gelatin sheets then add it to the warm juice, and stir to dissolve and combine. Add the remaining juice and leave to cool to room temperature.

2 Remove the jello mold from the freezer, scatter in the pomegranate seeds, and pour in 1 inch of the liquid jello. Pop into the fridge to lightly set, about 30 minutes.

3 Remove from the fridge and scatter the blueberries over the set jello. Pour on half the remaining liquid jello, then return to the fridge to set.

4 Finally, finish off with raspberries and the remaining jello. Chill for about 4 hours to set properly, or preferably overnight.

Tip If you want to be a touch more professional, swirl the jello around the chilled mold before putting in the fruit to coat the mold with jello all over; this gives the jello a better look.

Amount per portion
Energy 130 cals, Protein 2.6g, Fat 0.1g, Saturated fat 0.0g, Carbohydrate 31.6g, Total sugars 31.6g, Fiber 0.9g, Salt 0.03g, Sodium 10mg

Fruity Cream Cheese Cup

I wanted to include a trifle in this book so I opted for this fabulous tasting version that is lower in calories than a traditional trifle.

Serves 4
¼ lb raspberries
¼ lb blueberries
1 cup strawberries, quartered
juice and zest of 1 orange
1 cup low-fat cream cheese
3 teaspoons sugar or low-calorie granulated sweetener
6 mini whole wheat cereal, crumbled
1 tablespoon maple syrup
1 tablespoon toasted almonds, to garnish

1 Mix together all the berries, stir in half the orange juice, and set aside. Combine the cream cheese with the remaining orange juice, the zest, and the sugar or sweetener.

2 Put four large wine glasses or tumblers on your work surface. Put a spoonful of the berry mix in the bottom of each, followed by a spoonful of cream cheese, and then sprinkle on some of the cereal. Repeat all the layers then drizzle with maple syrup and sprinkle with almonds.

Amount per portion (low-calorie sweetener)
Energy 166 cals, Protein 6.8g, Fat 8.5g, Saturated fat 4.1g, Carbohydrate 16.2g, Total sugars 11.7g, Fiber 2.3g, Salt 0.59g, Sodium 230mg

Amount per portion (sugar)
Energy 180 cals, Protein 6.8g, Fat 8.5g, Saturated fat 4.1g, Carbohydrate 19.8g, Total sugars 15.2g, Fiber 2.3g, Salt 0.59g, Sodium 231mg

Rhubarb and Yogurt Crunch

This fruity favorite is tasty for breakfast, but it does require a bit of preparation.

Serves 4
4 rhubarb stalks, destrung and cut into 1in pieces
2 teaspoons sugar or low-calorie granulated sweetener
½ cup fresh orange juice
13oz non-fat Greek-style yogurt
1¼ cups unsweetened muesli
2 teaspoons honey

1 Preheat the oven to 400°F.

2 Spread out the rhubarb on a roasting pan, sprinkle with the sweetener, and pour over the orange juice. Bake for 15 minutes without stirring, or you will break up the rhubarb. Leave to cool.

3 Spoon a little yogurt into the bottom of four glass tumblers or wine glasses, cover with a layer of muesli, and then top with some rhubarb pieces. Repeat the layers, finishing with rhubarb, then drizzle with a little honey.

Amount per portion (low-calorie sweetener & no added sugar muesli)
Energy 164 cals, Protein 12.2g, Fat 2.0g, Saturated fat 0.3g, Carbohydrate 25.9g, Total sugars 12.1g, Fiber 2.5g, Salt 0.2g, Sodium 78mg

Amount per portion (sugar & no added sugar muesli)
Energy 173 cals, Protein 12.2g, Fat 2.0g, Saturated fat 0.3g, Carbohydrate 28.3g, Total sugars 14.5g, Fiber 2.5g, Salt 0.2g, Sodium 78mg

Carrot and Pineapple Cake

This moist, luscious cake is a real treat, filled with carrots, nuts, and spices. It also freezes well.

Serves 8 to 10
1lb whole wheat self-rising flour
2 teaspoons baking powder
½ tablespoon ground cinnamon
½ teaspoon grated nutmeg
½ teaspoon ground allspice
½ cup dark muscovado sugar
½ cup light olive oil
2 eggs, lightly beaten
¾ lb carrots, grated
½ cup walnut pieces
¾ cup raisins
⅓ cup desiccated coconut
9oz pineapple, crushed, in natural juice
confectioners' sugar, for dusting

1 Preheat the oven to 350°F. Grease a 10-inch spring-release pan and line its base with parchment paper.

2 Mix all the dry ingredients together in a large bowl. Add the remaining ingredients and mix well until evenly combined.

3 Transfer the mixture to the prepared pan and level the surface. Bake in the center of the preheated oven for about 1 hour until risen and golden and a fine metal skewer comes out clean when inserted in the cake.

4 Cool in the pan for 15 minutes then transfer to a wire rack until completely cold. Dust with confectioners' sugar and serve.

Amount per portion (serves 8)
Energy 514 cals, Protein 10.9g, Fat 23.7g, Saturated fat 4.8g, Carbohydrate 68.6g, Total sugars 32.5g, Fiber 7.2g, Salt 0.41g, Sodium 163mg

Amount per portion (serves 10)
Energy 412 cals, Protein 8.8g, Fat 19.0g, Saturated fat 3.8g, Carbohydrate 54.9g, Total sugars 26.0g, Fiber 5.8g, Salt 0.33g, Sodium 130mg

Summer Bread Pudding

Berries are one of the best low GI fruits, so by using multigrain bread and a low-calorie sweetener, this dessert makes a perfect fruity treat. If you need an accompaniment low-fat yogurt or low-fat ice cream is better than cream.

Serves 4
sunflower oil, for greasing
¾ cup redcurrants
¾ cup blackcurrants
1lb raspberries
4 tablespoons low-calorie granulated
    sweetener
1 loaf of multigrain bread, thinly sliced,
    crusts removed and discarded,
    cut into triangles

1 Lightly oil a 1-quart pudding basin, then line it with plastic wrap, leaving plenty overhanging.

2 Place the fruit and sweetener to a saucepan and add ½ cup of water. Bring to a boil, then remove from the heat. Transfer the fruit into a sieve placed over a bowl to catch some juices—only remove the excess juice, as you need the fruit to be quite wet.

3 Dip the bread triangles into the saved juice then use to line the prepared pudding basin, overlapping each piece of bread slightly. There will be some bread left, which will be needed later.

4 Set the pudding basin on a tray to catch any juices. Spoon the fruit to the top of the basin, pour in a little juice, then cover with the remaining bread. Cover the top with the overhanging plastic wrap, then with a saucer or plate that fits inside the rim of the bowl, and set a heavy weight such as a few canned goods on top. Refrigerate for up to 2 days to completely set.

5 Remove the weight and saucer and peel back the plastic wrap. Invert the pudding on to a plate. To serve, cut into wedges.

Amount per portion
Energy 284 cals, Protein 10.2g, Fat 3.7g, Saturated fat 0.6g, Carbohydrate 56.0g, Total sugars 12.0g, Fiber 9.6g, Salt 1.02g, Sodium 405mg

Strawberry and Mint Tea Jello

This is one for the adults, or perhaps the sophisticated child. I've chosen mint tea because the flavor goes well with the strawberries, but there are a whole host of different teas you could try, such as jasmine and lapsung souchong.

Serves 8
1 quart mint tea, hot
4 teaspoons sugar or low-calorie granulated sweetener
juice of 2 limes
9 gelatin sheets, soaked for 6 to 8 minutes in a small bowl of cold water to soften and bloom
1 cup strawberries, sliced or diced

1 Place a jello mold in the freezer to chill. Combine the tea with the sugar or sweetener and lime juice. Remove the gelatin from the water and squeeze out any excess moisture, then stir it into the tea to dissolve and blend.

2 Now you've got two options in how you prepare the set jello. You can go all cheffy and pour a little jello into the frozen mold, swirl it around to give a thin coating, and then stick slices of strawberry to the set jello; pour in a bit more jello with some strawberries and allow to set, then repeat 2 or 3 times until the mold is full. This way you get strawberries throughout the jello. Or, you can simply spoon strawberries into the mold then pour on the jello—the strawberries will float up, not as professionally pretty as with the cheffy method, but it has the same fantastic taste. Chill in the fridge for a few hours to set.

3 Turn the set jello out by dipping the mold in warm water for a few seconds, then turn it out on to a serving dish.

Variation Make individual jellies that you don't have to turn out at all by filling wine glasses or tumblers that you can bring straight to the table.

Amount per portion (low-calorie sweetener)
Energy 11 cals, Protein 1.1g, Fat 0.0g, Saturated fat 0.0g, Carbohydrate 1.7g, Total sugars 1.7g, Fiber 0.2g, Salt 0.01g, Sodium 5mg

Amount per portion (sugar)
Energy 20 cals, Protein 1.1g, Fat 0.0g, Saturated fat 0.0g, Carbohydrate 4.1g, Total sugars 4.1g, Fiber 0.2g, Salt 0.01g, Sodium 5mg

Melon Dessert

If you are going to choose a dessert, try and opt for a fruit based one. This Italian treat should add a little twist to your normal repertoire as the infusion of spice with jasmine tea and orange flower water is a beautiful combination with chocolate, fruit, and nuts.

Serves 4

1 Galia or Cantaloupe melon, rind and seeds removed
4 tablespoons low-calorie sweetener
2 tablespoons cornstarch
pinch of grated nutmeg
¼ cup + two tablespoons brewed Jasmine tea, leaves strained
½ teaspoon orange flower water
1½ oz dark chocolate, grated or finely chopped, plus extra shavings to serve
2 teaspoons chopped pistachio nuts, plus extra to serve
1½ oz candied lemon peel, finely chopped

1 Cut the melon into chunks and process to a fine purée in a food processor. Pass through a sieve into a bowl.

2 Whisk a little of the melon juice with the sweetener and cornstarch to a smooth paste, then place in a saucepan over low heat and stir in the remaining juice little by little. Slowly bring to a boil, stirring regularly, then remove from the heat. Stir in the nutmeg, jasmine tea, and orange flower water. Leave to cool.

3 When the mixture is hand-hot, fold in the chocolate, pistachios, and candied peel and divide between individual glass bowls or tumblers. Refrigerate until ready to serve. Just before serving, decorate with chocolate shavings and chopped pistachios.

Amount per portion
Energy 150 cals, Protein 1.6g, Fat 4.3g, Saturated fat 1.7g, Carbohydrate 27.8g, Total sugars 22.3g, Fiber 1.4g, Salt 0.19g, Sodium 76mg

Middle Eastern Fruit Salad

This fruit salad makes a beautiful dessert, of course, but it's also great in the morning scattered over granola or oatmeal or served with a dollop of low-fat Greek yogurt.

Serves 4

½ cup dried apples
½ cup dried apricots
¼ cup dried figs
¼ cup dried pears
¼ cup dried peaches
1 strip fresh or dried orange peel
1½ in piece of cinnamon stick
2 cloves
1 star anise
1 teaspoon honey
pinch of saffron
2 teaspoons pomegranate molasses (see Tip on page 165)
¼ cup toasted almond flakes
3 tablespoons chopped pistachios
½ teaspoon orange flower water (optional)
1 tablespoon fresh pomegranate seeds, to garnish

1 Place all the ingredients except the almonds, pistachios, orange flower water, and pomegranate seeds in a saucepan and just cover with water. Bring to a boil, then reduce the heat, cover, and simmer for 20 minutes. Leave to cool, then gently stir in the nuts and orange flower water. When ready to serve, sprinkle with the pomegranate seeds.

Amount per portion
Energy 216 cals, Protein 4.6g, Fat 7.4g, Saturated fat 0.9g, Carbohydrate 34.9g, Total sugars 34.4g, Fiber 5.3g, Salt 0.06g, Sodium 26mg

Minty Melon and Strawberries

Keep it simple, keep it fresh, as the Australians do; the mint adds a refreshing point of difference.
I've chosen Charentais melon, but feel free to mix and match: a combination of watermelon, Charentais, and honeydew makes for great color.

Serves 6
2 teaspoons sugar or low-calorie
    granulated sweetener
leaves from 1 small bunch mint
2 Charentais or Galia melons, seeded
1 cup strawberries, hulled and halved

1 Heat 1 cup of water with the sugar or sweetener and half the mint, stir to dissolve the sweetener, and simmer for 10 minutes. Strain and leave the syrup to cool. Chop the remaining mint leaves and add them to the syrup.

2 If you have a melon baller, scoop out balls from the melon flesh; otherwise, dice the melon into bite-size pieces. Mix together with the strawberries. Chill the fruit salad, then pour over the mint syrup and stir to coat the fruit.

Variations Mint goes well with all sorts of fruit, such as peaches, pears, and nectarines, so experiment with different combinations.

Amount per portion (low-calorie sweetener)
Energy 55 cals, Protein 1.2g, Fat 0.3g, Saturated fat 0.0g, Carbohydrate 12.5g, Total sugars 12.5g, Fiber 1.2g, Salt 0.16g, Sodium 62mg

Amount per portion (sugar)
Energy cals 61, Protein 1.2g, Fat 0.3g, Saturated fat 0.0g, Carbohydrate 14.1g, Total sugars 14.0g, Fiber 1.2g, Salt 0.16g, Sodium 62mg

Char-grilled Peaches with Honey and Vanilla Yogurt

I love cooked peaches, as in this Italian dessert, but it's getting increasingly hard to find sweet-tasting ripe peaches, with most having a cardboardy texture; the same goes for nectarines and apricots. At least when you cook these fruit, you intensify the natural sweetness they do have.

Serves 4
spray sunflower oil
4 ripe peaches, halved and pitted
½ cup fresh orange juice
1 tablespoon honey
½ cup non-fat natural yogurt
1 teaspoon vanilla extract
1 teaspoon sugar
⅓ cup chopped pistachios, to garnish

1 Preheat the oven to 400°F. Spray oil in the bottom of a ridged grill pan or frying pan, heat, then add the peaches cut-side down and cook for 5 minutes over high heat. If using a griddle pan, turn the peaches sideways by 45° halfway through cooking to create patchwork markings.

2 Set the peach halves cut-side up in a roasting pan, pour the orange juice around them, then drizzle the cut surfaces with the honey. Roast for 10 to 15 minutes, depending on their ripeness—you want the peaches soft but not collapsed.

3 Meanwhile, combine the yogurt with the vanilla and sugar. Place the peach halves into individual warmed bowls cut-side up, spoon on a dollop of yogurt, and scatter with the pistachios.

Tip If possible buy "freestone" peaches rather than "clingstone" ones. Your local supermarket may not know what on earth you are talking about, but freestone, as the name suggests, are much easier when trying to remove the pit. Basically, if the peach twists easily it's freestone, if you have to cut the flesh from the pit it's not.

Amount per portion
Energy 147 cals, Protein 5.8g, Fat 5.7g, Saturated fat 0.7g, Carbohydrate 19.5g, Total sugars 19.0g, Fiber 1.7g, Salt 0.1g, Sodium 38mg

Mango Lassi

In India, variations on this yogurt drink are popular for any time of the day. This version should be a regular on your breakfast menu.

Serves 4
2½ cups non-fat natural yogurt
2 mangoes, coarsely diced
2 tablespoons bran
3 tablespoons pomegranate seeds
1 tablespoon honey
12 ice cubes

1 In a smoothie machine or food processor, process all the ingredients (except the ice) together until well blended. Pour into 4 glasses and serve immediately over ice.

Amount per portion
Energy 195 cals, Protein 10g, Fat 1g, Saturated fat 0g, Carbohydrate 40g, Total sugars 35.7g, Fiber 5g, Salt 0.37g, Sodium 146mg

Old-Fashioned Barley Water

When I saw the recipe for this drink in one of the cookbooks my aunt put together a long time ago, I knew I had to put it in this book. As long as you use low-calorie sweetener, the rest of the drink is nothing but healthy.

Serves 4
1½ cups pearl barley, washed
grated zest and juice of 6 oranges
grated zest and juice of 3 lemons
low-calorie sweetener

1 Place the barley in a saucepan and add 2½ quarts of water and the orange and lemon zests. Bring to a boil, reduce the heat, and simmer for 1 hour. Strain the liquid and leave to cool.

2 Stir in the citrus juices and sweeten to taste. Decant the barley water into bottles or a jug and refrigerate. Drink within 3 days.

Tip Think thrifty—the discarded barley would be useful added to another dish, such as a soup.

Amount per portion
Energy 85 cals, Protein 1.9g, Fat 0.2g, Saturated fat 0.0g, Carbohydrate 20.2g, Total sugars 9.7g, Fiber 0.1g, Salt 0.01g, Sodium 4mg

Index